"At a time when the mixture of religion and politics seems to generate much more heat than light, Amy Black's primer is a most welcome exception. Her book's account of political complexity and Christian responsibility is clear, thoughtful, calm, and brimming with insight. For Christian believers who want to understand contemporary American politics, and for those who wish to take part, there is no better place to begin than *Beyond Left and Right*."

—**Mark A. Noll**, Francis A. McAnaney Professor of History, University of Notre Dame

"Puzzled by politics? This clear, easily understood introduction by an expert on politics is what you need."

—**Ronald J. Sider**, president, Evangelicals for Social Action; professor of theology, holistic ministry, and public policy, Palmer Theological Seminary; author, *The Scandal of the Evangelical Conscience* and *Rich Christians in an Age of Hunger*

"For those of you have been frustrated or disappointed by the behavior of some Christians in the political arena, Amy Black may provide some insights into how you can work to avoid those mistakes and actually serve as a positive voice in the process.

"Imagine people watching you in the political arena and observing, 'Wouldn't I love to have the character and frame of mind of that person! What do they have that I might want?' The answer is, 'The confidence that we're all created in the image of God and that we're learning from each other, through the lens of Christ, why he's put each of us where we are and how we can serve him.'

"The challenge Amy offers each of us is to exhibit humble behavior in an environment in which humility is a scarce commodity."

—**Pete Hoekstra**, U.S. Representative (R-MI)

"Amy Black's *Beyond Left and Right* reveals the touch of a gifted teacher. She interprets competing points of view with clarity, fairness, and insight, respecting her readers' ability to arrive at their own conclusions. Her book will be an inspiration and a helpful guide to those seeking to relate their faith to the complexities and challenges of politics."

—**David Price**, U.S. Representative (D-NC)

"A wise voice sounds through the pages of Amy Black's primer for Christian participation in American democracy. It is uncommon to hear calm pleas for civility and respect for complexity in this age of instapundits. This call to temper political zealotry with love of God, neighbor, and enemy will be of use to churches and academies alike."

—Jason Byassee, assistant editor, *The Christian Century*

"At a time when overheated rhetoric about Christians and American political life can be heard everywhere, Amy Black has written a superb primer, informed by careful scholarship and firsthand experience of the political process. This book would be ideal for use in small groups—especially leading up to November 2008."

—John Wilson, editor, *Books & Culture*

"An enormously helpful and timely introduction to important principles of Christian political participation, to the nature of the American political system, and to the role of Christians in contemporary American politics. Christians of all political stripes and colors can learn and benefit from its discussion and analysis."

—Corwin Smidt, director, the Paul B. Henry Institute for the Study of Christianity and Politics, Calvin College

"Professor Black has written an excellent primer on American politics for serious Christians. It will be invaluable for novices, but even experienced citizens will learn something from this brief, informative, and insightful book."

—John C. Green, distinguished professor, political science; director, Ray C. Bliss Institute of Applied Politics, University of Akron

BEYOND
LEFT AND RIGHT

HELPING CHRISTIANS MAKE SENSE
OF AMERICAN POLITICS

AMY E. BLACK

BakerBooks
Grand Rapids, Michigan

Published by Baker Books
a division of Baker Publishing Group
P.O. Box 6287, Grand Rapids, MI 49516-6287
www.bakerbooks.com

Second printing, August 2008

Printed in the United States of America

Library of Congress Cataloging-in-Publication Data
Black, Amy E.
    Beyond left and right : helping Christians make sense of American
politics / Amy E. Black.
        p.   cm.
    Includes bibliographical references and index.
    ISBN 978-0-8010-6726-6 (pbk.)
    1. Christianity and politics—United States. I. Title.
BR516.B5155 2008
261.70973—dc22   2007036399

For Daniel,
with gratitude for his wisdom and love

Contents

Acknowledgments

Many wonderful friends, students, and colleagues contributed to this book. It seems only fitting to first acknowledge Mark Amstutz, whose enthusiasm for Wheaton students and our department convinced me to apply for my current job. I would not be at Wheaton if not for his insistent recruiting, and I would not have written this book without the opportunities for intellectual and spiritual growth my Wheaton position has provided.

In much the same way, I am indebted to my students, especially those who have shared the journey of the political science capstone seminar on Christianity and politics. Their questions keep me constantly on my toes, their energy is infectious, and their insights inspire me. Much of the material in this book grew directly out of my experiences talking with Wheaton students about how our faith can inform our political lives.

This book would not have been possible without the particular encouragement of Bob Fryling, who first asked me to teach an adult education course on Christianity and politics and then convinced me that the course should be expanded into a book. I am privileged to count Bob and his wife, Alice, as cherished friends and spiritual mentors.

As is so often the case, current and former Wheaton colleagues were great resources. Thanks to Mark Noll, Tim Larsen, and Vince Bacote for their willingness to read and comment on chapters in progress. I am indebted to Steve Spencer for his insights and voluminous library, both of which helped me write chapter 9. Despite my colleagues' many efforts to keep me focused, there may be some remaining mistakes, for which I accept all responsibility. So many other friends contributed along the way. Tat and Jo Ebihara provided a dining room table that inspired many rounds of edits and meals that kept us fed in the final weeks of writing; Jan Miller kept me well supplied with purple pens; and the women in my Bible study and the couples in our covenant group supported me in prayer.

My work also benefited from the suggestions of my editor, Chad Allen, and the assistance of Bobbi Jo Heyboer, Adam Ferguson, Lauren Forsythe, Jessica Miles, Kim DeWall, and the entire team at Baker Books. When I began this project, I counted Chad among my close friends; happily, the friendship remains intact after months of work and rounds of editing. Additional thanks are due to Josh Magnusson, Katy Crosby, Jon Flugstad, and Jennifer Aycock for their capable research assistance and support of the project, and to Daniel Treier, Jo Ebihara, and Jan Miller for their careful editing. David Malone and his colleagues at the Wheaton College Archives and Special Collections provided me a sabbatical office and a warm welcome. I am grateful to Corwin Smidt, Ellen Hekman, and the Paul B. Henry Institute for the Study of Christianity and Politics at Calvin College for providing the index. This book would not be possible without support from the G. W. Aldeen Fund and the Wheaton College sabbatical program.

No project in my life, big or small, would be the same without the encouragement of my family. My parents, sister and brother-in-law, and in-laws are great sources of strength and joy. I am thankful most of all, however, for my husband, Dan, whose entrance into my life forever changed my understanding of theology and whose love and support mean more than my simple words can express. Our respective loves of politics and religion may not make us particularly welcome dinner party guests, but they do inspire our teaching and writing. It is to him that I lovingly and gratefully dedicate this book.

Introduction

Politics determines your temporal life and religion determines your
eternal life, so what else is there to talk about?

—Activist Paul Weyrich's father on why people
should discuss politics and religion at dinner

One need not be well versed in the intricate details of proper
etiquette to know some basic truths about the unspoken rules of
"polite" conversation. Two topics are forbidden among polite
guests at a dinner party: politics and religion.

Although Miss Manners may warn against discussing either
of these subjects, the purpose of this book is to defy those rules
of etiquette and encourage you to bring these taboo topics to the
table. This book will help you find appropriate ways to break
from the social convention and talk more, not less, about politics
and religion.

Why might etiquette books warn people to steer clear of these
subjects? I think the answer is straightforward: people often have
very strong, deeply held beliefs about them. Because the subject
matter can be intensely personal and quickly divisive, discussions
of both topics can quickly reach an impasse. Instead of initiating a
conversation that could lead to frustration and even anger, it seems
wiser to avoid such subjects. Yet if we can find a way to think and
talk about religion and politics that doesn't automatically cause

friction, perhaps we can bring these topics to the table and begin a constructive and valuable dialogue.

The impetus for this book comes primarily from two sources: an adult education course I taught at my church in the fall of 2004, and the capstone seminar I have the joy of teaching to senior political science majors at Wheaton College. Those who attended the class at the church brought a beautiful range of perspectives to the subject and helped me think through the relationship between Christianity and politics in new ways. The class was also a good reminder that some folks need a quick refresher on the basics of American politics. Once reminded of some aspects of "Politics 101," they were ready to ask deeper questions and share new insights about what it means to be faithful in politics. One might think that college students in the very last stages of completing their political science major would have lots of answers, but many of them found themselves still asking questions as they wrestled with what it really means to let their faith inform their civic lives. I too find that the more I research and teach about religion and American politics, the more questions I ask. It is much easier to study political science than it is to wrestle with the reality of solving complex problems in a messy and broken world.

In the midst of these intellectual journeys, I have encountered much frustration, but I have also discovered unspeakable joy. In my own life and in the lives of my students, I have seen God lend us constructive ways for the depth of our faith to inform even something as complicated and messy as politics. At that proverbial dinner party, in our churches, or even in the comfort of our own homes, it won't always be easy or comfortable to talk about religion and politics. But the challenge is both worthy and worthwhile. Come join me as we bring the taboos to the table.

PART 1

THE BASICS

BEGINNING THE CONVERSATION

1

Who Speaks for God in Politics?

Where We Begin

One of the Ten Commandments is for us not to take God's name in vain. That means we are not to use his name in a way he has not authorized. We have to be careful about what we make him the patron for. We, on the left and the right, have made God some kind of mascot. Instead of a transcendent God who speaks to us, he's someone who sort of blesses our agenda and sanctifies our programs.

Michael S. Horton, J. Gresham Machen Professor of Systematic Theology and Apologetics, Westminster Seminary, California

A view of a church steeple, a bright blue sky, and Jesus's words recorded in Luke 6:31, "Do to others as you would have them do to you," fills the television screen. A Baptist preacher from Louisville, Kentucky, identified on the screen as Pastor Lou Phelps, asks viewers if they share the values of Wal-Mart. The screen fades to black as Phelps lists concerns about the retail giant's child labor practices, gender discrimination lawsuits, and lack of health coverage for many employees. The camera moves to the inside of a church building, where Phelps stands in front of a stained-glass window and asks, "As we celebrate Christmas together, search your heart. If these are Wal-Mart's values, would Jesus shop at Wal-Mart? Should you?"

In the same town, prominent national religious leaders address a crowd of thousands assembled in the Highview Baptist Church auditorium on a Sunday evening. The message is simulcast so hundreds of thousands more can gather to watch the broadcast in their sanctuaries across the country. The Senate majority leader speaks via satellite to encourage fellow Christians to unite in support of conservative judges, while organizers sound the refrain to "stop the filibuster against people of faith."

Can a Christian shop at Wal-Mart? Must all Christians support conservative judicial nominees? To hear much of the popular rhetoric, one can easily conclude that God is a Republican, while other signals send an equally clear message that all good Christians should vote Democrat. At the same time that many Christians publicly proclaim the "correct" Christian view of various public policy issues, others forcefully argue that Christians should stay as far away from politics as possible.

In a theme that echoes from casual conversations at the water cooler to the *New York Times* bestseller list, religion appears to be a source of division and contention, not consensus. From mainstream media portrayals that don't seem to understand religion to caricatures of Christians as single-minded ideologues, popular notions of faith and politics are often oversimplified and flawed. Compounding this problem, some churches preach ideology and single-issue politics instead of training parishioners to think biblically and theologically about politics and public policy. In the midst of so much confusion, American Christians have very few resources to help them develop a thoughtful and informed approach to political issues and elections.

As a scholar of American politics teaching at a Christian college, I constantly examine the intersection of religious and political perspectives. Although tackling these subjects is not always comfortable and easy, such conversations are not only valuable; they are essential. To understand American politics today, one needs to understand the ways in which religious values and beliefs inform political behavior. To contribute productively to political debates about candidates and public policy, one needs a working knowledge of the structure and limitations of American government.

This book is designed to help you navigate the rocky waters of religion and politics, providing tools and information for addressing questions such as the following: How should Christians respond to this confusing mix of seemingly contradictory views about Christianity and politics? Why does religion seem to cause so much division? Should Christians just avoid politics all together? Does anyone really speak for God in politics? How should my faith affect my voting decisions and political participation?

Instead of offering one set of definitive answers to these and other questions, the goal of this book is to educate and equip you to answer them for yourself. On this journey, you will learn more about how the American political system works, gaining insights and tools to help you better understand and interact with government.

A Few Assumptions Up Front

Anytime we enter a conversation about a serious topic, it is useful to know where everyone is coming from. We cannot help but bring our own perspectives and life stories into a discussion; that is, we begin with suppositions about how the world works and what is important. If three people are discussing effective parenting techniques, it is useful to know that one has three teenagers, the other has two toddlers, and the third has no children. Each person can contribute important insights to the conversation, but their views will likely reflect their personal experiences in part.

In a similar way, political scientists often begin their analyses by listing their underlying assumptions about how the political world works. This practice provides a foundation for further discussion, establishing the starting point from which to begin a deeper analysis. Thus, before I begin navigating the waters of religion and politics, it seems wise for me to explain my central assumptions about the role of religion in a democracy—and in the United States in particular—that will guide the discussion in the rest of this book.

The United States Is, and Always Has Been, a Pluralistic Nation

Any honest discussion of religion in contemporary American politics must begin with the recognition that this nation is not, nor ever has been, exclusively Christian. From the earliest (and short-lived) government created by the Articles of Confederation, and continuing to the current structure established in the Constitution, the United States has been a democratic nation that protects individual freedoms. Freedom of religion, one of those cherished liberties, is a foundational principle of our democracy.

People from a wide diversity of faiths live in the United States and participate in American politics. Data from a comprehensive survey of American religion reveal a complex religious landscape. According to the American Religious Identification Survey, an estimated three of four adult Americans identify themselves as part of the Christian tradition, but dozens of other religions also have a place in the cultural landscape. Consider one example: the number of Americans identifying themselves as Muslims, Buddhists, and Hindus has more than doubled in the past decade alone. These three religions combined now represent about the same percentage of the population as Jews. Perhaps the most striking finding in recent surveys of religion is the rapidly increasing number of Americans who say they are not religious at all. In 1990, an estimated 14.3 million Americans did not identify with any religion; by 2001 that number had increased to 29.4 million, representing 14 percent of the population.[1] If these trends continue (and all recent data suggest that they will), the United States will become increasingly more religiously diverse, and Christianity will likely lose its status as the majority religion.

This book approaches the subject of religion and politics in the United States with a keen awareness of and appreciation for our nation's religious diversity. Just as I want the government to protect my freedom to worship as I choose, so I must promote policies that respect others' rights to their religious practices. Furthermore, the religious diversity of the United States demands that we not expect everyone to accept or embrace political arguments that appeal exclusively to Christian principles and doctrine. Religious views and traditions will inform your political perspectives; indeed, the purpose of this book is to help you apply your faith to your politics with care and discernment. But even as we approach the public square with a particular faith perspective, we need to be aware that our conversations take place in an increasingly secular and religiously diverse nation.

Religion Affects Everyone's View of Politics

A second underlying assumption builds from the first. Although some people may think they don't mix their religious views and their thoughts on politics, in practice this is rarely, if ever, the case. A person's view of religion and the supernatural and questions of ultimate reality will affect his or her politics, either directly or indirectly.

Consider a few examples of religion directly influencing politics. Some pastors, priests, rabbis, and other religious leaders teach their faithful to support particular political issues and candidates. Many people talk informally about politics when they gather for worship or congregation-related events. At some houses of worship, interest groups distribute voter guides that "compare" candidates for office on a few select issues, leaving little ambiguity about which candidate deserves the vote.

Even those who would rather avoid the combination of politics and religion will find the task difficult if not impossible. As we will see, religion has a central role in the political culture of the United States. Throughout American history, elected officials have sprinkled their public statements with God talk, biblical references, and religious appeals. Almost every political speech seems to end with some version of "God bless America." Most Americans expect their leaders to evoke biblical imagery and religious themes, so politicians comply. Not all voters appreciate such public displays, but they likely cannot escape the pervasive reach of religion. If voters react against politicians' overt religious appeals, ironically they too are demonstrating how religion affects their political behavior.

Most fundamentally, religious beliefs provide a basis for morality. Just as religious teaching is helpful for discerning right from wrong in one's everyday life, so religion can offer a framework for evaluating a legislative proposal, comparing candidates for office, or assessing the latest actions of the local school board. Even those who do not identify with a particular religion still uphold some form of moral code that, much like an explicitly religious worldview, will affect their evaluations of political questions.

Honoring God in Faith and Politics

So how should a Christian approach faith and politics in a pluralistic democracy? If religion really affects our views of politics

Religious Appeals in Presidential Speeches

Throughout history American presidents have employed religious imagery to communicate with the American people, especially in times of crisis. Here are a few examples:

Rarely are we met with a challenge, not to our growth or abundance, our welfare or our security, but rather to the values and the purposes and the meaning of our beloved Nation. The issue of equal rights for American Negroes is such an issue.

And should we defeat every enemy, should we double our wealth and conquer the stars, and still be unequal to this issue, then we will have failed as a people and as a nation. For with a country as with a person, "What is a man profited, if he shall gain the whole world, and lose his own soul?"[2]

—Lyndon B. Johnson, Special Message to Congress: The American Promise (asking for passage of the Voting Rights Act), March 15, 1965

The crew of the space shuttle *Challenger* honored us by the manner in which they lived their lives. We will never forget them, nor the last time we saw them, this morning, as they prepared for their journey and waved good-bye and "slipped the surly bonds of earth" to "touch the face of God."[3]

—Ronald Reagan, Address to the nation on the *Challenger* disaster, January 28, 1986

Let us teach our children that the God of comfort is also the God of righteousness. Those who trouble their own house will inherit the wind. Justice will prevail.

Let us let our own children know that we will stand against the forces of fear. When there is talk of hatred, let us stand up and talk against it. When there is talk of violence, let us stand up and talk against it. In the face of death, let us honor life. As St. Paul admonished us, let us not be overcome by evil, but overcome evil with good.[4]

—Bill Clinton, speech honoring those killed in the Oklahoma City bombing, April 23, 1995

The course of this conflict is not known, yet its outcome is certain. Freedom and fear, justice and cruelty, have always been at war, and we know that God is not neutral between them.

Fellow citizens, we'll meet violence with patient justice—assured of the rightness of our cause, and confident of the victories to come. In all that lies before us, may God grant us wisdom, and may He watch over the United States of America.[5]

—George W. Bush, Address to the Nation (in response to the events of September 11), September 20, 2001

but we don't all share the same religious views, how do we reach enough agreement to govern effectively? Although the context of American politics makes it difficult to reach democratic consensus, I believe that Christians can serve important roles in shaping and guiding both politics and the wider culture. These beliefs lead to my third assumption, one based not on my understanding as a political scientist but instead on my perspective as a Christian.

The Ultimate Christian Calling Is to Love God and Follow Him

Although cultivating an understanding of politics and government is an indispensable tool for civic engagement, politics should never be an end in itself. Political power is enticing and potentially very dangerous; the lure of power can quickly turn us away from serving God. In politics, as in all endeavors, Christians must not lose sight of their ultimate purpose to love God and follow him.

In his classic writing *On Christian Teaching*, Augustine writes to a young church trying to interpret Scripture correctly and avoid heresy. At the heart of his argument, he extols love as the guiding principle of Christianity, reminding his readers of Jesus's explanation when asked what was the greatest commandment: "'Love the Lord your God with all your heart and with all your soul and with all your mind.' This is the first and greatest commandment. And the second is like it: 'Love your neighbor as yourself.' All the Law and the Prophets hang on these two commandments" (Matt. 22:37–40). Keeping in mind what Augustine calls the "double love" of God and neighbor will help Christians discern God's truth from false teaching and provide a guide for Christian thought and action.

A Blueprint for Politics in the Old Testament

When seeking guidelines for engaging with the political system in ways that honor God and demonstrate love for our neighbors, we need not look any further than the Ten Commandments. The first commandment calls us to worship God alone, and the second follows from it, prohibiting idolatry:

> You shall have no other gods before me. You shall not make for yourself an idol in the form of anything in heaven above or on the earth beneath or in the waters below. You shall not bow down to them or worship them; for I, the LORD your God, am a jealous God, punishing the children for the sin of the fathers to the third and fourth generation of those who hate me, but showing love to a thousand (generations) of those who love me and keep my commandments.
>
> Exodus 20:3–6

Only the one true God is worthy of worship, yet other gods capture our attention and seem to take his place. Political power is one such potential idol. If Christians lose confidence in God's sovereign control and instead place their primary confidence in politics as the path to cultural restoration, they make government into an idol.

Likewise, the third commandment reminds us of the power and holiness of God and his perfect name: "You shall not misuse the name of the LORD your God, for the LORD will not hold anyone guiltless who misuses his name" (v. 7). Far more than just an indictment of swearing, this commandment warns against invoking God's name for anything that is not truly from him.

Instead of using God's name in an attempt to validate merely human pursuits, we should follow the principles of the third commandment, using God's name with utmost care and reverence. As one expositor noted, "God's answer to a world that blasphemes His name is a community who honors His name. Honoring the Lord's name is our highest calling. Christ will be honored when the world sees a community of people who show awe and affection for Him."[6] In politics, as in all spheres of life, we should honor God and serve as a light to the world.

A Blueprint for Politics in the New Testament

In much the same way that the first three commandments offer principles to guide Christians in approaching politics and government, New Testament passages provide important insights. Many commentators rightly direct Christians to Paul's discussion of authority in Romans 13: "Everyone must submit himself to the governing authorities, for there is no authority except that which God has established. The authorities that exist have been established by God. . . . Give everyone what you owe him: If you owe taxes, pay taxes; if revenue, then revenue; if respect, then respect; if honor, then honor" (vv. 1, 7). This passage is instructive and important to help us understand God's provision for government, but when I am asked what biblical text I find most useful for developing a Christian approach to politics, I point to a different passage: 1 Corinthians 12 and 13.

In his first letter to the Corinthians, the apostle Paul exhorts and instructs the church in Corinth, a church struggling with internal division and with a culture that places great value on status and power. As one commentator describes, "Paul's purpose is not to correct their theology but to get them to think theologically so they would respond properly to their polytheistic, pluralistic culture."[7] We too can find guidance in this letter to help us think theologically about interactions with politics and government.

Chapters 11 through 14 of the letter offer Paul's teaching on worship, living in community, and spiritual gifts. He is concerned that some in the church are too prideful, and he writes to correct them. In a short digression from the specific topic of spiritual gifts, Paul reminds the Corinthians of the centrality of love as a guiding principle for interaction with God and with one another. Toward the end of this famous description of God's unconditional love, Paul exhorts believers:

> Love never fails. But where there are prophecies, they will cease; where there are tongues, they will be stilled; where there is knowledge, it will pass away. For we know in part and we prophesy in part, but when perfection comes, the imperfect disappears. When I was a child, I talked like a child, I thought like a child, I reasoned like a child. When I became a man, I put childish ways behind me. Now we see but a poor reflection as in a mirror; then we shall see face to face. Now I know in part; then I shall know fully, even as I am fully known.
>
> And now these three remain: faith, hope and love. But the greatest of these is love.
>
> 1 Corinthians 13:8–13

Even as we are reminded of the power and depth of God's love, we are also cautioned about our human limitations. We should not get trapped in spiritual pride, Paul warns, for we all "see but a poor reflection as in a mirror" (v. 12). Our own sinfulness and the fallen state of nature cloud our vision. We can claim the promise that we will one day "see face to face" and "know fully," for everything will indeed be clear once we are in God's eternal presence. But in the meantime, life this side of heaven will be marked by ambiguity and uncertainty.

A Framework for Thinking about Politics

So how might politics look different if viewed through the prism of the first three commandments and 1 Corinthians 12 and 13?

Let me suggest four principles to guide Christians developing a framework for thinking about politics.

1. We all *"see but a poor reflection as in a mirror"* and therefore should exercise genuine humility when discussing politics.

When politicians speak, they typically speak with great certainty and clarity. We expect our elected officials to act decisively, and their rhetoric reflects these expectations. But certainty can quickly devolve into arrogance, especially when combined with religious language. Critics will often say of someone who holds an opposing view: "Who does she think she is? God?"

Paul's teaching to the Corinthians suggests a very different framework for talking about politics. If indeed we know in part and we see in part, it follows that a Christian perspective on politics should begin in a context of love and humility. As limited humans, we don't have all the answers. Instead of cloaking our politics in arrogance, we should approach this subject, as all others, with awareness of our limits and with reliance on God's love and wisdom. We can speak from our religious convictions in a context of love and humility, arguing our views with passion but also respect for others.

2. The diversity of the body of Christ makes room for Christians to disagree on many political matters.

God creates each man and woman as a unique bearer of his image, giving each person a distinct set of talents that glorify him. As Paul reminded the church in Corinth, "In fact God has arranged the parts in the body, every one of them, just as he wanted them to be. If they were all one part, where would the body be? As it is, there are many parts, but one body" (1 Cor. 12:18–20). We are created to live and serve in community, so it makes sense that Christians work best when they combine their perspectives and gifts to work together for the common good. Each person can offer a valuable contribution.

Since we all have imperfect knowledge this side of heaven and we are each created to serve different functions in the body of believers, it follows that Christians may disagree on political issues. One person might have a special concern and care about education, while another is a strong advocate for the environment, and yet another has a passion for tax policy. We can celebrate these passionate concerns as gifts from God.

Let's take the argument even further. Perhaps God even impresses on the hearts of two Christians political views that seem, from our limited perspective, to be in direct opposition to one another. Through constructive dialogue and honest listening, Christians with opposing political views can sharpen one another and help inform each other's political perspectives. Think of how discussions of politics within our churches would change if we started conversations with the recognition that our own view on a political issue is imperfect, and that other people who hold a seemingly opposing view might also have insight due to their gifts from God.

3. The label "Christian" is for God and his work, not to validate human endeavors like politics.

Responding to the question of whether Christians in the United Kingdom should start a Christian political party, C. S. Lewis answered an emphatic no. Invoking the third commandment, Lewis noted the danger of misusing God's name by labeling a particular political group "Christian":

> The principle which divides [a "Christian" party] from its brethren and unites it to its political allies will not be theological. It will have no authority to speak for Christianity. . . . It will not simply be a *part* of Christendom, but *a part claiming to be the whole*. By the mere act of calling itself the Christian Party it implicitly accuses all Christians who do not join it of apostasy and betrayal. It will be exposed, in an aggravated degree, to that temptation to which the

Devil spares none of us at any time—the temptation of claiming for our favourite opinions that kind and degree of certainty and authority which really belongs only to our Faith.[9]

When we label as Christian that which is not from God but from our own limited vantage point, we claim for ourselves an authority that rightfully belongs to God alone.

The label "Christian" is also dangerous in that it uses God's perfect name as a descriptor for something imperfect. In my work on Capitol Hill, I occasionally encountered activists from "Christian" groups behaving in ways that maligned the name of Christ. In one particularly embarrassing episode, representatives of a Christian interest group came to thank a congresswoman for her sponsorship of legislation important to their agenda. At the start of the meeting, the congresswoman inadvertently offended the organization's leader by asking her to introduce herself. The simple question so wounded the leader's pride that she instructed an assistant to call the office and cut off all further cooperation and communication with the congresswoman and her staff. This encounter with public Christians was a harmful witness; indeed, the incident turned the label "Christian" into an object of ridicule among some staff members.

4. Politics can and should be a means for demonstrating love in action and building the body of Christ.

Unfortunately, far too many discussions of Christianity and politics end in shouting matches instead of constructive dialogue. An environment that encourages simplifying controversies into two positions, "us" versus "them," creates instant enemies, as if anyone expressing an opinion on a political question must be preparing for war. When Christians speak hatefully of another believer, they sin against their Christian brother or sister and erode the unity of the church. When Christians speak with hatred toward someone outside the church or intentionally cause dissension, they harm the reputation of the church as a community of love in the world.

Instead of demonizing those who disagree with us, we should approach them in Christian love. In this age of negative campaigning and personal-attack politics, it is almost impossible to imagine a political world modeled after the love described in 1 Corinthians 13. How would the tenor of politics change if political opponents actually interacted with patience, kindness, trust, and hope? How different would political advertisements look if they did not "delight in evil but rejoice[d] with the truth"? Although Christians are not likely to change the nature of political discourse overnight, it is indeed possible and commendable to justify political positions in a manner that is not boastful, self-seeking, or rude. If Christians viewed politics as a means for demonstrating love in action as a witness to the world, the nature of political discourse could change. More important, we could live the gospel by demonstrating the transformative power of love in action. Politicians might not be as successful on the campaign trail, but then again, winning office is not the ultimate goal of the Christian life.

Where Do We Go from Here?

Having explained my assumptions and offered a framework to help Christians approach politics, it is time to look at the journey ahead. The next two chapters bring a few more basics to the table. Chapter 2 highlights the benefits of compromise. Chapter 3 discusses the use and misuse of ideological labels.

Once we have these basics behind us, we'll move to part 2 of this book. In chapter 4, we'll look back to the founding of America and consider some of the arguments for and against the concept of the United States as a Christian nation. Chapter 5 looks at more recent history, describing various relationships between religion and voting.

Do you ever wish that you had a better understanding of the difference between the Senate and the House of Representatives or how legal cases make it to the Supreme Court? Just in case you weren't giving your undivided attention in government class or you need a quick refresher, part 3 gives you a crash course in American politics. Chapter 6 explains why the United States has a two-party system and why that matters, tracing the recent rise in partisanship among elected officials. Chapter 7 introduces separation of powers, comparing the strengths and weaknesses of the three branches of the federal government. Chapter 8 reveals common myths about the Constitution and separation of church and state, explaining what the Constitution really says about religion and politics and why the Supreme Court is so influential on this topic.

Part 4 will give you tools and resources to help you apply your faith to politics in constructive ways. Chapter 9 presents and evaluates different Christian approaches to politics and to the relationship between the church and the state. Chapter 10 discusses the roles of ends and means when tackling political problems and offers suggestions for fostering constructive political dialogue. Chapter 11 looks at a complex public policy problem, poverty, as a case study to show different ways Christians might address a political issue. Chapter 12 offers a few pointers before you go to the ballot box, suggesting ways to evaluate candidates and campaigns to help you make an informed voting decision. As voting is only one way to participate in American politics, chapter 13 looks at other practical ways your faith can inform your political activity.

After that whirlwind tour of Christianity and politics, we'll slow down the pace a bit in chapter 14. In looking back on our journey, this final chapter will conclude with a few more reflections on how we can truly love God and neighbor through political words and deeds.

Political scientist Harold Lasswell inadvertently created a new definition of politics with the subtitle of his classic book first published in 1936: *Politics: Who Gets What, When, and How.* At its core, politics is all about people and meeting their needs, so politics and government offer Christians a means to live out the commandment to love our neighbors. In the pages that follow, you will learn more about American politics and ways your faith can inform your participation in it. By the time you reach the end of this book, my hope is that you will be better equipped to serve God and others. So let's begin.

2

When It's No Sin
to Compromise

From Black-and-White to the Real World

All legislation, all government, all society is founded upon the principle of mutual concession, politeness, comity, courtesy; upon these everything is based. . . . Let him who elevates himself above humanity, above its weaknesses, its infirmities, its wants, its necessities, say, if he pleases, I will never compromise; but let no one who is not above the frailties of our common nature disdain compromises.

Henry Clay (1777–1852),
speaker of the house and secretary of state

Those who are prone by temperament and character to seek sharp and clear-cut solutions of difficult and obscure problems, who are ready to fight whenever some challenge comes from a foreign Power, have not always been right. On the other hand, those whose inclination is to bow their heads, to seek patiently and faithfully for peaceful compromise, are not always wrong. On the contrary, in the majority of instances they may be right, not only morally but from a practical standpoint. How many wars have been averted by patience and persisting good will!

Sir Winston Churchill (1874–1965),
British prime minister

In January of 2001, in the wake of the roller-coaster presidential election results and the contentious Florida recount, I began work on Capitol Hill as a legislative aide. The U.S. Senate was split evenly between the two parties, with fifty Republicans and fifty Democrats; Republicans controlled my side of the Capitol complex, the House of Representatives, by a razor-thin margin. Tensions between the two political parties were high.

Entering the fray was my boss, newly elected Republican Melissa Hart, who had just arrived in Washington DC after serving a decade in the Pennsylvania senate. Although the political environment was difficult, she was determined to work across the party aisle and find ways to partner with Democrats on issues of mutual concern. One issue of particular concern to Hart and her constituents was abortion. Hart had already established a strong pro-life voting record, and she wanted to continue pressing this agenda in the House of Representatives.

Although pro-life and pro-choice activists fundamentally disagree on issues such as legal access to abortion, Hart knew from experience that people could work together across political fault lines and find areas of common ground. Concerned about incidents of parents abandoning their babies, leaving helpless infants to die if not discovered in time, Hart asked me to help her write legislation designed to stop this horrific practice and help parents in crisis.

Hart eventually introduced a bill, the Safe Havens Support Act, which drew support from some of the most conservative and some of the most liberal members of the House. Many passionate pro-life and pro-choice legislators were willing to work together to support a cause with which they all agreed: saving the lives of newborns. A few interest groups objected to the bill; one pro-family organization claimed it encouraged infant abandonment. But most saw the bill as its author intended—as a good-faith effort from people on both sides of a controversial issue who could work together on a problem of mutual concern.

Hart succeeded in shepherding the key provisions of the Safe Havens Support Act through the legislative process; they eventually became law. Although her work on this bill required compromise and willingness to work with legislators who held very different views, the compromise achieved important goals. Hart didn't find a way to end the practice of abortion with this particular bill, but she never compromised her pro-life commitment. By seeking common ground, she found a way that she and those who appeared to be her political opponents could work together and save lives.[1]

Black, White, and Shades of Gray

Some observers of the political process argue against political compromise, contending that devotion to a cause requires a firm stand. But the case of saving abandoned infants is just one example of seeking common ground and holding firm to principles at the same time. Why are so many people opposed to compromise? Is it possible to hold strong convictions but also be willing to bargain? In this chapter, we'll consider first why the combination of faith and politics seems to make compromise so troubling, and then we'll explore some situations in which compromise may be the best means for loving God and neighbor.

Religion in Black-and-White

Religious identity cuts to the very heart of who we are and how we view the world. It provides a foundation for morality, offers answers to questions about the meaning of life and death, and shapes our views of how we should interact with one another and with the divine. Religious views offer a framework for determining what is true, beautiful, and good, so many people naturally think and talk about religion in black-and-white terms.

Religious worldviews often make truth claims, and some truth claims are by definition exclusive. This is certainly the case with Christianity. Jesus teaches with the strongest of moral clarity, stating emphatically, "I am the way and the truth and the life. No one comes to the Father except through me" (John 14:6). Not only does he *speak* truth, Jesus also tells his followers that he *is* truth. As the incarnate Son of God, he has the ultimate authority, offering the gift of salvation and providing the foundation for Christian morality. The vantage point of Christian belief often presents two options: God's way or the wrong way.

Although religion often appears black-and-white at first glance, the application of divine teaching is rarely so straightforward. We need only look to church history to see this principle in action. From as far back as New Testament times, groups of believers have split over differing interpretations of how to live out the faith. It is all too easy to confound the moral clarity of the Word of God with flawed human attempts to apply biblical principles to everyday living.

Political Ideology in Black-and-White

Just as religion engenders deeply held values, so can political or ideological identity signal deeply held beliefs about the world and one's place in it. Political ideology reflects and shapes our understanding of the role and functions of both the government and the private sector, provides a framework for prioritizing political problems, and offers guidance for what government should (or should not) do to address issues. Chapter 3 will talk about political ideology in greater depth.

For many Americans, political views are in part inherited, passed from generation to generation. Families and peers contribute to political socialization—that process through which each person first learns about government, political parties, candidates for public office, and the role of elected officials. For example, while some people can recall talking about politics at family meals from their earliest memories of childhood, others may have equally vivid memories of never discussing politics.

Especially for people schooled in a particular political ideology from birth, political perspectives may be part of their identity. It is no wonder that many people hold black-and-white views of politics. They know what they believe, and they hold strong convictions.

Practical Politics in Shades of Gray

Although many people perceive their own religious and political views in black-and-white terms, the everyday practice of politics is shaded with gray. At its heart, politics is the result of compromise; it is a rather messy process of give and take. Ultimately, people resolve extreme differences one of two ways—through violence or through politics. Thus, the real work of politics is seeking common ground, finding a way for people of various and often widely divergent beliefs to live peaceably with one another. When viewed through this prism, compromise, the central mechanism of politics, can be an instrument of love.

In a modern democracy like the United States, elected officials must work together to craft acceptable solutions to complex problems, bargaining and compromising as needed to create policies that at least a majority can support. At the same time, elected officials juggle multiple responsibilities. They need to represent broadly the concerns of their entire constituency—not just the people who voted for them or agree with them—while being responsible to listen to their own conscience.

The framers of the Constitution would be proud—they designed our system of separate institutions sharing power to be slow and deliberate, and they succeeded. If you think of how long it can take three or four people to agree on a DVD at the local video store, imagine the complexity of getting 218 or more members of the House of Representatives, or even just 60 senators, to agree on the exact wording of complex legislation! Add in the president, who must also concur, and one begins to wonder how any bill ever becomes a law.

Politics is all about managing competing interests. To begin with, legislators must try to balance their personal values and perspectives with the needs of their constituencies. At the same time, voters, interest groups, businesses, and other concerned activists exert pressure on elected officials to address their particular needs. All of these different voices raising competing concerns create an intense and high-pressure environment. In the end, policymakers must reach a decision through bargain and compromise, creating policy that accomplishes some of their goals but is unlikely to satisfy everyone.

Black-and-White Ideals in a Gray-Shaded World

If indeed many people perceive religion and politics in black-and-white terms and the day-to-day work in politics necessarily involves shades of gray, it's no wonder combining these subjects can create such tension. When passionate activists with deeply held beliefs about right and wrong pressure legislators working in an unwieldy democratic system that succeeds primarily through compromise, the sparks are sure to fly.

To complicate matters, many politicians and political activists intentionally frame issues with sharp contrasts as a technique to rally their supporters and gain credibility. If voters begin to perceive a political issue as a moral question, their concern and engagement

Voting Your District or Voting Your Conscience?

Elizabeth Anne Oldmixon's book, *Uncompromising Positions: God, Sex, and the U.S. House of Representatives*, examines how legislators approach three categories of moral issues—abortion and reproductive policy, gay and lesbian rights, and school prayer—on the congressional agenda. Her findings suggest that many members of Congress weigh voting decisions on so-called moral issues differently than other policy issues. Consider how one Republican representative explained how he decides which way to vote:

> If my district indicates, and I have a pretty good idea that this is a fair representation of my district, if they indicate somewhere between 45 and 55 percent on a certain issue, I vote the way I want to. If it gets between 40 and 45, 55 and 60 percent on an issue, I begin to really weigh what they think,

if it happens to be different from mine. I factor that in. If it's over 60 percent I factor what they think heavily into my decision-making process, and if it's more than that I generally vote with them. . . . But on moral issues, this is the thing that I am getting to: I decided before I came [to the House of Representatives] that I was going to vote exactly the way I thought I should vote, regardless of what everyone thought about it, and let the chips fall where they may.[2]

Oldmixon's interviews with legislators suggest that most lawmakers defer to their own values and beliefs when deciding how to vote on moral issues such as abortion and gay rights. These findings highlight an interesting irony: outside pressure on legislators seems to be least effective precisely where voters and activists are most passionate and strident.

with the issue will likely intensify. Similarly, when leaders argue their case with moral clarity and impassioned speech, citizens are more likely to respond. Conservative activist Paul Weyrich described this phenomenon from his own experience building support for political causes: "One thing I had learned over the years is that if you sound as if you are morally certain, people will tend to believe you. So whether or not I know what I am talking about, I always try to sound morally certain."[3]

Finding a Way Forward: Thinking about Compromise

Given the potentially combustible combination of religion and politics, Christians should approach these realms with great care. If indeed our goal is to love God and neighbor as we consider these issues, in what ways might we want to rethink our views of compromise? In what ways can we hold to black-and-white truths in a political arena shaded with gray? Let's begin with a few basic pointers.

1. Recognize that religion and politics will often exist in tension.

Perhaps the first step is admitting the problem. As Christians, we should expect our religious beliefs and principles to inform our societal perspectives, so our faith will likely have an important influence on how we view political problems. But if we bring simplistic black-and-white views into a complex process shaded with gray, tension is inevitable.

People motivated by strong religious convictions can indeed have a significant influence on politics, but they must work within the confines of our pluralistic democracy. Even if motivated to action in pursuit of what we think is right, we must keep in mind the demands of the democratic political arena. Not everyone will share the same views, so policymakers will reach their decisions by weighing many competing interests, including ours. Furthermore, elected officials often need to negotiate and bargain. If we enter the political arena expecting lawmakers to translate our specific views directly into public policy, we will almost always leave disappointed. If instead we keep in mind that compromise is likely necessary to reach peaceable agreements, we are more likely to accept the tensions inherent in the process.

2. Government cannot solve every problem, but it can help with some.

Similarly, we need to recognize and accept the limits of government itself, not expecting more from the political system than it can offer. Government has already fixed the problems that are easy to solve. For example, Americans take for granted access to drinking water, public utilities, and a sophisticated transportation network of highways, railroads, and airports. The issues that remain on the political agenda are therefore the most complex and vexing problems that likely do not have simple, straightforward solutions. Government cannot solve every problem, nor should we expect it to do so. But government can address certain issues and provide services better than any other institution.

Perhaps the first question we should ask when seeking a political solution to a problem is: "Is this a problem government *should* help address?" Certain categories of issues seem a natural fit for public policy. National security, public health and safety, and infrastructure such as roads and bridges are three examples of collective goods government provides for the benefit of all. In general, we can think of law and policy as regulating simply those areas of life that affect the public good, leaving individuals otherwise free to live their lives as they choose. For example, the state does not require that I drive a car or tell me what kind of vehicle I should purchase, but it does make provisions to ensure that I know how to operate a car, that I follow traffic regulations designed to make the roads safe, and that I carry insurance in case I damage someone else's property.

A second question worth asking follows from the first: "Is this a problem government *can* help address?" Government power, at its heart, orders our communal lives by compelling behavior and punishing those who disobey. Through the creation and enforcement of law, government attempts to compel action. Laws regulate behavior, but they cannot control hearts and minds. Unfortunately, many people look to the political process to solve problems that it has no ability to address. In their zeal for what is right and true, some Christians blur the distinctions between the kingdom of God and the kingdom of man, expecting more of government than it can deliver. As the late Congressman Paul Henry observed:

> Nothing is so frustrating to me as a public official as to hear the clergy decry the "decline of values in our society," and turn to the Congress for social salvation! The role of government—at least in a constitutional system—is not that of "making new men," but addressing the conflicts between them. Government is not responsible for the human condition, it responds to it.[4]

Government cannot change hearts, but God can and does. We need to approach politics with keen awareness of the strengths and limits of democratic government, not expecting more from the political process than is possible.

3. We can uphold truth in an arena of compromise.

The limited role of government and the need for bargaining to reach democratic compromise create frustrations for many

Christians seeking change. In particular, a central tension for many is finding a way to uphold truth in an arena of compromise. If the Bible teaches truth and provides a moral framework for ordering life, don't Christians risk abandoning their principles if they enter the political arena?

Although some forms of compromise are indeed problematic, at its core the principle of working alongside others to reach agreement and solve problems can be a practical way to demonstrate love for neighbor. Much of the suspicion of compromise likely stems from confusing compromise on public policy with compromise of one's principles. In the political arena, where bargaining is often necessary, elected officials often conclude that getting part of what they want is better than nothing at all. Political observers Stephen Monsma and Mark Rodgers call this type of bargaining a "half-a-loaf compromise" and contend that such deals are often necessary in a fallen and imperfect world. Legislators who choose such tactics need not compromise their fundamental beliefs, nor do they necessarily lose sight of God's truth. As Monsma and Rodgers explain:

> God's word is truth. Biblical principles are absolute. But our applications of God's truth are often fumbling and shrouded in the fog produced by extremely complex situations, missing facts, and the pressures of limited time. All this means that when one is asked to compromise by accepting only some of what one is seeking to achieve, one is not being asked to compromise absolute principles of right and wrong. . . . One is being asked to compromise groping, uncertain applications of biblical principles.[5]

In many situations, Christians will seek change based on principles grounded in biblical truth. Yet even when we know our principles are right, we still must apply them in the context of an imperfect political system with finite knowledge, seeing only "a poor reflection as in a mirror."

At times, however, elected officials face temptation to put aside their moral and ethical principles in order to achieve personal or political gain. If, for example, a legislator trades votes with a colleague, agreeing to support a bill that goes against her beliefs in order to secure that fellow legislator's assurance of his vote for her bill, she has sacrificed her principles for political gain. This type of compromise is very different and dangerous. Instead of

Compromises to Save Lives: The Global HIV/AIDS Pandemic

Estimates of the prevalence and scope of the global HIV/AIDS crisis are staggering. More than forty million people currently live with the disease. In the coming year, another five million will likely contract the virus, and an estimated three million will die from complications from AIDS. With no known cure and with many of the world's poor unable to access treatment, contracting the virus is a death sentence.

Assessing the gravity of the current situation, a report from the President's Emergency Plan for AIDS Relief noted, "Prevention represents the only long-term, sustainable solution to turn the tide against HIV/AIDS. Treatment and care are necessary, vital, life-extending services that greatly mitigate the impact of HIV infection and AIDS. But unless the world can reduce the number of new infections, we will be running a race we cannot win."[6] Indeed, almost all experts agree that the only hope for curtailing the loss of life is preventing infections in the first place.

But consensus quickly erodes when discussing prevention programs. Because AIDS is a sexually transmitted disease, the three most common steps toward prevention are promoting abstinence, encouraging sexual fidelity, and distributing condoms to the most vulnerable and those likely to engage in risky behavior. The Christian who believes that abstinence outside of marriage is God's plan will likely support the principles behind the first two steps but may disagree in principle with the third. Yet another principle is also at stake—the belief in the sanctity of human life. Since condoms help save lives by reducing the risk of transmission by 80 to 90 percent,[7] perhaps compromise makes sense. So-called "compromise," in other words, sometimes can actually promote balance between biblical values on occasions when they appear to be in tension.

For some of those most at risk of infection—young girls and women forced into prostitution, spouses of an infected partner, victims of abuse—abstinence is likely not an option; access to potentially life-saving protection offers some defense from further victimization. In such cases, providing condoms seems a small compromise in the name of human dignity.

Considering condom distribution for others at risk because of their own lifestyle choices raises more difficult moral questions. Yet even in this case, the "compromise" of one set of important values for the goal of saving lives seems worth the price.

upholding the principle of love for God and neighbor, the legislator is willingly acting against what she believes is right, exchanging the truth for a lie. The political world is full of temptations; many principled men and women have justified unethical behavior with claims of serving a greater good. Such abandonment of principles in the name of compromise is perilous.

As we have seen, compromise can be a tool for good or a pathway to temptation and sin. Not all compromise is wise or God-affirming, but many forms of day-to-day bargaining are actually opportunities to love our neighbor by seeking solutions to problems and serving others. Seeking the compromise necessary to maintain a functioning democracy is rarely easy, but it is an essential task.

With these reminders about the complexities of politics and some of the ways to love God and neighbor in our political endeavors, we are almost ready to begin our journey through the contours of American politics. But before we begin thinking about how to apply our own religious views to politics, one more background piece remains: learning the vocabulary. It is to this essential task that we now turn.

3

Is *Liberal* a Bad Word?

Understanding Political Labels

If you take away ideology, you are left with a case by case ethics which in practice ends up as me first, me only, and in rampant greed.

Richard Nelson, U.S. playwright

A liberal is a person who believes that water can be made to run uphill. A conservative is someone who believes everybody should pay for his water. I'm somewhere in between: I believe water should be free, but that water flows downhill.

Theodore H. White, political journalist

When visiting a foreign country, travelers may encounter difficulties if they cannot speak or read the native language. Even the most mundane tasks—asking for directions, reading traffic signs, or ordering from a menu—can become quite complicated in a different tongue. So it is with politics. Just as tourists find knowledge of a foreign language helpful for their travels, so outsiders to the political system would benefit greatly from learning at least some of the language of politics.

American politics has its own lexicon; that is, elected officials, journalists, and other political observers use various phrases and jargon to explain political activities and experiences. At just that moment when the public finally becomes comfortable with a term, politicians are likely to craft new phrases, replacing old words with new ones. Adding to the bewilderment, a word used in one context may have a different or even opposite meaning in another context. To help you better understand American political lingo, this chapter explores the meaning of some common political labels.

Is Ideology in the Eye of the Beholder?

Chapter 2 briefly described the role of political ideology, which refers to a set of values and beliefs about politics and government that provides a framework for approaching politics. Theoretically, ideology is consistent and stable: a person's views hold together tightly and coherently, remaining the same for a lifetime. In practice, however, most people's belief systems are not so well defined. Some people discover that their political views change over time. Others may hold consistent ideological views about one set of policies yet seem to have haphazard, unrelated perspectives on other issues. Many may not know or care about every issue that arises along the political spectrum.

Part of the confusion likely is due to inconsistencies in public discussions of ideology. The terms and definitions used vary over time and across political issues. For example, the hallmarks of a political conservative were somewhat different four decades ago than they are now. Meanwhile, "liberal" has become such a loaded term that many politicians now prefer to speak of "progressive" views instead.

In the Beginning . . . We Were All Liberals

Perhaps the place to begin our discussion of ideological labels is with the founding of America. At that time, liberalism was the political philosophy that inspired the demand for democracy. Drawing from the writings of John Locke, Thomas Hobbes, John Stuart Mill, and other Enlightenment philosophers, liberalism emphasized the rights of individuals, free markets, and limited government. As one political scientist explains:

> Originally the term Liberal referred to the political and economic ideal of liberating individuals from unrepresentative and arbitrary governments. Early liberalism set in motion patterns for the rule of law that would guarantee individual rights, representation in law making, access to the courts, and protection of private property.[1]

Almost all Americans are liberals in this original usage of the term. Rejecting monarchy or totalitarian power, we believe in limited government whose authority comes directly from the people. Although modern-day liberals and conservatives will disagree on the scope and role of government and on many specific policies, almost all maintain support for liberal government in this classical sense.

With roots in the Progressive Era reforms at the turn of the twentieth century, and culminating with Franklin D. Roosevelt and the New Deal coalition, the meaning of the term *liberal* was redefined to describe the ideology typically associated with the Democratic Party. Now the word *liberal* had two possible meanings. To resolve this confusion over the use of terms, most contemporary observers describe the liberalism associated with America's founding as *classical liberalism*.

How Ideology Works Today

The two most common ideologies in contemporary American politics, liberalism and conservatism, both draw upon the broad principles of classical liberalism. As we will see, these variant perspectives differ in their emphasis on liberty or equality, the role of government in society, and the role of private enterprise.

On the Right: Contemporary Definitions of Conservative Ideologies

According to strict definition, *conservatives* want to "conserve" things as they are; that is, they seek to preserve established tradition and advocate incremental change only when necessary. Conservatives place great value on individual rights and responsibilities. Holding a more pessimistic view of human nature, they are likely to view government as a necessary evil to preserve law and order. From this viewpoint, government best serves the people by restraining evil, protecting citizens, and providing laws and moral codes that serve as a foundation for society. Otherwise, government should leave the people free to make their own choices. If individuals make poor decisions, they must accept the consequences.

Conservatives are often suspicious of government trying to do too much, generally preferring free enterprise over government regulation, and advocating lower taxes. According to this perspective, markets serve a positive role in restraining unwise business practices; too many government policies may interfere with free enterprise and harm the economy. To the extent that government is necessary, the decision making should be as close to the people as possible to protect their freedom. Thus, conservatives typically prefer that state and local governments have more control than the federal government. Traditionally the party of businesses, lower taxes, law and order, and a strong defense, the Republican Party is the most natural home for conservatives in the United States.

To the political right of conservatism is *libertarianism*, a political philosophy that opposes almost all government regulation. Libertarians uphold the supremacy of individual freedom, maintaining that each person should have the liberty to do anything that does not take away the liberty of others. As such, libertarians advocate freedom of markets and of individual choices. A traditional libertarian would therefore disagree with government programs that redistribute wealth to aid the poor as vehemently as they would dispute laws regulating narcotics or abortion.

Adherents of another variant of political conservatism in the United States are the *neoconservatives*, often called *neocons*. The origin of the term is a reference to liberals who became conservatives;

however, in contemporary usage the word is typically connected to a particular set of policy views. In general, neoconservatives favor tax cuts in the name of economic growth, distrust international institutions, and support an aggressive foreign policy that places a high value on spreading democracy.[2]

On the Left: Contemporary Definitions of Liberal Ideologies

Liberals, in the contemporary usage of the term, emphasize community and equality, typically holding a more positive view of government than conservatives. This viewpoint argues that individuals on their own will not necessarily act in ways that serve the common good, so government is necessary to promote equality and justice. Government is a positive institution for change; public policy is an instrument to help institutions and individuals make progress. Thus, liberals advocate an approach to governing that addresses structural and institutional problems in society—problems they contend will not go away without government help. As such, liberals support government policies and programs to meet essential needs such as education, health care, and housing. Believing that unchecked free enterprise fosters inequality, liberals are likely to favor market regulations designed to protect workers, civil rights, and the environment. Given its history of implementing broad-based government programs, the Democratic Party is the natural home for most liberals.

In recent years, the term *liberal* has become more politically charged. Conservative candidates and media personalities have found great success demonizing the word, so many left-leaning politicians now try to avoid it. Because of their ideological emphasis on progress, some traditional liberals prefer the label *progressive* as a better descriptor of their views.

To the political left of liberals are *socialists*, who advocate greater redistribution of wealth and increased government control of the economy. In contrast to liberals who advocate working within the market economy, socialists believe that the means of production should be under community, or government, ownership and control.

In the Middle: The Role of Political Centrism

Although not an ideology in the technical sense of the term, some elected officials and many voters are *centrists*, or moderates;

that is, their view of government and political issues tends to be in between that of conservatives and liberals. As we will see in chapter 7, the number of moderate elected officials, especially within the House of Representatives and the Senate, has declined sharply in recent decades. Among everyday Americans, however, an increasing number find themselves between the two major ideologies. Not comfortable with the labels *conservative* or *liberal*, such voters may describe their political views as *moderate*.

Political centrism in the Unites States typically takes one of two forms. Many people are centrists because they find that their political perspective generally falls between liberals and conservatives on most issues. Such moderates seek to find a "middle way" with public policies, trying to find a balance between alternatives supported by strong partisans on either side of a debate. A second form of political centrism includes those whose views differ from issue to issue, who advocate a more liberal policy to address one problem but hold conservative views for others. Those in this category are liberal *or* conservative, depending on the issue, so they may find that their beliefs defy any simple ideological categories.

Many ideological moderates do not describe themselves as Democrats or Republicans, preferring instead the descriptor "Independent." In practice, however, survey data show that most Independents tend to vote fairly consistently with a party, even if they are unlikely to accept the party label.

By the Numbers: Ideology and the American People

So how do the American people describe themselves? Do these ideological labels work in practice? To answer these questions, we can look to the American National Election Study, a nationwide survey that political scientists have conducted every two years for more than half a century.

In one question, the survey asks respondents to place their political views on a seven-point scale ranging from extremely liberal to extremely conservative, with "moderate, middle of the road" in the center. To discourage people from giving a reply when they don't actually have an opinion, the survey asks, "Where would you place yourself on this scale, or haven't you thought much about this?" The data suggest that some Americans have difficulty identifying with this terminology. Since the survey began including the question in 1972, an average of one in four respondents say they have not thought enough about ideology to place themselves on the scale. The responses of those who do choose an ideological label have remained quite consistent over the past twenty years. About 25 percent describe themselves as liberal, about 40 percent identify as conservatives, and the remaining third say they are moderates.[3]

The same survey also asks participants the question, "Generally speaking, do you usually think of yourself as a Republican, a Democrat, an Independent, or what?" Respondents seem to find this question easier, with almost everyone providing an answer. In the 1950s, slightly less than half of the respondents said they were Democrats, slightly more than one in four were Republicans, and about one in five described themselves as Independents. Over the past few decades, the patterns have shifted slightly as more Americans describe themselves as Independents and fewer say they are Democrats. The average result from the past decade of surveys suggests that 35 percent of Americans describe themselves as Democrats, 27 percent as Republicans, and 37 percent as Independents.[4]

These data suggest that more Americans can connect their political views with a party than with a political ideology. Furthermore, the data show a fairly even distribution of political views—no single party or political ideology dominates.

The Problem with Labels

Ideological labels can be helpful for understanding basic differences between political perspectives, but, like so many other ways that people tend to categorize and stereotype, such terms have only limited usefulness. First and foremost, labels can be reductionist. Because words like *conservative* and *liberal* describe a complex and diverse set of ideas, if we are not careful, we can distort and obscure their meaning. Particularly in the midst of heated political debate, some will use ideological labels as weapons, attempting to discredit an opponent with a dismissive turn of phrase. Following the command to love God and neighbor, we should exercise great caution when using simple labels to describe complex ideas.

Another problem with ideological labels is that their meaning and application can vary over time and across issues. Consider a few examples. The party of Abraham Lincoln, the Republicans, was the party of civil rights for almost a century. By the mid-1960s, however, the issue positions reversed, with the Democratic Party becoming the strongest advocate for civil rights. Traditionally, conservatives favor limited government and local control, whereas liberals prefer a more active government with policies that reach broadly across the nation. In the contemporary debate over abortion and gay marriage, however, the roles sometimes reverse. Conservative activists back constitutional amendments to define marriage across the nation, while liberal activists promote local gay rights ordinances. Supporters of the conservative, pro-life position advocate more government regulation of abortion, just as those on the liberal, pro-choice side of the debate argue for individual freedom. As these examples illustrate, many political issues do not fit neatly into either a conservative or a liberal box.

Another possible source of misunderstanding is the emergence of competing ideological camps within each of the major political parties. Because the United States has a two-party system (we'll talk about this in more depth in chapter 7), both the Republican and Democratic parties seek to build broad enough coalitions to win the support of a majority of Americans. Some voters care most about abortion, sex education, gay marriage, and similar debates over so-called social issues. Others are most concerned about tax policy, trade, and government budgeting—what we often deem economic issues. Yet a third camp gives priority to foreign policy, viewing relations with other countries and international institutions through an ideological lens. Thus, party leaders must work to appeal broadly to several different camps of conservatives or liberals. Such outreach is not without cost, however, as broad coalitions will likely include groups of supporters with competing interests and concerns. Activists who connect to a party because of shared values on social issues may end up fighting against those concerned most about economic issues, vying for the party's attention and resources. Party infighting between the different camps further muddles the practical meaning of ideological labels.

To add to the confusion, the words *liberal* and *conservative* are also used to label theological positions, potentially leading Christians to believe that they should approach their faith as if it were a political ideology. (We explore the use of theological labels in more depth in the sidebar "Same Words, Different Verse.")

Same Words, Different Verse: Theological Labels

We use words like *conservative* and *liberal* in multiple ways and in many situations. Much like in politics, theology has a prominent place for these labels, all too often for the sake of attacking opponents.

Liberal theology is a fairly precise term referencing a particular school of thought that originated in Germany and Britain during the late 1700s and early 1800s. Celebrating God-given human freedom, liberal theologians felt that certain traditional Christian doctrines needed some reinterpretation. Moreover, Christians needed the freedom to reinterpret the Bible so that their teaching could account for developments in modern science.

A key foundation for liberal theology was the doctrine of creation. Accounting for the possibilities of reason meant focusing on what was universal. For example, if people could agree on certain basic beliefs that every rational person should hold, then that might reduce religious warfare caused by particular disagreements. Liberal theologies therefore celebrated God as the one Creator of all. They handled the identities of Jesus Christ and the Holy Spirit, along with issues of salvation, in a variety of ways—tending, though, to emphasize human dignity in their interpretations.

From a traditional Christian perspective, the weaknesses of liberal theology became clear over time: a tendency to lose the doctrine of the Trinity in favor of Unitarianism, a tendency to keep reinterpreting more and more traditional beliefs, and a tendency to be too optimistic about human nature (especially in light of two world wars). Some wanting to critique liberal theology described their own views as "conservative." Beyond association with orthodox Christian beliefs, the label *conservative* is also used by more progressive thinkers to attack those with whom they disagree.

Because the terms *liberal* and *conservative* are used in both politics and theology, many people confuse the two or assume that they must go together. Although many theological conservatives are politically conservative as well, the two perspectives are distinct and need not be interrelated. In addition, there is now so much variety within liberal theology (as well as within the more conservative counterparts) that these labels often may be more confusing than clarifying.

Daniel J. Treier

On one hand, this is indeed true and even inescapable, as the Christian faith provides intellectual and ethical guidelines useful for evaluating and interpreting all other ideologies. On the other hand, if we try to apply our faith in such a way that it becomes just another form of political ideology, we risk confusing divine teaching about Christian life and service with specific prescriptions for crafting public policy.

Christians and Ideology

As we have seen, political labels can create a useful framework for thinking about public policy. At the same time, however, they are often the source of confusion and divisiveness, which can quickly get in the way of our love for God and our love for neighbor. Looking beyond labels for others and ourselves is important to our Christian witness, for it reflects a commitment to seeing one another as bearers of God's image.

Stereotypical assumptions about others based on their political ideology—or even just how others label them—fall short of the command to love our neighbors. Instead of quickly dismissing people because they do not appear to share our views, engaging them in meaningful conversations will allow for dialogue and foster mutual respect. Similarly, we should refuse to use labels in a demeaning or insulting manner. Glib remarks such as "conservatives hate poor people" or "those godless Democrats" make a mockery of broad categories of people, showing contempt instead of love for others. Former Republican senator John Danforth reflects on some problematic uses of ideological labels in the church, explaining:

> The problem is not that Christians are conservative or liberal, but that some are so confident that their position is God's position that they become dismissive and intolerant toward others and divisive forces in national life. . . . It is no advance to supplant the self-confident religious agenda of the Right with a religious agenda of the Left.[5]

Ideological commitments in and of themselves are not problematic. The problem arises when ideological labels create a barrier between us and those we are called to love and serve in God's name.

In the same way that we should exercise caution when interacting with people who may not share our views, so should we be careful about the role of political labels in our own lives. Ideology and its role in structuring political perspectives can be powerful and enticing. Such frameworks offer quick shortcuts for choosing sides on political issues and for selecting candidates. But the quest for ideological purity can supplant the desire to serve God first in our political discussions. Thus, engaging in an ongoing process of self-reflection will help us to determine which is coming first: our Christian commitments or our ideological commitments.

These first chapters provided a framework for beginning the task of making some sense of American politics. The next three sections of this book will give you more tools to help you approach politics first and foremost as a follower of Christ. With the basics behind us, we are ready to look to the past—first to the American founding and then to more recent elections—to learn more about the relationship between religion and politics in the United States.

PART 2

LOOKING BACKWARD

HINTS FROM HISTORY

4

Is the United States a Christian Nation?

Separating Truth from Myth

Christians rightly aspire to be salt and light in the world and to counteract the evil of their day. But mistaken views of history frustrate, rather than aid, the fulfillment of these aspirations.

Mark Noll, Nathan Hatch, and George Marsden

God, country, community. These are quintessential American consistencies, quintessential American prayers, and they point up the nation's strengths as well as its fault lines. . . . These incantations are important not because they are true but because their performance is so consistent, so popularly sanctioned. Their regular pursuit makes a people a people and gives them political identity.

Roderick Hart, *Campaign Talk*

The front page of a Sunday edition of the *New York Times* (July 30, 2006) ran a story that captured media attention nationwide. Laurie Goodstein told the story of Rev. Greg Boyd, a pastor from suburban Minneapolis, whose teaching from the pulpit drove almost one thousand of the church's five thousand members to leave the church.

What was the subject of the six-part sermon series that sent almost 20 percent of Boyd's congregants packing? In his words, Boyd sought to "expose the danger of associating the Christian faith too closely with any political point of view, whether conservative or liberal."[1] He argued that the idea of a Christian America was a myth and that the church was losing its focus on the gospel message, allowing patriotism and desire for political power to devolve into idolatry.

Clearly Boyd's views on Christianity and politics touched a nerve. Interpreting his preaching as arguing against good citizenship or as an indictment of the Republican Party and conservative political positions, many families left. Others expressed appreciation at hearing a message they thought was long overdue.

The controversy ignited by Boyd's sermon series helps illustrate the power of Americans' beliefs about God and nation. For many, notions of citizenship and religion are so deeply interconnected that it is all but impossible to think of one without the other. This chapter looks back in history for evidence of Christian imprints on American government, helping you separate truth from myth. After considering the historical record on the role of religion in the founding of America, we will explore the notion of civil religion and its continued influence—both positive and negative—on American politics.

Religion and the American Founding

Depending on your sources, you are likely familiar with one of two competing narratives about the founding of America. Proponents of the Christian America thesis thread together a vast array of quotations in books and multimedia presentations to make their central claim: the United States is a Christian nation founded by committed believers following God's direction. As one pastor argues:

> There is no doubt that this is indeed a nation that was built upon a foundation of faith and the belief that the Lord is indeed the God of this nation. The great charters and founding documents proclaim that America was conceived upon the principles of God's Word,

upon the teachings of Christianity, and for the advancement of the kingdom of Christ. But all of that is under attack today, as it has been for at least three decades.[2]

Because opponents of Christianity want to remove all influence of America's Christian heritage and values, adherents explain, faithful Christians must join together to reclaim our godly heritage and thus renew society.

Opponents of this perspective contend the founders could have created a Christian government but intentionally did not. For example, Americans United for Separation of Church and State maintain: "The U.S. Constitution is a wholly secular document. It contains no mention of Christianity or Jesus Christ. . . . Had an officially Christian nation been the goal of the founders, that concept would appear in the Constitution. It does not. Instead, our nation's governing document ensures religious freedom for everyone."[3] According to Cornell professors Isaac Kramnick and R. Laurence Moore, "The U.S. Constitution, drafted in 1787 and ratified in 1788, is a godless document. Its utter neglect of religion was no oversight; it was apparent to all."[4] The framers debated both the role of religion in the new republic and if the new document should mention God or Christianity, a discussion that Kramnick and Moore label "one of the most important public debates ever held in America over the place of religion in politics. The advocates of a secular state won, and it is their Constitution we revere today."[5]

As Christians, what should we make of these competing narratives that appear to have such power over Americans? In what ways, if any, might it be accurate to describe the United States as a Christian nation? To answer these and related questions, we need to look at the historical evidence from the time of the founding. In particular, this chapter will consider what is known about the religious beliefs and practices of the Founding Fathers as well as the religious imprints they left on the government they formed.

Faith and the Founding Fathers

The Founding Fathers—those men who encouraged revolt against Great Britain and gathered to debate and craft the earliest documents of American government—were not a monolithic group. The founders shared many general goals and a broad outlook; they valued ideals such as personal liberty, equality, rights of the individual, respect for the common person, governmental checks and balances, and popular sovereignty (the concept that government gets its power from the people). Collectively they worked to achieve these common goals, but individually they differed in priorities and held a range of views on the best way to form a government. They found inspiration in various places—some in personal religion, others in political philosophy, still others in the promise of human reason. Attempts to generalize about the motivations or values of such a diverse group of people will inevitably fall short.

Numerous authors have written about the faith of the Founding Fathers with varying levels of academic precision and faithfulness to the historical record. Some writers simply count religious-sounding words in speeches and letters, as if word count alone could determine one's religious outlook. The Bible was a common text in colonial times; almost everyone would have recognized biblical allusions and religious imagery. In much the same way that people today quote lines from popular movies and television shows, so would the colonists have referenced and quoted the Bible as a shared, familiar source.

In colonial America, as in modern times, more people professed belief in God than actually practiced a particular religion.

Although only God can know what a person truly believes, we can devise ways to examine the historical record and make reasoned judgments about a person's probable religious views. Religious historian David Holmes suggests a four-part classification scheme for reaching such conclusions about the Founding Fathers: (1) look at their actions, especially the frequency of their church attendance; (2) look for evidence of participating in the sacraments, notably confirmation and communion; (3) measure the extent of religious activity or inactivity; and (4) consider their use of religious language.[6]

The overwhelming consensus of those scholars who evaluate the faith of the Founding Fathers by careful examination of their words and actions is that few, if any, of them would qualify as "evangelicals" in the current use of the term. Some of the Founding Fathers appear to have held orthodox Christian beliefs, but most of the Founding Fathers (including the most famous) are best described as Deists in some form. In modern usage, Deism refers to a belief in a distant god who created the universe, set things in motion, and no longer intervenes. At the time of the founding, however, Deism was a growing movement, one that typically included five elements: "(1) there is a God; (2) he ought to be worshipped; (3) virtue is the principal element in this worship; (4) humans should repent of their sins; and (5) there is a life after death, where evil will be punished, and the good rewarded."[7] Many Deists believed in some of the general tenets of Christianity, especially traditional Christian morality, but they disavowed the particulars such as the divinity of Christ, the doctrine of the Trinity, and divine revelation.

The historical evidence suggests that many of the Founding Fathers did not hold orthodox Christian beliefs, but most of them appear to have shared general beliefs in God, the sinfulness of humanity, the need for repentance, and an afterlife. A range of religious ideas and values likely had a profound influence on their viewpoints and the government they established, but a careful review of the historical record finds little evidence that the United States was founded to be an explicitly Christian nation.

Christian Influences on the Structure of American Government

Even though orthodox Christianity was out of favor with most of those who helped craft the Constitution, several central concepts borrowed in part from Christianity and its doctrines had a profound influence on the structures of American government. Consider a few examples.

Covenant theology has been imprinted on American politics since the earliest stages of colonization. The idea of individuals entering into a covenant for self-government follows from the idea of covenants with God and from social contract theory, which suggests that people willingly accept the restrictions of government to establish order and meet societal needs. In somewhat the same way that the sinner receives eternal life through a covenant with God, so could individuals agree to contract with government to provide for the common good. The very first formal document in American political history (and the first historical template for a written Constitution), the Mayflower Compact of 1620, was a covenant between God and the Puritan settlers and between one another, establishing their government.

The two most foundational documents in American government, the Declaration of Independence and the Constitution, reflect aspects of covenantal theology. The Declaration includes several deistic mentions of God, referencing "the separate and equal station to which the Laws of Nature and of Nature's God entitle them," describing the people as "endowed by their Creator with certain unalienable Rights," and closing "with a firm reliance on the protection of Divine Providence." Although the Constitution never directly mentions God, it does create an agreement between the people and their government that many approach with a sense of sacred obligation.

Another significant Christian principle, the doctrine of human sinfulness, was an important premise for the design of governing institutions. The founders believed that government was necessary to control sinful people, but they also mistrusted a government that placed power in the hands of sinful people. James Madison outlined this perspective in Federalist #51, an essay written in defense of the Constitution:

> But what is government itself, but the greatest of all reflections on human nature? If men were angels, no government would be necessary. If angels were to govern men, neither external nor internal controls on government would be necessary. In framing a government which is to be administered by men over men, the great difficulty lies in this: you must first enable the government to control the governed; and in the next place oblige it to control itself.[8]

Because of this concern that humans are far from angels, the framers of the Constitution created a multilayered system of government with separation of powers to control a government comprising sinners that, in turn, needed to restrain sinful people. (We will explore these concepts in more detail in chapter 7.)

A third example of Christian influence is the common association of law and morality. Borrowing in large part from the heritage of the Puritans, American politics is "infused with a moral architecture that still guides the conduct of American political life."[10] The political culture places great value on the rule of law: good citizens follow the law, play by the rules, and live upright lives. For many, the law is an important reflection of public morality; laws provide a collective means of determining right from wrong and holding people accountable for their actions. Thus, the stakes seem extremely high in policy debates that advocate legal change. Viewed from this perspective, a proposed statute to legalize gay marriage would not be merely an issue of changing the legal standing of particular couples; its passage or failure would represent a public statement about the morality of homosexual behavior.

Religion in the American Political Culture

As we have seen, the system of government created in the Constitution drew upon both secular and religious ideas. Some of the Founding Fathers appear to have been deeply religious men, while one or two others renounced almost all formal religious beliefs. Although the idea of recapturing the explicitly Christian heritage of the United States is based largely on myth, in certain important ways the United States can be described loosely as a Christian nation. Notions of God and country abound in the United States. Politicians and everyday Americans speak of God's provision and blessing. Many civic ceremonies and government activities begin with prayer, and many houses of worship display the flag. In these and other ways, religion continues to shape and define American identity.

The Influence of Civil Religion

Likely the most enduring imprint of religion in American politics is the cultural phenomenon scholars call *civil religion*. Examining references to religion in political speech throughout American history, renowned sociologist Robert Bellah explained, "The words and acts of the founding fathers, especially the first few presidents, shaped the form and tone of the civil religion as it has been maintained ever since. Though much is selectively derived from Christianity, this religion is clearly not itself Christianity."[11]

The term *civil religion* originated in the writings of political philosopher John Jacques Rousseau. Offering a contrast to theocracy, Rousseau advocated dividing the basic elements of religion into two parts: those held in common as a nation and those held privately as individuals. Civil religion, from his perspective, includes those "social sentiments" that serve the collective good by providing a basis for good citizenship and respect for the rule of law:

> The dogmas of civil religion ought to be few, simple, and exactly worded, without explanation or commentary. The existence of a mighty, intelligent and beneficent Divinity, possessed of foresight and providence, the life to come, the happiness of the just, the punishment of the wicked, the sanctity of the social contract and the laws: these are its positive dogmas. Its negative dogmas I confine to one, intolerance.[12]

The other aspect of religion—what Rousseau calls the *religion of man*—includes one's more particular beliefs, that is, a person's individual identity with a specific religion and its doctrines. According to Rousseau, states should allow individuals freedom of religion "so long as their dogmas contain nothing contrary to the duties of citizenship."[13]

Although the American system does not follow the exact pattern Rousseau described, we do have a long tradition of civil religion. In particular, Rousseau's description of two kinds of "religion"—which distinguishes personal religious beliefs from national, nonsectarian beliefs, rituals, and creeds—is a foundation of the American political culture. As two religion-and-politics scholars explain: "At the core of the rich and subtle concept of civil religion is the idea that a nation tries to understand its historical experience and national purpose in religious terms."[15] What this means, in practice, is that most Americans overtly or inadvertently appear to mix religious notions into their understanding of national identity, combining religious or transcendent ideas with the concept of a secular state. Civil religion is not a formal written statement of what a nation or government believes, nor is it a government-sanctioned church. Instead, the concept refers to a shared understanding of citizenship and patriotism that uses religious language and symbolism without direct ties to one particular religion or sect. Thus, when we refer to the Constitution as a "sacred" document or express concern over the

Code Words or Culture?

During the 2000 presidential campaign, *New York Times* reporter Frank Bruni wrote a piece describing candidate George W. Bush's folksy affect. As an example of Bush's down-home style and casual talk, Bruni opined: "Mr. Bush also offered an interesting variation on the saying about the pot and the kettle. 'Don't be takin' a speck out of your neighbor's eye,' he told the audience, 'when you got a log in your own.'"[16] What the reporter heard as an "interesting variation" on a common metaphor, most Christians would recognize as Jesus's parable from the Sermon on the Mount. Explaining his use of biblical allusions in speeches, former George W. Bush speechwriter Michael Gerson explained: "I've actually had, in the past, reporters call me up on a variety of speeches and ask me where are the code words. I try to explain that they're not code words; they're literary references understood by millions of Americans. They're not code words, they're our culture."[17]

desecration of an American flag, our patriotism evokes similar emotions as religion.

While we find examples of civil religion throughout American history, the fusion of religion and patriotism escalates at times of crisis and war. The most recent formal additions to the civil religion lexicon came in the 1950s as the Cold War struggle between the United States and the Soviet Union intensified. On June 14, 1954, President Eisenhower signed a bill into law that added the phrase "under God" to the Pledge of Allegiance, reminding Americans of the importance of calling upon God in troubled times: "In this somber setting, this law and its effects today have profound meaning. In this way we are reaffirming the transcendence of religious faith in America's heritage and future; in this way we shall constantly strengthen those spiritual weapons which forever will be our country's most powerful resource in peace and war."[18] Two years later, Congress passed a resolution to replace the original national motto, *E Pluribus Unum*, translated "out of many, one" with a new motto: "In God We Trust."

Recognizing that civil religion is a significant aspect of our political culture does not imply that *all* Americans think of the nation in religious terms, but many or most do, often without even recognizing that they are making such connections. In the aftermath of the events of September 11, for example, we were far more likely to hear and sing the hymn "God Bless America" than the much more secular national anthem.

God Talk and Politics: Religion and Campaigns

Religion also shapes the American identity on the campaign trail. Americans do not all share the same religious values and beliefs, but most appear comfortable with—and may even demand—the subtle infusion of politics with religion. In political campaigns, candidates sprinkle their public comments with references to civil religion, evoking God and country, often to thunderous applause. Most public events and political speeches end with some version of the phrase "God bless America." A large majority of Americans seem to like religious rhetoric. In a 2004 Pew Research Center poll, for example, about a third of the respondents said that "there has been the right amount of expressions of religious faith and prayer by political leaders," and almost as many (31 percent) complained there is too *little* religious expression.[19]

Is religious talk in campaigns something new? To answer this question, political scientist Roderick Hart analyzed the words used in more than twenty thousand speeches, debates, advertisements, and news stories from five decades of campaigns. The results were quite clear: candidates and news coverage in every campaign consistently included references to God, religion, and the Bible. But this religious rhetoric has a particular tone, as if following unwritten rules: "It must be heartfelt but not confessional, frequent but not cloying; pointed but never sectarian. In the United States, at least, political rhetoric must avoid being overly religious, and religious rhetoric overly political."[20] When politicians stray from these expectations, the public notices and reacts negatively—complaining on the one hand if they appear godless or on the other hand if they come off as preachy.

Successful candidates quickly learn that appeals to civil religion are great crowd pleasers, and wise politicians have answers ready, expecting at least a few reporters to ask questions about their religion. Sometimes the preparation backfires, however. During Howard Dean's quest for the Democratic presidential nomination in 2000, he told a reporter that his favorite book of the New Testament was Job.

God and the Bully Pulpit: Religion and the Presidency

Although we can see its elements in every sphere of American politics, civil religion especially shapes public expectations of the president. In speeches and other public appearances, presidents routinely appeal to civil religion and reference divine power; throughout history they have incorporated biblical references into their public addresses.[21] Especially in times of grief or national crisis, the president is expected to calm the nation with comforting religious words and the promise of God's blessing. These expectations are as old as the office. Studies of presidential rhetoric throughout American history reveal fairly consistent patterns of references to God, biblical stories and verses, and other civil religious language.

The American people don't want their presidents just to talk religious talk; they seem to expect presidents to be at least nominally religious and, up to this point in history, to be Christian. Consider the story of Dwight Eisenhower's decision to join a church once he was a candidate: "In 1952 when he began to run for president, he called up Billy Graham and asked him if he should join a church. And Graham told him yes and suggested the Presbyterian Church, and that's how Ike became a Presbyterian."[22] So as not to be seen as making a political statement, however, Eisenhower waited until after the election to be baptized and join the church. Every president yet inaugurated has identified in some way with the Christian tradition and in some manner with a particular denomination. This is likely not just an accident of history, for many Americans seem hesitant to vote for candidates from other religious backgrounds. In a 2003 poll, half of those surveyed said they would not vote for a well-qualified atheist for president, a number that has remained relatively steady for the past quarter of a century. Almost two of five voters (38 percent) expressed reluctance to vote for a Muslim presidential candidate, and one in ten said they would not vote for someone Jewish.[23]

Christian America or American Christianity?

As we have seen, religion has influenced American politics from the founding to the present day—although not necessarily in the ways you might expect. The United States is not nor ever has been a Christian nation in the popular use of the term. Biblical concepts and Christian doctrines were among the many ideas that inspired the Founding Fathers as they crafted a new form of government, and aspects of our religious heritage continue to shape the role and function of governmental institutions. But above and beyond the historical legacy, the most enduring imprint of religion on contemporary American politics has been cultural.

Generic religious imagery has a central and enduring place in American political rhetoric and national observances. Yet it is

A Presidential Prayer

At his first inaugural, Dwight D. Eisenhower began his remarks by reading from a slip of paper he had tucked in his pocket—words aides later told biographers the president penned himself:

> MY FRIENDS, before I begin the expression of those thoughts that I deem appropriate to this moment, would you permit me the privilege of uttering a little private prayer of my own. And I ask that you bow your heads:
>
> Almighty God, as we stand here at this moment my future associates in the Executive branch of Government join me in beseeching that Thou will make full and complete our dedication to the service of the people in this throng, and their fellow citizens everywhere.
>
> Give us, we pray, the power to discern clearly right from wrong, and allow all our words and actions to be governed thereby, and by the laws of this land. Especially we pray that our concern shall be for all the people regardless of station, race or calling.
>
> May cooperation be permitted and be the mutual aim of those who, under the concepts of our Constitution, hold to differing political faiths; so that all may work for the good of our beloved country and Thy glory. Amen.[24]

important for Christians to realize that this public religion is only a pale shadow of the true gospel message. It is easy to confuse these public displays with meaningful Christian faith. When evoking God and country or God and politics, Christians must walk a very careful line. Associating the message of Christ with the actions of a secular state ultimately dilutes the gospel and may adversely affect our Christian witness. It seems wise to approach political discussion with great care and tact, resisting the temptation to play the "God card" as a cover for seeking to further our own political interests.

Like so many other good things, devotion to nation can turn into idolatry. As we will see in more detail later in this book, government has a rightful place, and Christians have a role participating in it. But the temptations are great to look to government as a source of renewal, shifting focus away from the true source of renewal—Jesus Christ and his saving grace.

Having looked at the past for evidence of Christian influence on government, we now move forward on the historical timeline. The next chapter looks at the influence of religion on politics in more recent decades, exploring some of the connections between religion and voting behavior.

5

Are All Christians Republican?

Christians and Voting

Although he is regularly asked to do so, God does not take sides in American politics.

George J. Mitchell, former U.S. senator

America is not like a blanket—one piece of unbroken cloth, the same color, the same texture, the same size. America is more like a quilt—many patches, many pieces, many colors, many sizes, all woven and held together by a common thread.

Jesse Jackson, Address to Democratic National Convention, July 17, 1984

"Where will you spend Sunday morning? Will you go to church or Home Depot? Sing in the choir or play golf? Answer that question and you've given the most reliable demographic clue about your vote on Election Day."[1] In the months leading up to the 2004 presidential election, political journalist Susan Page made this point in one of the many news stories that called attention to a trend in voting behavior nicknamed the "religion gap" or the "God gap." This new term refers to the phenomenon that grew most pronounced in the 2000 and 2004 presidential elections—when frequency of attendance at religious services was a better predictor of how someone would vote than age, income, gender, or education level. Regular churchgoers are likely to be Republican voters; Sunday morning shoppers and golfers are probably Democrats. Although religiosity is only one of many factors that help Americans form their political views, the widening gap in the voting behavior of those who are highly religious and those who are more secular has brought issues of religion into the spotlight of politics in new and important ways.

In this chapter we will explore the emergence of this "God gap" and other ways that religion helps shape the context of American elections. First, we will introduce survey research, the primary means by which political scientists gather information about religion and voting. Then we will look at the data and ask in what ways religion appears to affect voting behavior. Finally, the chapter will consider ways politicians may use religious appeals to attract voters.

Reading the Public's Mind: Measuring Political Attitudes

Before we examine connections between religion and voting, it is probably wise to take a step back and think about how we measure such relationships in the first place. Where do experts get the data to tell us what Americans think about politics? Is this research really reliable?

Opinion polling (also called survey research) is the most common source of data about political attitudes. Starting from the premise that the best way to learn what people think is to ask them, researchers create questionnaires that give respondents an opportunity to express their opinions on a range of topics. Researchers collect data by asking questions about a particular subject of interest—shopping patterns, political beliefs, health and diet, to name a few—and end the survey by asking for demographic information such as age, race, gender, and income. After compiling the data, pollsters can group responses by demographic category to look for interesting patterns that may help explain behaviors or trends. A researcher could ask, for example, if exercise rates vary between men and women or if younger or older people are more likely to vote. As we will see, surveys have weaknesses as well as strengths, but they are likely the best tool available for finding out what the public thinks about an issue or policy at a given time.

Scientific Opinion Research vs. Nonscientific "Polls"

Not all surveys are created equal; indeed, the most common "polls" are actually a form of entertainment or marketing, not a scientific measurement of true opinion. When local news programs ask you to call a phone number to register your opinion, Internet websites urge you to click a button in response to a question, or a reality television show encourages you to vote for your favorite competitor, the results of these kinds of "polls" only show a rough estimate of the opinion of those people who had enough interest and chose to respond. A very enthusiastic person may call or click repeatedly, thus "voting" multiple times, as if representing many people. Others who have strong opinions may not have access to a phone or the Internet or may not be aware of the opportunity to express their opinions.

Survey research, in contrast, uses a variety of techniques and safeguards to measure opinion accurately and minimize bias. The essential first step for rigorous data collection is using scientific sampling procedures. All polling begins with identifying the *population* (the group of people whose opinions you want to measure) and then designing a method for choosing a *sample* (a portion of the population who will accurately represent the rest). When a cook stirs a pot of soup and then tastes a spoonful to see if it is warm enough, he can make a good judgment with just one taste. In much the same way, a survey researcher can use mathematical tools to create a sample of adult voters that will allow her to measure the political temperature rather accurately even if asking only a small group of people.

The most common tool for creating telephone survey samples is called random digit dialing (RDD). In this usage, *random* does not mean "haphazard"; the statistical term refers to occurring by chance and without a discernible pattern. Survey researchers use computer programs to generate and dial phone numbers—random sequences of numbers that equalize the possibility of reaching almost any household in the country. Because such scientific sampling gives every person with a telephone the same possibility of inclusion in the group receiving phone calls, a small set of voters surveyed are likely representative of the entire voting population.

The Answer Depends on How You Ask the Question

Survey respondents can answer only the questions asked of them, so the exact wording of polling questions can influence the results. Different polling organizations can elicit seemingly contradictory results by asking about related issues in different ways. Consider the following survey questions on attitudes toward abortion, both asked to a nationwide sample of adults in January 2006. [2]

According to this question, a majority of Americans (53 percent) described themselves as pro-choice on abortion:

"With respect to the abortion issue, would you consider yourself to be pro-choice or pro-life?"

Pro-Choice:	53%
Pro-Life:	42%
Mixed/Don't Know/Unsure:	5%

Source: CNN/*USA Today*/Gallup Poll, Jan. 6–8, 2006. N=1,003 adults nationwide. Margin of sampling error +/- 3 points

A different survey asked respondents their views on abortion, giving three possibilities—making the procedure generally available, restricting it more, or not permitting abortion at all:

"Which of these comes closest to your view? Abortion should be generally available to those who want it. OR, Abortion should be available, but

under stricter limits than it is now. OR, Abortion should not be permitted?"

Generally Available	38%
Stricter Limits	39%
Not Permitted	21%
Unsure	2%

Source: CBS News/*New York Times* Poll, Jan. 20–25, 2006. N=1,229 adults nationwide. Margin of sampling error +/- 3 points

Respondents to this question needed to answer based on their own knowledge of existing abortion restrictions, and they did not have the option to say that they wanted to continue existing abortion policies. The reported results of this survey could vary widely: one activist could interpret these results to say that 77 percent of Americans want abortion to be legal and thus are "pro-choice"; another could rely on the same data to say that 60 percent of Americans favor stricter limits on abortion and thus are "pro-life."

A third survey conducted about the same time also probed abortion attitudes, again offering no response for keeping the status quo while offering different options:

"What is your personal feeling about abortion? (1) It should be permitted in all cases. (2) It should be

By definition, samples include part but not all of the population. Survey researchers compute a statistic called *margin of sampling error*, which estimates the difference between the "true" answer if everyone in the population were polled, and the reported answer based on just the sample of respondents. Although this is not the

▶

permitted, but subject to greater restrictions than it is now. (3) It should be
permitted only in cases such as rape,
incest and to save the woman's life. OR,
(4) It should only be permitted to save
the woman's life."

Permitted in All Cases	27%
Greater Restrictions	15%
Rape, Incest, Woman's Life	33%
Only Woman's Life	17%
Never (vol.)	5%
Unsure	3%

Source: CBS News Poll, Jan. 5–8,
2006. N=1,151 adults nationwide. Margin
of sampling error +/- 3 points

Note how the slight wording change shifts the pro-choice response: results from the previous survey suggest that 38 percent of Americans support making abortion "generally available," but only 27 percent in this study agreed with the more absolutist wording that abortion "should be permitted in all cases." Analysts could interpret these results to show that 55 percent of Americans are strongly pro-life or that 70 percent support the pro-life cause of increasing abortion restrictions. The broadest interpretation of the results finds only 42 percent of Americans holding pro-choice views, an exact reversal of the pro-choice/pro-life self-identification question in the CNN/*USA Today*/Gallup poll.

only source of potential error in surveys, it is one that can be quantified based on the size of the population and the size of the sample. Reputable pollsters always report the margin of sampling error. A common margin, +/– 3 points, means that researchers are 95 percent confident that the "true" response of the entire population is within a range of 3 percentage points higher or lower than the number reported in the poll. Thus, a survey reporting that 52 percent of Americans support a particular candidate is saying that the true level of support is very likely within the range of 49 to 55 percent. In very close elections, the differences between the candidates are within the margin of sampling error; although media reports may claim one person is leading the other, survey researchers would tell you the race is a statistical dead heat.

Another hallmark of scientific survey research is *uniform administration*, which means that every survey should be distributed in the same way, asking the same questions and following the same procedures. Some pollsters train teams to ask questions in person, others to mail written questionnaires to the members of the sample, and still others to conduct phone interviews. To keep the procedures uniform, however, pollsters should choose one format for everyone. Differences in wording can also have powerful effects on responses (see the sidebar "The Answer Depends on How You Ask the Question"), so surveys need to ask each question with the same wording, and typically in the same order, for each respondent. If each person hears or reads the same questions presented in the same format, the results will be more trustworthy.

Are Poll Results Reliable?

Perhaps the best way to evaluate polls is to ask if they appear to work. The answer seems to be a qualified yes. In the past few decades, results of most reputable preelection polls have a solid track record of predicting outcomes within the margin of sampling error. It is important to remember, however, that polling is not a perfect science; the results give us good measures of opinions and attitudes, but there remains plenty of room for error. The famous photograph of a triumphant Harry S. Truman holding up the *Chicago Tribune* emblazoned with the headline DEWEY DEFEATS TRUMAN is a reminder that pollsters can miss the mark. Although survey methods have improved greatly in the intervening decades, even the best polling organizations will make mistakes.

In general, when evaluating polling data, look for reports from reputable survey research companies that will uphold the highest standards of professionalism. All of the major national news organizations hire such companies to conduct surveys on their behalf, so the data they report are usually reliable though still subject to interpretation. If you read a report about a recent poll that says nothing about the sample size, margin of sampling error, dates conducted, and other basic methodological information, be wary of the source.

By the Numbers: Religious Identity and Voting Behavior

Having briefly explored the hallmarks of survey research, we are now ready to use polling data to understand more about religion and politics. Does religion have much of an impact on voters' choices? Do Catholics, Protestants, and Jews tend to vote alike? Recent data comparing voting patterns of different religious groups will help answer these and related questions. As we will see, religious identity does appear to influence the choices voters make at the ballot box, although it is only one of many factors that affect people's vote.

As survey research has developed, researchers have improved the quality of their surveys, refining question wording and adding new questions to learn more about respondents' opinions. Questions about religious belief and practice reflect this trend. Early polls asked very few religion questions; a typical survey would offer voters only a short list of choices, asking if they were Protestant, Catholic, or Jewish. In the past few decades, scholars of religion and politics have convinced survey organizations to expand their questionnaires to provide more detailed data on religion. As a result, several of the most important sources of political opinion data go more in depth with religious questions, even probing Protestant respondents to name their specific church denomination.

Using these more complete responses, scholars of religion and politics can group voters into different categories of religious adherents. The most common groupings include Mainline Protestant, Evangelical Protestant, Black Protestant, Catholic, Jewish, Other Religious, and Seculars.

The first common category of religious adherents is *Mainline Protestant*. Defined as those who worship in the historic Protestant churches in the United States, this group currently comprises about one-fifth of the electorate. Sometimes called *liberal Protestantism* to signify the dominant theology in these churches, mainline Protestantism includes denominations such as Disciples of Christ, the United Methodists, the Episcopal Church, the Evangelical Lutheran Church of America, and the Presbyterian Church (USA). Churches within this tradition emphasize the role of Jesus as the model for Christian morality and accentuate the need to combat corporate sin, the call to love one's neighbor, and the desire to transform society. Thus, it is not surprising that mainline calls to political action often emphasize social justice, equal rights, and combating racism. The voting behavior of this group in recent elections has been closely divided between the two major parties. An estimated 53 percent of mainline Protestants voted for Bush in 2000; 55 percent of them supported Bush in 2004.[3]

A second group of Protestants, *Evangelicals*, includes almost one of four voters. Although precise definitions of the term vary, *evangelical* usually refers to those whose views include four elements: (1) an emphasis on the personal nature of salvation, (2) belief in the Bible as the ultimate source of truth and authority, (3) an emphasis on the death and resurrection of Jesus Christ,

Religious Data from the 2004 Presidential Exit Poll

A particular type of political survey, the *exit poll*, is an important source of data to help us understand voting behavior. This type of survey gets its name from the way it is administered: when voters exit polling places, a sample is asked to complete a short written form with a series of questions, including how they voted. Media organizations collect and use the data to predict the results of elections before all of the ballots are counted. If the results suggest one candidate has a particularly strong lead, news programs will declare the winner right after the polling places close. Although exit polls generally serve this purpose well, they sometimes fail, as in the 2000 presidential election,

when media organizations falsely declared a winner in Florida.

After the election, researchers examine exit polling data to learn more about who voted for whom and what reasons they gave for their choice. Respondents to polls conducted in the days and weeks following an election tend to slightly overreport voting for the winners; some people seem to want to say that they were on the winning side. Since exit polls are conducted on Election Day at the polling place, participants are more likely to report their voting accurately.

Here are the results of some of the responses to questions about religion, compiled from the exit poll conducted for the 2004 presidential election:

Religion among Whites

	% Total	Kerry Voters	Bush Voters
White Protestant/Other Christian	41	32	67
White Catholic	20	43	56
White Jewish	2	75	24
White something else	4	65	33
White none	8	64	36
Non-white	26	69	29

White Evangelical/Born-again Christians

	% Total	Kerry Voters	Bush Voters
White Evangelical/Born-again Christians	23	21	78
All others	77	56	43

How often do you attend religious services?

	% Total	Kerry Voters	Bush Voters
More than once a week	16	35	64
Once a week	26	41	58
A few times a month	14	49	50
A few times a year	28	54	45
Never	15	62	36

Source: MSNBC politics webpage, data from the National Election Pool Exit Poll, conducted by Edison/Mitofsky. Accessed at http://www.msnbc.msn.com/id/5297138.

and (4) the desire to evangelize, that is, to share one's faith with others. When working with survey data, many pollsters apply the label *evangelical* as a broad, catch-all phrase for theologically orthodox Christians, including evangelicals and fundamentalists. Researchers typically identify evangelicals in one of two ways. Some surveys simply ask respondents if they describe themselves as evangelical or not. More often, though, researchers use church affiliation to categorize evangelicals, selecting respondents from denominations whose teachings generally reflect evangelical principles, such as Assembly of God, Lutheran Church Missouri Synod, Southern Baptist Convention, and Presbyterian Church of America. Compared to their mainline counterparts, evangelical Christians are more likely to emphasize individual sin and each person's need for conversion. Politically, this theological focus often translates into concern for what many call "family values" issues—those issues of moral conduct often connected to individual behavior, such as abortion and homosexuality. In the past two decades, evangelicals have been a very strong voting bloc for the Republican Party. An estimated 68 percent of evangelicals voted for Bush in 2000; in the 2004 election, more than three of four (78 percent) voted to reelect the president.

Because of the unique history and traditions of African American churches, commentators typically separate *Black Protestants* into a distinct religious category representing about 8 percent of the American electorate. Most of the current denominations whose members are predominantly African American arose in response to racial discrimination. Black worshipers who were excluded from religious communities created their own separate churches and denominations by necessity; over time these churches became institutional centers of culture and community for African Americans, offering help to meet their spiritual, material, and social needs. Black Protestants are known for their theological conservatism and political liberalism. Their theological views are closely in line with those of white evangelicals, but their voting behavior is much different. As two sociologists have summarized, "The same religious principles that lead whites to the right lead blacks to the left."[4] More politically conservative on social issues and more politically liberal on economic issues, they have developed into a very solid Democratic voting bloc, which began in the New Deal and solidified by the 1960s, when Democrats emerged as the national party in support of civil rights. In the 2000 election, for example, about nine out of ten black Protestants (91 percent) voted for Al Gore. Perhaps due in part to the attention given to social issues in general, and gay marriage in particular, the numbers dipped slightly in the 2004 election when John Kerry received 86 percent of the Black Protestant vote.

A broad category of Christian voters, *Roman Catholics*, currently comprises about one-fourth of the American electorate. Catholics tend to emphasize family and community as well as deep concern for the poor, generally holding a more positive view of human nature than conservative Protestants. Traditionally a voting bloc that tended to favor Democrats, the Catholic vote has shifted in recent decades so that it is now split more evenly between the two parties. The official teachings of the Catholic Church include issue positions typically connected to the Republican Party (such as opposition to abortion and gay marriage) as well as those more often identified with the Democrats (such as combating poverty and protecting the environment), so neither party reflects most of the official church positions on public policy. Political scientist John DiIulio summarizes the current situation: "Catholics come as close as any religious cohort in the country to mirroring the American electorate politically. Catholics come near to being the nation's typical, average, or—to use the term that many political scientists prefer—median voters."[5] In the 2000 election, 47 percent of Catholics voted for Bush. Although 2004 Democratic nominee John Kerry was a practicing Catholic, his positions on some high-profile political issues differed from his church and may have hurt him in his attempt to appeal to Catholic voters. In 2004, Bush won a slim majority (52 percent) of the Catholic vote.

The final two religious categories include voters who tend to support the Democratic Party. *Jews*, who comprise about 2 percent of the electorate, are a strong Democratic voting bloc. Almost four of five Jewish voters (79 percent) voted for Gore in 2000, and Kerry received 74 percent of their votes.

Although the number of Americans describing themselves as belonging to a religion other than Christianity or Judaism is increasing, their small percentages in surveys provide too few cases to allow for aggregate data analysis. Thus, most political profiles of American voters compare just the five Judeo-Christian groups and seculars.

Secular identifiers—those individuals who say they do not identify with any religion—represent about one in ten voters. (Many calculations add to this group the voters who say they never attend religious services; thus defined, seculars comprise close to 15 percent of the voting population.) Wanting to guard against religious influence on civic and political life, many seculars raise concerns about candidates and campaigns that seem to take political cues from religious leaders. Likely partly a reaction against the Religious Right, seculars tend to vote Democratic, with recent elections showing significant gains for Democrats within this group. In 2000, 61 percent of seculars voted for Gore; Kerry received 67 percent of the secular vote in 2004.

The God Gap

Clearly, religious identity offers important clues about voting behavior, but other related measures are also important in understanding the relationship between religion and voting in the United States. The survey question that is often described by the shorthand phrase *church attendance* asks all voters, irrespective of religious background, how often they attend religious services. As mentioned at the beginning of this chapter, this question has been one of the best predictors of how someone will vote in each of the federal elections since 2000. Christians, Jews, and Muslims who frequently attend religious services are likely to vote for Republicans, and Christians, Jews, and Muslims who rarely or never attend are more likely to vote for Democrats. Journalists coined the catchy phrase "the God gap" to describe this division between voters based on church attendance.

In the 2000 and 2004 presidential elections, for example, more than three of five voters (63 percent in 2000 and 64 percent in 2004) who attended religious services more than once a week voted for George W. Bush, and similar percentages (61 percent in 2000 and 62 percent in 2004) of voters who reported never attending religious services voted for the Democratic candidate.[6] As you can see in Table 5.1, the same patterns hold in congressional elections. The percentages of votes for Republicans increase with frequency of worship attendance, and Democrats receive larger percentages of votes as reported attendance decreases. In addition, the God gap seems to be widening: voters who never attend worship are increasingly more likely to vote Democrat.

Reaching across the God Gap

At times, politicians can find ways to blend religion and politics that overcome partisan stereotypes.

Discussing the God gap phenomenon, Democratic senator Barack Obama argues that his fellow partisans should recognize and even embrace the role of faith in Americans' lives:

> Democrats, for the most part, have taken the bait. At best, we may try to avoid the conversation about religious values altogether, fearful of offending anyone and claiming that—regardless of our personal beliefs—constitutional principles tie our hands. At worst, there are some liberals who dismiss religion in the public square as inherently irrational or intolerant, insisting on a caricature of religious Americans that paints them as fanatical, or thinking that the very word "Christian" describes one's political opponents, not people of faith. . . . But over the long haul, I think we make a mistake when we fail to acknowledge the power of faith in people's lives—in the lives of the American people—and I think it's time that we join a serious debate about how to reconcile faith with our modern, pluralistic democracy.[7]

Speaking to an audience gathered for the Global Summit on AIDS and the Church, Republican senator Sam Brownback spoke against judging others, calling instead for people to work across party lines.

> Now what do we have to do? At a governmental level, we do have to reach across the aisles, and we have to engage. And there's nothing political about dealing with malaria and global HIV. This is just something American and it's something from the church of God here to do. We can do this, and we've got to reach across the aisles.
>
> And I've worked on some topics like this. And it's basically a two step process. Number one, you got to reach out. You got to say, "OK, who is it that's willing to work with me on this topic?" And number two, you've got to look at the other person and instead of us—and this is something I struggle with—judging them, you've got to love them.[8]

Table 5.1
Church Attendance and the Vote for U.S. House of Representatives

Church Attendance	2006 Dem	Rep	2004 Dem	Rep	2002 Dem	Rep
More than weekly	38	60	37	61	37	61
Weekly	46	53	42	57	41	57
Monthly	57	41	50	49	52	46
A few times a year	60	38	55	43	50	47
Never	67	30	60	36	55	41

Source: Adapted from "Religion and the 2006 Elections," Pew Forum on Religion and Public Life, http://pewforum.org/docs/print.php?DocID=174.

This relationship between religiosity and voting behavior has created a stereotype of Republicans as the "party of God" and Democrats as the "party of the godless." Indeed, recent elections show that religious voters now comprise a key Republican voting bloc, and seculars are an equally important part of the Democratic Party coalition. But both parties find pockets of support from active churchgoers and those who never attend. This religious divide means that each party treads carefully. Republicans try to maintain the support of religious conservatives without ostracizing less religious voters who share the party's goals, and Democrats want to communicate with voters in a way that shows respect for religion without pushing away the seculars who provide an important base of party support.

Voting and Religious Groups: Lessons and Limits

Grouping voters by religious tradition can help us understand general patterns of voting and shifts in group allegiances over time, but these data have limits. Aggregate data mask the diversity within religious groups and encourage stereotyping; that is, such results tell us nothing about how a particular person voted, nor do they tell us what all members of a particular religion think. When more than three of four evangelicals cast their ballots for a Republican candidate, as they did in the 2004 presidential election, they indeed comprise a significant component of the Republican political base. But these numbers still leave almost one in four evangelicals who chose the Democrat instead. Even though the white evangelical who chooses a Democrat and the Black Protestant who chooses a Republican cast votes differently than the data would predict, their decisions do not imply that religion is unimportant to them. Believers can and do appeal to the same theological principles yet reach different conclusions about how to vote.

In addition, the five religious categories are very broad and will fit most, but not all, respondents. Most forms of analysis, for example, would incorrectly categorize someone who describes herself as evangelical but attends a mainline church. Other voters may not follow religious cues when voting. Although these and other problems remind us that data sets have limitations, survey research remains a useful tool to help us understand broad connections between religious traditions and voting patterns.

As we have seen, survey research is a helpful (albeit imperfect) tool for measuring political attitudes. Analysis of recent survey data confirms that both religious identity and frequency of attendance at religious services influence voting behavior. Religion helps shape the context, influence the content, and determine the outcome of elections in the United States, so any serious discussion of campaigns and elections that does not consider religious variables will necessarily be incomplete.

Reach Out and Touch Someone: Politicians and Religious Appeals

When 90 percent of American voters identify with a religious tradition, and the data like those presented in this chapter show strong relationships between religious identity, observance, and voting, it makes perfect sense that religion plays an important role in political campaigns. Civil religion is an essential part of the American political culture, so voters expect and even demand that politicians make broad religious appeals. But what happens when candidates reach out to particular groups of religious voters? How might voters respond to and interpret overtly religious rhetoric?

A likely first step is separating generic appeals to civil religion from more direct references to particular religious traditions and beliefs. As described in more detail in chapter 4, generic religious rhetoric is a staple of American political life, as common as campaign signs printed in some combination of red, white, and blue. Appeals to civil religion, such as talking about God's hand of protection or ending a speech with the perfunctory "God bless America," reveal little to nothing about the speaker's actual religious views.

Most politicians will speak about religion in ways that move beyond the typical patriotic gloss. First and foremost, it is natural to expect candidates to discuss their own faith tradition as part of their personal story. In the same way that voters learn about politicians' marital status, education, and family background, so we learn about their faith-oriented activities. It seems reasonable to expect political candidates to be candid about their religious affiliation. On the other hand, politicians' willingness to speak at length about their religious beliefs will vary widely, in part due to political strategy, but also—and perhaps most significantly—depending on their religious tradition. For those steeped in certain denominations that emphasize personal piety, for example, the inner life of a Christian is primarily kept between oneself and God; talking about personal religious practice risks committing the sin of pride. In other Christian traditions, public discussion of personal religion is not only acceptable but even expected as a sign of true commitment and effective witness. When evaluating politicians' religious rhetoric, it is helpful to bear in mind that they may not share the norms of your particular religious tradition.

It makes sense to consider politicians' religious views as one of many factors that may influence your judgment of them. Although you may prefer to support politicians from your religious background, this connection alone may not be sufficient. If a particular candidate appears to share your religious views yet does not hold your positions on most major policy issues, religiosity may not be the most important factor that determines your support. Indeed, it may not even be relevant.

Politicians are well aware of the data on religion and voting behavior; shrewd campaigners design ways to appeal directly to these key voting constituencies. Thus, a great challenge for people

of faith who follow politics is to try to discern the difference between genuine expression and calculated pandering to religious
voters. Unfortunately, this is much easier said than done. One
way to evaluate candidates that may help minimize distortions is
to consider the totality of the evidence. Instead of picking apart a
single speech, event, or advertisement in isolation, it makes sense
to evaluate the campaign as a whole by asking questions such as:
What are the central themes? What kind of tone did the campaign
set? What messages are repeated consistently? After answering
these questions, you may then be in a better position to evaluate the
politician's tone and message in light of your religious values.

As one Christian who both studies politics and advises political
campaigns warned, "Political talk, whether on the campaign trail
or inside government, is not only very cheap, but also not always
highly predictive regarding what people actually believe or really
will do."[9] Successful politicians quickly learn to say what appeals
to voters; translating those words into actions is far more difficult.
This continuous struggle leads to another way to evaluate religious
appeals, one that is effective only after the fact. Once elected officials win office, you can hold them accountable for their actions,
not just their words.

In these last two chapters, we have looked a bit at the past,
considering some of the history of religion in American politics
to help us understand the current political environment. In the
next section of this book, we will focus on the nuts and bolts of
American politics. For those of you who didn't pay attention in
American Politics 101 or may not remember it all, these next three
chapters will reintroduce some of the basics of how our system
operates.

PART 3

HOW IT WORKS

HIGHLIGHTS FROM AMERICAN POLITICS 101

6

Good Guys and Bad Guys?

Understanding Our Two-Party System

The more you read and observe about this Politics thing, you got to admit that each party is worse than the other. The one that's out always looks the best.

Will Rogers (1879–1935)

David Duke, white supremacist and former Ku Klux Klan leader, entered electoral politics in 1975 as a Democrat, running unsuccessfully for a seat in the Louisiana state senate. More than a decade later, he once again sought public office, this time running in a few of the 1988 Democratic presidential primaries. He garnered few votes and little media attention. After this failed attempt, Duke switched to the Republican Party and sought a seat in the Louisiana state house. Republican Party leaders refused to support Duke, campaigning heartily for another Republican who was also vying for the seat. In the end, Duke narrowly won the election, receiving 51 percent of the vote.

Two years later, David Duke ran for governor, again using the Republican Party label. Reporter David Maraniss described the election as "the most closely watched gubernatorial campaign in modern American history," noting the attention given to Duke, "who has emerged as a strong new voice of white racism and economic resentment across the nation and a force within the Republican Party, whose leaders are embarrassed by his past and want nothing to do with him."[1]

In the final gubernatorial election, Louisiana voters chose between the former Klansman and a former governor, Democrat Edwin Edwards, who had been acquitted of racketeering charges two times. A popular bumper sticker at the time summarized a popular sentiment: "Vote for the Crook. It's Important." In the end, Edwards won the governorship.

David Duke's career illustrates one of the peculiarities of political parties in the United States—they are completely voluntary. Anyone can claim to be a Republican, just as anyone can claim to be a Democrat. If, like David Duke, you decide you don't like one party anymore, you can switch allegiance to another at any time. Although party organizations can choose which candidates they assist in campaigns, they have no direct control over individuals who claim their label. Republicans in Louisiana and across the nation disavowed Duke and his controversial views, but nothing could stop him from running for office as a Republican.

Voluntary association—and all of the complications it can create—is just one of many hallmarks of American political parties. What then are some of the other characteristics of parties and the party system in the United States? What are the benefits and drawbacks of party loyalty? This chapter explores these and related questions. After considering the role of parties in elections and government, we will examine some of the reasons why the United States has only two major parties. Finally, the chapter will look at the effect of partisanship on American politics and the challenges it poses to Christians.

Political Parties: What They Are and What They Do

Perhaps the best place to start our exploration of political parties in the United States is with a basic textbook definition, which describes them as "organizations that seek political power by electing people to public office so that their positions and philosophy become public policy."[2] Parties are different from other groups trying to influence politics because their goal is winning office in order to shape public policy. Not content just to communicate their views, parties want to govern. In American government, parties are most significant in helping structure elections and organizing governing institutions.

Parties in Elections

Even though most voters will never see their behind-the-scenes work or realize its importance, parties are central to the election process. As soon as the results of an election are announced, party organizations begin their work preparing for the next one. The first step is recruiting and training strong candidates. Some people decide to run for political office on their own, but often the best candidates are those specifically chosen and groomed by party leaders. Seasoned party operatives know what qualities, background, and experience work best for each elected office; they know what the voters like, and they know the ingredients necessary to win. In the same way that successful college sports programs send scouts to find and recruit the most promising high school players to join their team, effective party leaders look for charismatic and talented men and women whom they can train and mentor to run one day for elected office. Ultimately, a political party is as strong or as weak as its team of candidates for office, so effective recruitment is essential to a party's success.

In preparation for elections, parties help candidates by raising money and mobilizing voters. Even seemingly small races such as those for local office can cost tens of thousands of dollars, so fund-raising is crucial for any campaign. Parties solicit their own donations that can indirectly help candidates, and they connect prospective donors to candidates, helping fill their campaign coffers.

Political parties simplify elections through the nomination process. Most elections in the United States occur in two stages. First, the parties hold contests between party candidates to select one person to represent them. (The sidebar "Narrowing the Field" describes the two most common methods of nominating candidates: primaries and caucuses.) In the second stage, the general election, voters choose from a shorter list of candidates, and the winner assumes elected office. Ballots that list candidates and their party affiliations provide cues to guide voters' decision making. Even if you know nothing else about a candidate except party affiliation, you can make a reasoned choice. In chapter 12, we'll explore in more detail how party labels help voters make decisions.

Narrowing the Field: Primaries and Caucuses

If so many people want to run for Congress or the presidency, how do we narrow the choices? Ultimately, each political party must find a way to select only one nominee to stand in the general election. Although the process is not uniform across every state, the most common methods political parties use to nominate candidates are primary elections and caucuses.

Primaries are in-party elections used to determine party nominees for the general election. A typical primary election would look like this: voters go to the same voting locations and cast ballots in the same manner as they would in the general election. Instead of choosing between the Democrat, the Republican, and nominees from other parties, however, primary voters select from a list of people in the same party. The person with the most votes wins and becomes the party's nominee for the final, or general, election.

Caucuses are party meetings held for the purpose of selecting nominees for elected office. Unlike primary elections where voters show up anytime on a given day and cast their ballots in secret, caucuses meet at a set time (usually on a weekday evening) and are open discussions. Supporters may give speeches in favor of candidates; participants are free to change their minds during the course of the event. When the evening's discussion concludes, registered voters present at the caucus choose a candidate, and the convener records the results.

Sometimes supporters offer incentives that encourage caucus attendees to choose their candidate. For example, at the Iowa precinct caucuses for the 2004 presidential election, Kerry organizers offered bottled water, donuts, and—for at least one gathering—pizza to woo supporters.

Since the 1970s, Iowa and New Hampshire have become extremely important for narrowing the field of presidential candidates. Democratic Party leaders in Iowa scheduled the 1972 caucuses in January, thus making their state first to choose candidates. Once Iowans realized the power of "first in the nation" status, party leaders made sure to schedule their caucuses before any other state. In 1977, New Hampshire passed a law that says their presidential primary must occur at least seven days before those in any other state, establishing a pattern for New Hampshire to hold the first primary.

Candidates also rely on political parties in the final days before the general election to assist with "get out the vote" efforts. Research shows that people are much more likely to vote if they are reminded in the days and hours before an election. Thus, parties and campaigns develop voter databases to identify likely supporters and persuade them to vote. If you have ever wondered why perky volunteers call you on Election Day to tell you the seemingly obvious news that the polls are open, they are part of a voter mobilization effort and have reason to believe you will support their party's candidates. The call is their last effort to encourage more votes for their side.

Campaign organizations can and do work to get out the vote, but party organizations have greater resources and wider reach. Parties want to get their supporters to the polls to support candidates at all levels of office, so their mobilization efforts are likely to span an entire county or even an entire state. The Republican Party, for example, has developed a database called the "Voter Vault," which is described as the most comprehensive collection of voter data ever assembled. The database includes information on an estimated 165 million Americans, with entries ranging from voting frequency and intensity of party loyalty to more esoteric categories like whether or not voters own cabins or boats and what type of car they drive. Individual campaigns could never complete such a mammoth project on their own.

In addition to the practical ways parties participate in elections, they can also serve to unify voters. Parties bring different groups of voters together, building broad coalitions of supporters who collectively have the power to effect change. Although many voters are tempted to focus on one or two particular issues, political parties encourage voters to apply their ideology to a broader range of issues likely to face political decision makers.

Parties in Government

Elections are a means for political parties to achieve their fundamental purpose—making public policy. Once parties succeed in getting their candidates elected, they serve an additional function: organizing government institutions.

First and foremost, parties coordinate the work of government; that is, they provide a system of organization to make it work more effectively. A single individual can do very little in government, but groups of people can accomplish quite a bit. Knowing this law of practical politics, fellow partisans work together to coordinate government activities and achieve their policy goals.

The best example of party coordination is Congress. Members of the House and Senate make their own rules for how they will conduct business, and party is at the center of it all. Legislators have discovered that parties are an effective way to organize each chamber and provide leadership. Before a new session of Congress,

The Power of Party: Tales from the Frontline

Party leaders often apply intense pressure to make sure members vote with them. Consider the experience of two different legislators when the Republican Party held the majority in the House of Representatives.

One member campaigned for the chairmanship of a key House committee. The Republican leadership had implemented new rules to determine committee chairs. Interested members competed for the post by presenting party leaders with their vision for the committee's organization, policy programs, and communications strategy. Although known for his conservative voting record, this legislator was also on the record expressing reservations about key legislation that was slated for the committee's agenda. No surprise to him, he lost the chairmanship race to a more loyal supporter of the upcoming bill.

Another member had received a spot on the coveted Energy and Commerce committee, one of the most powerful committees in the House. As the committee was working on a major bill, the vote was tight. It looked like the bill would need almost every Republican vote to pass favorably out of the committee, so Republican leaders warned their members that they would lose their seats on the committee if they voted against the party. This member of the Energy and Commerce committee, who had serious reservations about the bill, spent a restless night worrying about the vote. The next day he voted against the party's wishes even though he knew he would likely lose his powerful committee assignment as a result. In the end, party leaders did not follow through on their threat, and he remained on the committee.

Threats from party leaders may be empty rhetoric, or they may foreshadow disciplinary actions. But legislators from both parties realize that they risk their power and position when they veer from the party line.

members of each party gather together to select their leaders. Once the session begins, they meet weekly to plan their legislative agenda and strategy. These sessions are so essential that even the members of Congress elected as Independents join with the party closest to their views. The party with the most members, and therefore the most votes, leads the chamber and selects committee chairs.

Because party is the central organizing tool in Congress, each party's leadership has power over its members. Parties bestow or withhold favors—choosing what legislation reaches the floor for debate, helping with fund-raising for the next campaign, assigning members to coveted committees—so members have strong incentives to tow the party line. Members who go against the party do so at their own risk. Former Democratic Representative Jim Traficant learned this lesson. When the House assembled at the beginning of the 107th Congress for the formal vote to elect the speaker, Traficant voted for the Republican's candidate, Dennis Hastert. The Democratic leadership responded swiftly to his recalcitrance, stripping Traficant of all his committee assignments.

Party leaders have many tools to help keep members of their delegations in line, but legislators are free to ignore efforts to pressure them. Because partisan identity is ultimately an individual's choice, leaders must take care not to anger rank-and-file members too much. Elected officials can change party at any time. Senate Republicans saw this danger firsthand when then-senator Jim Jeffords left the Republican Party in May 2001, changing the balance of power in the chamber to the Democrats.

In addition to organizing government, parties also work to translate election results into policy. If you listen to the political analysis in the days following most federal elections, pundits will likely discuss who has a "mandate" from the people to implement new policies. Although analysis of polling data rarely reveals evidence to support such posturing, politicians nonetheless act as if the voters speak collectively through elections in support of particular issue positions. If partisan control of the presidency, the House, or the Senate changes from one party to the other, leaders usually interpret the result as a demand for change. After the Democratic Party won back control of the House and Senate in the 2006 election, for example, newly elected Speaker of the House Nancy Pelosi claimed a mandate. In her first official speech from the rostrum, she trumpeted, "The election of 2006 was a call to change, not merely to change the control of Congress, but for a new direction for our country."[3]

At the same time the party in power tries to carry out its agenda, the party out of power serves as the "loyal opposition," proposing alternative policies, critiquing the current policy agenda, or providing some mixture of the two. Particularly at times when the margin of party control in Congress is slim and presidential elections are decided by tiny margins, members of the minority party look ahead to the next election with the hopes of regaining power.

They Came Two by Two: The Two-Party System

As we have seen, political parties play important roles in structuring American elections and governing institutions. Although they have been a significant factor for most of our political history, the Constitution makes no mention of them. The founders were well aware of parties, but they mistakenly thought the Constitution created a new form of government that would not need or foster the development of parties.

In his Farewell Address of 1796, George Washington made an impassioned call for national unity and a government in service to all. He echoed the sentiments of many who feared the effects of parties, describing them as "likely, in the course of time and things, to become potent engines, by which cunning, ambitious, and unprincipled men will be enabled to subvert the power of the people and to usurp for themselves the reins of government, destroying afterwards the very engines which have lifted them to unjust dominion."[4] Only four years after Washington issued his warning, political parties had already found their way to the center of American politics.

Why Two Parties?

In most democratic countries, multiple political parties compete for power. In the United States, however, only two parties regularly contest elections. Why might this be the case? Although several factors likely contribute to the trend, two factors in particular seem to explain much about the emergence and continuation of the two-party system.

One part of the explanation is the role of tradition. In an ironic twist, the earliest American parties developed along the political lines drawn in the debate over ratification of the Constitution. Supporters of ratification and of a strong central government became the Federalists, and those who raised the most concerns about the Constitution, the Anti-Federalists, formed the basis of the nineteenth-century Republican Party, later called the Democratic-Republicans. In every federal election from 1800 forward, two dominant parties have helped structure American elections. Whenever a third party has emerged to challenge the status quo, it has either been subsumed into one of the two existing parties or has replaced one of them. In either case, the balance of power quickly returns to two parties.

A second contributing factor is the structure of the American political system. Many aspects of our political institutions provide incentives for voters to align their preferences with two, and only two, parties. Elections typically follow the *single member, simple plurality* system. *Single member* means that each electoral district includes only one member. In countries with multiple-member systems, voters choose several people to represent their district. In a three-person legislative district, then, the three candidates receiving the most votes would each win a seat. The second hallmark of our system, *simple plurality*, is often described as "first past the post" and means that the person who receives the most votes wins. A candidate does not need a majority, half plus one, but merely a plurality, more than the others. When you combine these two factors—only one winner and whoever receives the most votes wins—voters and politicians quickly find strong incentives for only two parties. If many parties competed for a single seat, a person could win office with 20 percent, 15 percent, or even fewer votes, leaving most voters without their preferred choice.

The structure of presidential elections also contributes to two-party dominance. As we were reminded in the 2000 election, Americans do not directly elect their president. Although ballots typically list the names of each party's presidential nominee, voters actually choose electors, individuals selected at the state level whom we collectively call the *Electoral College* and who officially select the president.[5] According to federal law, electors gather in their respective states in mid-December for a formal vote. By tradition (and by state law in some cases), the electors cast their ballots for the person who wins the most votes in their state.[6] Each state then sends its results to Congress, where the electoral votes are officially tallied on January 6. On the night of each presidential election, national networks track the results by lighting up large maps of the United States. If the Republican candidate has the most votes in a state, the networks color the state red; if the Democrat secures the most votes, they color the state blue. Once a candidate wins a majority of votes in the Electoral College, the networks declare the winner.

If no candidate wins a majority of votes in the Electoral College, the Twelfth Amendment provides a mechanism for the House of Representatives to determine the winner, an event that has occurred only twice in American history. Many Americans were upset when Al Gore won a majority of the popular vote in 2000 but did not win a majority of the electoral vote. We can only imagine the response if the House were to decide a presidential election now! When more than two serious presidential candidates contend in the general election, the chance of any one winning a majority of the electoral

And Then There Were Two

Political parties may not be mentioned in the U.S. Constitution, but they have been part of the American political landscape since the election of 1796. The present two parties, Democrats and Republicans, have dominated for the past 150 years. Because the structure of our governmental and electoral systems fosters a two-party system, third parties have found limited success. From the inception of our nation, only five political parties have won multiple elected offices, including the presidency.

1. *Federalists* (1792–1816). America's first political party was composed of those who defended the federal Constitution during the ratification debates. This group represented only a small portion of the electorate, however, as it appealed mostly to the educated elite and those of wealthy status in the Northeast.

2. *Democratic-Republicans*, also known as the *Anti-Federalists*, *Republicans*, and *Jeffersonians* (1796–1828). The party of Thomas Jefferson consisted of a majority of small farmers and lower-class citizens who united in collective opposition to the Federalists. They first won the presidency in 1800 and dominated the political scene until the party's dissolution in 1828.

3. *Democrats* (1828–present). Grounded in broad-based, popular political platforms, the Democratic Party originally consisted of less-privileged voters who opposed high tariffs and a national bank while welcoming new immigrants. It remains one of the two major contemporary political parties.

4. *Whigs* (1836–1856). The Whig party won two presidential elections during its short existence and pursued a host of interests first represented in the Federalist party. These included support for nativist immigration policies and the interests of big business.

5. *Republicans* (1854–present). The party of Lincoln was birthed from opposition to slavery as the Civil War approached. It absorbed the issues of big business and property interests from the Whigs. The GOP (Grand Old Party) acts as the primary competition to the Democrats in contemporary politics.

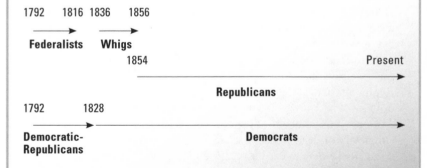

Jonathan Flugstad

votes narrows. When only two major parties nominate candidates, however, we usually know the winner on election night.

Americans are accustomed to quick and decisive election outcomes, so a two-party system works well for presidential elections.

The Persistence of Partisanship

In the rest of this chapter, we'll take a closer look at partisanship, describing first how political scientists measure it and then considering some of its effects.

Measuring Partisanship

Although we cannot quantify partisanship, we can estimate the influence of parties on legislative activity. By almost all the measures political scientists have developed, party appears to have a strong hold on members of Congress.

One way we measure the influence of party is to see how often the average member of Congress votes with his or her party. Higher percentages of party voting indicate fewer legislators who act independent of party wishes. Recent data on party voting are striking indeed. The 109th Congress (2005–2006) witnessed "the highest level of partisan voting ever";[7] members of Congress now vote with their party almost nine times out of ten. Congressional scholar Barbara Sinclair looked at other places where party might affect legislators' behavior, measuring partisanship levels in committee action, the floor process, and presidential/congressional agreement on legislation. She found consistent patterns of partisanship in every arena.[8]

Another way to measure partisanship is to look at the spectrum of ideological views within each party. When legislators in each party hold a wide range of views, they are more likely to work with colleagues across the party aisle. Conversely, the fewer moderates in each party, the greater the divide between them and the smaller the likelihood of bipartisan cooperation. In the past three decades, elected officials from both parties have grown increasingly polarized. In Congress, most Republicans are conservative and most Democrats are liberal; therefore, the number of moderates in both parties has declined sharply. The elections of 2006 only exacerbated

Bipartisan Isn't a Bad Word

Perhaps it is a sign of the times, but a common error I detect in early sessions of many of my classes is that students deride elected officials for being too "bipartisan." Unknowingly they confuse the term *partisanship* (fervent devotion to one party) with *bipartisanship* (working together across party lines). Maybe this confusion stems in part from their experiences. Displays of hyperpartisanship and political gridlock abound at almost all levels of government; contemporary American politics offers few examples of genuine bipartisanship and cooperation.

this trend; eight of the fifteen most moderate Republicans in the House lost reelection.[9]

Such partisan patterns can lead to gridlock. At a time of "party parity," in which defections by a few can change the outcome of a vote, the stakes are high for legislators to toe the party line. Narrow party margins lead to a perverse incentive structure. Because the next election could easily shift the balance of power, the party in control wants to claim all major policy victories for itself and not risk sharing credit with its rivals. In turn, the party out of power doesn't want to help the other party accomplish anything that might earn favor with the voters. Given the current stakes, members of Congress are usually willing to work across party lines to pass simple, noncontentious legislation, but they are far less willing to work together on significant policy matters.

Ironically, at the same time elected officials are growing more polarized, the general public charts a much more moderate path. The percentage of Americans who describe themselves as independent from either political party has grown over the past few decades and now eclipses the percentages of those who identify as Republicans or Democrats.[10] Even those voters within a party camp are typically more ideologically moderate than the elected officials who represent them.

Working in partnership with the other party may not be the current norm for high-profile legislation, but many congressional norms still rely on bipartisan cooperation. For example, almost all representatives and senators still follow the pattern of introducing legislation with a primary cosponsor from the other party. The goal with almost every new bill is to pair a Democrat and a Republican as the named sponsors. In addition, bipartisan caucuses are still a vibrant part of congressional politics. From the Congressional Ski and Snowboard Caucus to the Steel Caucus and everything in

Although many people contribute to partisan warfare, much of the strongest rhetoric comes via the broadcast media. Common culprits are ideological talk show hosts and political commentators, who are enlisted for the specific purpose of presenting their particular side of the issue. Two people expressing reasoned opinions and explaining the complexity of public policy can make for a boring broadcast, but opponents trading jabs and pithy responses capture the audience's attention by making sparks fly. Consider a few examples of rhetorical missiles fired during national broadcasts.

There are a lot of bad Republicans; there are no good Democrats.

Ann Coulter, conservative commentator, appearing on CNN's *Lou Dobbs Tonight*

Everything is such spin [for Democrats]. . . . Everything is such PR that they have to create false impressions and images of who they are and what they believe because to be honest about who they are and what they believe would really doom their electoral chances. Nobody wants liberals running the show. And liberals, to get back in power, are gonna have to deceive people as to who they are.

Rush Limbaugh, conservative radio talk show host

The Republican Party, their message and their policies of exclusion and the tilted playing field appeals to the dumb and the mean. There is no shortage of dumb and mean people in this culture. So, therefore, their message, the dumb and the mean find a nice home in the GOP.

Janeane Garofolo, actress, liberal radio station Air America commentator

The country is not yet a theocracy but the Republican Party is, and they are driving American politics, using God as a battering ram on almost every issue: crime and punishment, foreign policy, health care, taxation, energy, regulation, social services and so on.

Bill Moyers, television host, journalist

between, groups of legislators meet together and plan legislative strategy based on common interests.

The Perils of Partisanship

Allegiance to a political party is not necessarily problematic; indeed, as we have seen, parties contribute to the democratic process in many positive ways. For many Americans, party identification simplifies politics and provides them a framework for approaching government. But excessive devotion to party can create problems, complicating politics and community building.

Many observers argue that fervent partisanship decreases civility in political interactions. During the past few decades of rising

"I Read It on the Internet" and Other Horror Stories

In a recent conversation regarding illegal immigration, a friend shared his frustration with the United States "being *invaded* by illegal immigrants"—how they are "stealing jobs from U.S. citizens" and then finding the nerve to make "political demands." When I asked him about his sources, he responded with the token phrase that so often prefaces modern political debate: the ambiguous "I read it on the Internet."

Feeling inspired to do a little research, I was directed by a simple Google search to thousands of links, including sources that offered the following analyses:

"Thousands, perhaps hundreds of thousands, of Americans are right now sharing their identities with immigrants and don't know it. It is the dirty little secret of the immigration issue: By not dealing directly with the undocumented worker situation, the U.S. government is actually encouraging identity theft. In fact, one can argue that the origins of the identity theft epidemic can be traced to the immigration issue."[11]

"Our wide-open borders may be wonderful for trade and profit, but terrible for national security and the safety of our citizens. No sane person would put greed ahead of the safety of his family, but apparently our politicians and many of the bureaucrats who lead critical agencies that the politicians appoint to key positions are willing to do precisely that."[12]

Conversely, many other sites presented very different perspectives:

"Any position that denies amnesty to the millions of immigrants from around the world is borne out of bigotry, xenophobia, and racism."[13]

"As far as I'm concerned, no one who is truly conscious of human rights should be willing to compromise over the amnesty issue. For in its purest essence, bigotry is the denial of human rights based on an individual's natural condition . . . born . . . into poverty outside of the United States of America."[14]

Like the examples above, blogs are often ideologically driven. Those who care the most about a topic are most willing to offer an opinion in a public setting, and passionate views increasingly blend fact and fiction for the sake of scoring political points. Unlike news reporting in papers and magazines,

partisanship in Congress, insiders claim the tone has changed. Many long-serving members lament the lack of civility on Capitol Hill, complaining that heavy-handed politics and caustic rhetoric make it more difficult to work across party lines. Instead of relying on the impressions of partisan legislators, former Republican congressman Vin Weber talked to those he describes as "the true experts on the Congressional process, the Capitol police" to see if which undergo strict fact-checking as part of the editorial review process, most blogs are completely unchecked. Hiding behind a cloak of anonymity, bloggers can post almost anything they choose—even libelous statements. In an effort to sway opinion, bloggers have strong incentives to use inflammatory rhetoric and even overt bias. A well-balanced approach might help defuse complicated situations and provide much-needed nuance, but it is unlikely to capture as many readers' attention.

The rise of the Internet marks a dramatic transformation in how many Americans learn about politics, increasing opportunities for people to gather information and share opinions rapidly. For all its benefits, however, the Internet poses many problems for healthy and effective political dialogue. While many online sources provide timely, factual information, too many blogs simply magnify the polarization of political opinions, fueling partisan fires with overblown rhetoric and false information.

Jonathan Flugstad

they had seen a decline in civility. As Weber explains, "I talk to those folks [the Capitol police], the parking lot attendants, the people who really understand how government works, and they *all* will tell you that, yeah, the mood and the tone and the atmosphere of the House of Representatives, the Congress more broadly, has changed over time."[15]

Another potential danger of extreme partisanship is that of ascribing motives to political behavior. Instead of comparing positions in terms of ideological left and right, some people characterize positions as good and bad, claiming good motivations for their own party and views while demonizing their opponents for bad motives. As we will explore in more detail in chapter 10, almost all political differences are fundamentally disagreements about the best way to achieve similar goals. Politicians typically agree on what needs to change; they disagree on how to do it. Just because someone advocates a different policy path does not mean they have ill motives.

Partisan thinking also increases the risk of simplifying complex issues into only two sides, as if each political question has a stock Republican answer and obvious Democratic answer. The two-party system encourages Americans to think in dichotomous terms, but the reality of public policy is that few, if any, political issues are so simple. The reduction of problems into two sides fosters a mentality of "us versus them," complicating bargaining and compromise while decreasing incentives to deliberate about policy alternatives.

Parties can help voters think through complex issues, but excessive loyalty to party can cloud judgment. Princeton politics professor Larry Bartels offers several examples of partisanship serving as a "perceptual screen in people's understanding of all sorts of day-to-day events."[16] One example he cites, a 1988 election survey, asked respondents several questions about their perceptions of the American economy. Inflation had declined sharply during the Reagan years, but only 10 percent of the "strong" Democrats surveyed agreed that inflation had improved. About half of them answered that inflation was worse under Reagan.

The rise of twenty-four-hour cable news and the Internet has made it easier than ever for Americans to filter out information they don't want to hear. As a result, many people self-select and pay attention only to those news sources that reflect their particular partisan or ideological view. As columnist David Broder summarized, "People easily find reinforcement for their own political preferences by choosing the channels they watch or the publications they read."[17] Without the balance of multiple perspectives, it is difficult to make reasoned political judgments.

All of these trends only make the stakes higher for those who want to live in harmony with others. An increasingly partisan environment complicates political decision making and hinders constructive political dialogue.

Countercultural Christians in Partisan Times

As this chapter reminds us, political parties can be positive institutions that help government work more effectively and responsibly, or they can be negative forces that pull people apart. Party loyalty, however, should never get in the way of the desire to love and serve God and neighbor.

At its worst, allegiance to party can overshadow allegiance to Christ. Recent analysis of election data and voter opinions suggests that party is more likely to influence people's values than the other way around.[18] With this in mind, Christians need great self-awareness to make sure their religious views inform their politics.

Devotion to party can also distort our views of fellow believers. If you find yourself wondering, *How can he be a true Christian and think that way politically?* partisanship has probably gripped your life too strongly. Far too much of the contemporary religion and politics debate creates implicit expectations that "good" Christians ally with one political party or the other, in effect using a party platform instead of the historic creeds of the church as the mark of true Christianity.

Reflecting on his career in politics, former senator John Danforth challenges fellow Christians to be agents of reconciliation, not divisiveness. The path to reconciliation is not an easy one, for it requires a humility we rarely see modeled in public life.

> Reconciliation depends on acknowledging that God's truth is greater than our own, that we cannot reduce it to any political platform we create, no matter how committed we are to that platform, and that God's truth is large enough to accommodate the opinions of all kinds of people, even those with whom we strongly disagree.[19]

Now that we have surveyed the development of our two-party system, the role of parties in contemporary government, and the potential perils of partisanship, let's continue our journey through highlights of "Politics 101." The next chapter offers a whirlwind tour of the U.S. Constitution, briefly describing the structure and powers of American government and looking at who does what in government and why it matters.

7

Who Does What?

The Branches of Government and Their Powers

Many forms of government have been tried, and will be tried in this world of sin and woe. No one pretends that democracy is perfect or all-wise. Indeed, it has been said that democracy is the worst form of Government except all those other forms that have been tried from time to time.

> Sir Winston Churchill (1874–1965),
> British prime minister,
> speaking to the House of Commons,
> November 11, 1947

My opinion is, that power should always be distrusted, in whatever hands it is placed.

> Sir William Jones (1746–1794),
> English jurist

Strapped under the enormous weight of national debt with little hope of repayment, the young nation plunged deeper and deeper into economic depression. Soldiers weary from battle still awaited their back pay, joining a line of debtors that included merchants

The Constitution before the Constitution: The Articles of Confederation

Although many people think of the U.S. Constitution as the founding document of American government, another "constitution," the Articles of Confederation, actually preceded it. First submitted on July 12, 1776, adopted by Congress on November 15, 1777, and finally ratified on March 1, 1781, the Articles failed to survive even a decade.

The Articles established a confederal system of government. Under such a system, each state retained its own power and sovereignty, and the states entered into a "league of friendship" designed to address matters of concern to them all. This central government had such limited powers that George Washington described it as "little more than the shadow without the substance."

Under the Articles, the national legislature (called Congress) was a single body of members chosen by state legislatures, paid by the states, and subject to recall by the states at any time if the members' work was needed more urgently at home. Each state had one vote. The Articles offered no provision for permanent executive or judicial authority.

The central government had a few powers—it could declare war, engage in diplomacy, enter into treaties, coin or borrow money (but each state had its own currency), and regulate trade with Native Americans. More problematic, however, were the powers not granted: the central government had no taxing powers (but could request that states offer voluntary contributions), no army, and no power to regulate commerce between the states. Any amendments required a unanimous vote of the states, rendering change practically impossible.

who had supplied the troops. A weak government passed laws that states often ignored, entered a treaty but couldn't enforce compliance with it, and found itself powerless to stave off organized armed rebellions that threatened to spread across several states. Trade disputes sparked tariff wars between the states, and foreign incursions threatened the borders. A leading statesman at the time described this dire situation in a letter, writing, "The wheels of Government are clogged, and our brightest prospects, and that high expectation which was entertained of us by the wondering world, are turned into astonishment; and from the high ground on which we stood, we are descending into the vale of confusion and darkness."[1]

What statesman wrote such foreboding words? What nation faced such tremendous struggles? The writer was George Washington; the nation was the United States under the Articles of Confederation, our first governing document.

In the midst of fighting a war for independence from Great Britain and from what they perceived as the tyrannical rule of

King George III, the colonial leaders who shaped the original American government were extremely wary of concentrated power. Thus, the governing document that arose from their debate gave almost all powers to the colonies, now organized as states, and intentionally created a weak central government with very limited scope. (For more specifics on the government established in the Articles, see the sidebar "The Constitution before the Constitution.")

Within a few years of ratification of the Articles, however, many political leaders were arguing that the government was too powerless. Delegates convened in Philadelphia to amend the Articles and strengthen the weak central government, but they soon abandoned this pursuit. Instead, they decided to begin again and craft an entirely new document, the U.S. Constitution, which created a form of government never seen before. In this chapter, we will take a brief look at the government structures established under the Constitution, exploring the principle of separation of powers that forms its core. This overview will help you understand some of the reasons behind the constitutional design and who does what in American government.

Too Much Power, Too Little, or Just Right? Separation of Powers

As we saw in chapter 4, the founders distrusted human nature and feared the concentration of power. Since individuals are likely to seek their own self-interest, they argued, government and those who are governed must both be kept in check. Aware of the weaknesses of the Articles and the need to create a stronger central government, the founders still held strong convictions favoring the principle of limited government. In seeking the best way to structure a new system, they thus sought to balance two concerns: creating a government strong enough to succeed but not so strong as to tyrannize the people.

The solution to this quandary was granting more power to government while at the same time dividing power so that no one person or group could gain complete control. In so doing, the founders established a principle now known as *separation of powers*. The technical term usually refers to the distinctive roles granted to the three branches of government: the legislative that makes the laws, the executive that enforces them, and the judicial that interprets them. Within each of these branches, many layers of government officials carry out their work, further diffusing power among people who serve a variety of constituencies and reach power through different channels.

But dividing power between three branches of government is only one aspect of our limited government. Power is also separated in two more ways: first by establishing different modes of selecting public officials, and second by dividing authority between multiple layers of government.

Different modes of selection help diffuse power further. By design, different elected officials answer to and represent particular sets of voters. Members of the House of Representatives are chosen most directly, for they face the voters in individual electoral districts every two years. In contrast, the Constitution originally provided for state legislators to select senators for six-year terms, placing some distance between senators and the people.[2] As we saw in the previous chapter, the president is elected through a multiple-step process we call the Electoral College. In addition, some government officials are not elected at all but are political appointees; federal judges and high-ranking officials are chosen by the president and confirmed by the Senate.

The formal term for the multiple layers of government is *federalism*. As one popular textbook describes, "Federalism is a way of organizing a nation so that two or more levels of government have formal authority over the same area and people."[3] At the time, the founders would have known only two systems of government: a *unitary* system, in which a single central government has all the political authority, or a *confederal* system (like that in the Articles), which gives ultimate power to states or provinces. They designed a new hybrid form, a *federal* system, that balances and divides power between the national government and the sovereign states, reserving any powers not explicitly stated in the Constitution for the states. The national government has certain roles and responsibilities that govern the nation, but the states also have their own powers, functions, and laws. Citizens thus owe allegiance to both the state and the national governments and must abide by both sets of laws.

In daily life, we interact with the various levels of government without giving much thought to its federal structure. Consider just a few of your interactions with multiple levels of government as you begin a seemingly simple weekend road trip. When you fill up the gas tank, the price per gallon includes some combination of local, state, and federal gasoline taxes. As you strap a young child into a car seat manufactured to federal safety standards, you are complying with state child-restraint laws. Inside the glove compartment is the proof of registration and insurance required by state law. Obeying local traffic ordinances, you make your way to an interstate highway whose construction and maintenance is funded with a combination of state and federal dollars.

At its core, the system created in the Constitution includes many different ways to separate and diversify government power. Because no single individual, group, level, or branch of government wields much independent power, government cannot tyrannize the people.

The Lawmakers: The Legislative Branch

Now that we have a better sense of the underlying structure of American government, let's look at each of the three branches of the national government to see how they work. We'll begin where laws originate, the legislative branch. The framers expected Congress, the primary lawmaking institution of the national government, to wield the most power, so they divided it into two chambers: the House of Representatives and the Senate.

Elected to two-year terms to represent districts of roughly equal size, members of the House are expected to be the closest to the people and their local concerns. The Constitution provided for one representative to serve for every 30,000 people, but eventually population increases made that impossible. If we followed this prescription today, the House would include almost 10,000 members! Since 1911, the chamber has included 435 members; each member now represents about 650,000 people. With its large size, the House could easily become an unwieldy chamber, so strict rules help limit and shape debate, and party leaders try to exercise tight control over their delegations. Almost all significant legislative actions in the House require a simple majority vote for passage, so the party that controls the chamber usually gets its way.

The other chamber of Congress, the Senate, includes two members from each state, elected to six-year terms. With their longer terms and larger constituencies, senators are more distant from the people and thus freer to concern themselves with the national interest. The Constitution grants a few powers to the Senate alone; these include offering advice and consent on presidential appointments and voting on approval of treaties.

Unlike the House of Representatives, which often regiments debate with strict time limits, the Senate follows the tradition of unlimited debate. In practice this means that its members can speak on the floor of the chamber as long as they please. When senators delay or stop legislation with unlimited debate, we call this tactic a *filibuster*. A vote from sixty or more senators invokes *cloture*, a practice used to cut off debate and force a vote on the measure. Because of these practices, the Senate needs the cooperation of at least sixty members to do most of its business, so neither political party has held a true working majority in recent decades. These and other procedures give individual senators more power than individual representatives, so legislation usually moves much slower in the Senate. To accomplish their goals, Senate leaders have to rely more on consensus building and working across party lines than do their counterparts in the House.

Traditional legislation requires cooperation between the two chambers of Congress. With the exception of revenue bills that must begin in the House, legislators from either chamber can introduce proposals. For a bill to become a law, however, the proposal must pass in the House and the Senate in identical form before going to the president for a signature or veto. When you take into account that many bills are hundreds of pages long, one wonders how both chambers ever reach agreement on every single word.[4]

Congressional Powers

Article I of the Constitution enumerates several congressional powers, including taxation, borrowing money, regulating interstate commerce, coining money, creating courts, and declaring war. Only Congress holds the power of the purse; that is, its members decide how to spend all federal dollars. The president has a role in the process through submitting an annual budget request outlining his plan for federal spending, but members of Congress make the final decisions. Legislators also have significant (though shared) authority over economic, foreign, and domestic policy.

Congress was not a dominating force in national government for much of American history. The state of New York, for example, had a larger budget than that of the United States for most of the nineteenth century. As the size and scope of national needs grew, so did the role of Congress. Although Article I, Section 8, specifies particular congressional powers in sixteen clauses, the section ends with what has become known as the *elastic clause*, which empowers Congress "to make all Laws which shall be necessary and proper for carrying into Execution the foregoing Powers, and all other Powers vested by this Constitution in the Government of the United States, or any Department or Officer thereof."[5] Supreme Court decisions interpreted this and other clauses in ways that expanded the scope of congressional powers, so Congress can now enact legislation on a broad range of policies.

The Enforcers: Executive Branch

A second branch of government, the executive, includes its formal head, the president, and the several million individuals who work as part of the federal bureaucracy to enforce and administer the laws. We'll consider the powers of the president and the bureaucracy in turn.

The framers were gravely concerned about vesting too much power in a single person, so the presidency is the result of many compromises. Some of those gathered at the Constitutional Convention argued that multiple people should share the executive role, but the debate ended with the creation of a single-person office called the president. Over time, the office and its importance have expanded greatly, but at its creation it appeared to be a weak and limited position.

Presidential Powers

Article II establishes the American presidency in what early-twentieth-century scholar Edwin S. Corwin famously described as the "most loosely drawn chapter of the Constitution." The description of the president was deliberately left vague, most likely due to the framers' shared trust in George Washington. They all expected Washington to assume the office, and most trusted him to define and shape the role for future presidents. As a result, the Constitution says almost as much about the selection of the president as it does about his powers. Article II, Section 1, creates the office: "The executive power shall be vested in a President of the United States of America." Section 2 bestows national security powers, stating that the president "shall be Commander in Chief of the Army and Navy." A vague statement in section 3, often called the "take-care clause," gives the power to "take care that the laws are faithfully executed." Over time, presidents have used this clause to justify broadening their powers.

The Constitution delineates a few other areas of presidential authority. As the nation's chief diplomat, the president nominates and receives ambassadors and makes treaties (subject to Senate approval). Control over legislation is limited; presidents can recommend (but not introduce) legislation, report to Congress, convene special legislative sessions, and attempt to prevent bills from becoming law with a veto. The president nominates high-level executive branch officials and all members of the federal judiciary, but all such nominations require Senate approval.

Although the framers left some room for expansion of the office through the years, the presidency is an office of delegated powers. Ultimately, all presidential power comes from one of two sources—the Constitution and the laws—so the president has no independent base of power. Then-president Truman commented on retired general Dwight Eisenhower's candidacy for president: "'He'll sit here,' Truman would remark (tapping his desk for emphasis), 'and he'll say, Do this! Do that! *And nothing will happen.* Poor Ike—it won't be a bit like the Army. He'll find it very frustrating.'"[6] As Truman predicted and Eisenhower discovered, the president's power is limited and checked; even the so-called leader of the free world does not wield complete command and control.

Executive Branch Powers

Even though we look to the president as the symbol of executive power, in reality the president is just the highest-ranking person leading a multilayered bureaucracy. Immediately below the president are about three thousand political appointees who serve at the will of the president. Under them are roughly 2.7 million federal civil servants and another two million workers in the Defense Department. Members of the executive branch are *civil servants*, employees chosen and promoted based on merit, not political connections. As presidential administrations and their political appointees come and go, the workers at the heart of the bureaucracy remain, providing continuity for government and wielding considerable power.

The executive branch includes four types of institutions. The largest are the fifteen *cabinet departments*, administrative units in charge of broad policy sectors such as agriculture, housing, and commerce. The heads of each of these departments comprise the core of the president's cabinet. The other executive branch institutions include *independent agencies*, smaller organizations with more discrete tasks, such as the Central Intelligence Agency and the Peace Corps; *independent regulatory commissions*, agencies with expertise in particular policy areas that help write and enforce government codes, such as the Nuclear Regulatory Commission; and *government corporations*, units that operate more like businesses to provide public services, such as the U.S. Postal Service and Amtrak.

Although we typically don't think of government bureaucracy as a major power center, in actuality executive branch officials make decisions on a daily basis that directly affect our lives.

Once Congress passes a bill and the president signs it into law, members of the executive branch decide if and how they will implement it, writing and enforcing the codes and regulations that will determine how the law applies and whom it affects. Every time you board an airplane, you must first submit to screening by the Transportation Security Agency, submitting to rules and procedures that can and do change as situations warrant. International travelers have even more interaction with executive branch officials, following State Department procedures to ensure that they have a valid passport and obeying instructions to clear customs and immigration.

The Interpreters: The Judicial Branch

The legislative branch writes the law and the executive enforces it, but one more essential power remains. The judicial branch interprets the law, ensuring that the letter of the law and the means of enforcing it fit within the boundaries set by the U.S. Constitution.

Article III of the Constitution gives very little detail about federal courts, merely stating in Section 1 that "the judicial power of the United States shall be vested in one supreme Court, and in such Inferior courts as the Congress may from time to time ordain and establish." Congress moved quickly to fulfill this duty, creating the three-tiered federal court system in the Judiciary Act of 1789.

Judges have greatly expanded the power and role of the federal courts through their own rulings. In actions that culminated in the 1803 case *Marbury v. Madison*, the Supreme Court established the power of *judicial review*, the right of the courts to evaluate and potentially overturn actions of other branches of government or states. If the justices find that a law violates the Constitution, they throw it out. Legislators have few options if the Court invalidates a law; their best hope is rewriting the statute with changes that they think will address the justices' concerns.

Like other high-level appointments, the president selects and the Senate confirms judicial appointees, but unlike other positions in government, judges serve "during good behavior." In practice this means they have lifetime appointments that, at least in theory, give them independence from the whims of politics and public opinion.[7]

Types of Courts and Jurisdictions

Judicial systems include two types of courts: trial courts and appellate courts. *Trial courts* serve as the court of original jurisdiction, the place where all cases begin. These courts are the only places where judges hear evidence and listen to testimonies of witnesses; they are also the only courts that may have jury trials. *Appellate courts* have appellate jurisdiction, meaning that the losing side can ask a higher court to reconsider the lower court's decision. Every person is guaranteed the right to appeal to a higher court, but this guarantee does not ensure that the court will agree to hear his or her case. If an appellate court does hear an appeal, the proceedings include judges only—no juries, no new evidence, no witnesses—who evaluate the lower court's actions based solely on matters of law. If the appellate judges find that the previous judge made a legal error, they may send the case back to the trial court for further proceedings. In practice this means that judges do not overturn rulings of another court simply because they don't like the outcome; they must have a legal justification for their actions.

Because of the federal structure of the United States, we have two court systems: courts established in each state that hear 99 percent of all legal cases; and federal courts (sometimes called constitutional courts) that decide cases involving federal laws, treaties, or the Constitution, as well as some cases involving citizens of more than one state.

The lowest level, or trial, courts in the federal system are called *district courts*. Above these are the *U.S. Courts of Appeals*, and above those is the *Supreme Court*. The nine members who serve on the Supreme Court are called justices. Each term, they consider about eight thousand cases, agreeing to hear between seventy and ninety of them.

The Supreme Court and Its Powers

Since such a small number of cases are accepted each session, how do the justices decide which ones to hear? A handful of cases each year automatically begin at the Supreme Court because the Constitution gives the Court original jurisdiction over a few specific types of cases, such as disputes between states or cases involving a foreign ambassador or minister. The cases on the rest of the court's docket (the agenda of cases the Court will hear) are appeals.

The Long and Winding Road ... to the Supreme Court

Each Supreme Court term, at least a handful of cases seem to capture national attention as they set legal precedents concerning hot-button issues of the day. What begins the process of a case reaching the Court? Who chooses what issues will be decided in a given year? Let's follow a case from the 2003–2004 term to find out.

In the recent and controversial First Amendment case *Locke v. Davey*, Joshua Davey, a resident of Washington State, won a state-funded Promise Scholarship, which he used to attend Northwest College. To comply with the Washington State constitution, the Promise Scholarship program prohibited state funding of any student pursuing a degree in devotional theology. A student could use the scholarship to support the academic study of religion, but the state would not fund a program that encouraged and developed religious practice. When Davey added a major in pastoral ministries, he lost his scholarship. He sued the state, arguing that the law violated his rights under the First Amendment.

How did a college student afford to sue the state? Who paid the legal fees to argue his case all the way to the Supreme Court? Like most litigants in

high-profile cases that raise constitutional questions, Joshua Davey found help from a public interest law firm, a nonprofit organization that provided free legal representation. Aware that most Americans cannot afford the hundreds of thousands of dollars in legal fees to challenge laws and practices they think are unconstitutional, interest groups have formed legal organizations to represent clients in cases that they believe can be used to challenge a particular law and create new legal precedent. Although many people may request help, constitutional lawyers look for the ideal "test case"—a compelling story and facts that maximize the likelihood that the Court will support their side. Examples of influential public interest law firms include the NAACP Legal Defense Fund, the American Civil Liberties Union, and the Becket Fund for Religious Liberty.

The American Center for Law and Justice, a public interest law firm that specializes in religious liberty issues, agreed to represent Joshua Davey. The case began at the federal district court, where the judge ruled in favor of the state. Davey appealed to the Ninth Circuit Court of Appeals, who ruled in his favor. The state then appealed to

If the parties in a legal action did not like the lower court's ruling, they may request a *writ of certiorari*, a formal petition to the court to order records from a lower court for review. Like all appeals, such requests must argue for reconsideration based on a rule of law. The justices meet to review potential cases and vote the Supreme Court, who upheld the Washington law in a 7–2 decision. Davey's lawyers criticized the opinion for allowing religious discrimination; supporters of strict separation of church and state cheered.

By the time Davey's case reached the Supreme Court, he had graduated from college and was completing his first year of study at Harvard Law School. Whatever way the court ruled, he knew that the decision would have little direct impact on his personal situation. But the reason for pursuing the case through the court system was far larger than the specific situation of this one student; Davey and his lawyers chose the long and winding road to the Supreme Court because they wanted this case to make a difference.

Seeking redress through the legal system entails many risks. No one can guarantee that higher courts will accept appeals, and no one knows for sure how the judges and justices will rule. But if a case defies all the odds and makes it onto the Supreme Court docket, parties on both sides of the case know that the decision has the potential to change American history.

on which ones they will "grant cert," or agree to hear. In what is called the *rule of four*, only four of the nine justices must agree for a case to be accepted. Justices limit the cases they agree to hear, selecting only those that have the most legal significance. They are most likely to accept cases that conflict with previous Supreme Court decisions, cases that resolve conflicts and inconsistencies in lower court rulings, or cases that raise new issues the court has not addressed before.

The Court also hears petitions for a *writ of habeas corpus*, a legal protection that allows someone accused of a crime to appeal directly to the Supreme Court. This second channel to the Supreme Court when other appeals fail is designed to safeguard individual rights.

Although many people would like Supreme Court justices to advocate particular public policies in their rulings, the role of the Court is far different. The Court's opinions set precedent for all other courts in the United States, because they represent final verdicts for the judicial system that apply across the entire country. When the justices issue an opinion, they are usually concerned less with the individual details of a particular case than they are with creating standards that other judges can apply to a range of cases that raise similar legal questions. For this reason, justices may create legal "tests," sets of questions or criteria other judges can use to determine if a

Theory Meets Practice: Predicting How a Judge Will Rule

Each time the president seeks to fill a vacancy on the Supreme Court, observers try to predict how the new justice will rule on important cases. We wonder, how will the nominee decide cases that come before the Court? To what extent might personal or political beliefs affect the outcomes? Although there are no simple answers to such complicated questions, most justices are rather consistent in their approach to their work. If you know two things about nominees—their philosophy of jurisprudence and their theory of constitutional interpretation—you can often predict how they will decide future cases.

A first factor that influences judicial decision making is a *philosophy of jurisprudence*. Practically speaking, this means one's view of what role the courts should play. Those who advocate *judicial restraint* believe that the court should avoid overturning previous decisions if at all possible. In addition, since judges are not elected, the court should defer to legislative decisions whenever possible. On the other hand, proponents of *judicial activism* advocate a more proactive role for the court. At times, they argue, it is necessary for the court to overturn a law, reject a presidential action, or go beyond the specific words of the Constitution to address contemporary issues.

Judges often apply these philosophies using various theories of constitutional interpretation, that is, different methods of interpreting the text of the Constitution. According to one theory, *original intent*, judges should determine what the founders intended when they wrote the Constitution and use that rationale to answer legal questions. Advocates of the *plain meaning of the text* approach (sometimes called strict constructionists) make decisions based on what the wording of the Constitution obviously seems to say. A third method applies the *living Constitution* theory, which contends jurists must consider the law in the light of the total history of the United States, approaching the Constitution as a living document that is dynamic enough to be interpreted in the light of progress.

The next time the Senate Judiciary Committee holds hearings to consider a judicial nominee, pay attention to the proceedings. Watch how the senators ask questions about his or her philosophy of the law and views on constitutional interpretation. As part of the process of deciding how to vote for president, you may want to think about how you would approach these two elements of judicial decision making and choose the candidate most likely to nominate judges who hold similar views.

statute under review violates the Constitution. In the case *Miller v. California*, for example, the court had to decide if the First Amendment freedom of speech included obscenity. Ruling that states could indeed restrict obscene speech, they created a test to help judges and legislators differentiate between obscene and legitimate speech. One part of the test, called the *LAPS test*, asks if the content has literary, artistic, political, or scientific (LAPS) value. According to this test, an image of a nude human figure in an anatomy textbook would have scientific value and thus count as protected free speech, whereas an image in a full-color entertainment magazine would be classified as obscenity that could be regulated by government.

Forced to Work Together: Checks and Balances in Action

As we have seen, the Constitution established several mechanisms to divide and limit government power. But one more structural element remains: the system of checks and balances. Not only did the framers separate national government power into three branches, they also created overlapping powers between the branches, so that each could check and balance one another's power as a further safeguard against tyranny.

Who Has Power over Abortion Law? Checks and Balances in Action

A practical example can help us see how checks and balances work. Consider the current political debate over the regulation of abortion. Which branches and levels of government have influence over abortion policy? Who checks the power of whom? As we will see, these seemingly simple questions have rather complex answers.

For most of American history, abortion laws were determined exclusively by state governments. In our federal system described earlier, state governments retain many powers, including the creation and enforcement of most criminal laws. Abortion law was no exception. Each state had freedom to allow doctors to perform abortions, to subject the practice to regulations, or to forbid the procedure entirely.

The balance of power on this issue changed in 1973 with the Supreme Court ruling commonly known as *Roe v. Wade*. (See the sidebar "What Really Happened in *Roe v. Wade*?" for more details on the Court's opinion.) In the *Roe* decision, the Supreme Court ruled that many forms of abortion restrictions violated the Constitution and were therefore invalid. The Court's action was a potent check on the power of state legislatures, setting new boundaries for what kinds of laws they could and could not enforce. This action also changed the balance and focus of the abortion debate; previously state legislatures had set the standards, whereas now the issue is a national one.

Once abortion was no longer an issue addressed primarily by state governments, officials in national politics entered the debate. Presidential candidates began talking about the abortion issue, campaigning in support of pro-life or pro-choice policies. Presidents often campaign on the issue, but in reality the constitutional division of government powers gives the president very little independent power to affect abortion policy. Past presidents have issued executive orders permitting or forbidding federal funding of abortion services and abortion counseling, for example, but they do not have the power to change the legal status of abortion. Presidents can exert indirect influence on the policy debate, however, through their power to nominate Supreme Court justices. Although no one can guarantee how a justice will rule if confirmed, presidents have the power to select nominees who are likely to uphold or strike down *Roe v. Wade*.

Members of Congress have also entered the debate, looking for ways they can influence abortion policy. Like presidents, they find few venues for directly influencing abortion law. Senators share the president's indirect influence in the judicial confirmation process, for they can approve or deny a judicial nominee, thus checking and balancing presidential power. Congress has little hope of passing legislation that would either prohibit or guarantee national access to abortion; in our federal system, state governments determine most criminal laws, and Supreme Court abortion rulings provide an additional check. In practice Congress is limited to small and symbolic actions on this issue.

State legislatures still have some power to write and enforce abortion regulations, but their statutes must not conflict with the guidelines set in Supreme Court rulings. Many assume that if *Roe v. Wade* were overturned, abortion would be banned in the United States. In reality, if this were to happen, the balance of power would simply shift from the Supreme Court back to state legislatures, and each state would once again have the power to forbid, regulate, or permit abortion as they choose.

As the abortion example demonstrates, the different institutions of the state and national governments share power over public policy, and the balance of power shifts over time. When seeking policy change, keep in mind the principles of separation of powers and checks and balances, holding realistic expectations of what government can and cannot do.

Healthy Opposition

The founders designed American government to control and disperse power, and they clearly succeeded. Sociologist William Martin explains the reasoning of the founders this way:

> The system of checks and balances they built into the Constitution was informed not only by the recognition that good citizens may differ over the proper course of action, but also, at least in part,

by the biblical understanding of humans as fallible and prone to wrongdoing and therefore frequently in need of some healthy opposition from their fellows. Nobody, in their view, has a corner on Truth, Justice, and the American Way.[8]

The checks built into the structure of American government make quick and sweeping change almost impossible, but these safeguards also protect us. Although the complexity and limits of the system can frustrate legitimate desires to make a difference, perhaps our system that accommodates healthy opposition prods us to be humble.

Now that we have looked at the structures and institutions created in the Constitution, let's turn to another foundational document, the Bill of Rights. In particular, the next chapter will look at the First Amendment—what we think it says, what it really says, and why that distinction is so important.

8

Does the Church
Have Any Business in Politics?

What the Constitution Really Says

We are a nation of many nationalities, many races, many religions—
bound together by a single unity, the unity of freedom and equality.
Whoever seeks to set one nationality against another, seeks to de-
grade all nationalities. Whoever seeks to set one race against another,
seeks to enslave all races. Whoever seeks to set one religion against
another, seeks to destroy all religion.

Franklin Delano Roosevelt (1882–1945),
thirty-second president of the United States

The day that this country ceases to be free for irreligion, it will cease
to be free for religion.

Robert H. Jackson, associate justice, Supreme Court

An ad in the *Washington Post* read, "Congratulations, Congressman
Pete Stark." Below a large close-up picture of the congressman's face,
the ad told the legislator, "You're in good company," and displayed
smaller photographs of six other men and women. What honor placed
Stark in good company with Tufts philosopher Daniel C. Dennett,
journalist and author Barbara Ehrenreich, Harvard psychologist
Steven Pinker, comedienne and *Saturday Night Live* alumna Julia

Sweeney, novelist Kurt Vonnegut, and Harvard biologist Edward O. Wilson? The congressman admitted that he is an atheist.

The American Humanist Association ran the ad congratulating the congressman for "his historic decision to come out as the first openly nontheistic member of Congress."[1] Newspapers across the country carried stories about the thirteen-term legislator's admission that he did not believe in a Supreme Being. Why did Stark's description of his religious views capture so much media attention? His remarks made history because he became the highest-ranking politician in the United States to disavow publicly any belief in God.

Surely Stark is not alone among his peers in not believing in God, but what sets him apart is his public admission of this politically sensitive detail. As we saw in chapter 4, Americans expect their elected officials to have at least the appearance of religion. Article VI of the Constitution forbids the government from creating religious tests to determine qualifications for public office, but unofficially voters can and do impose such criteria. Citing recent polling data to show that about half the American electorate refuses to vote for an atheist for president, Fred Edwords of the American Humanist Association explained, "The fact that Pete Stark's public avowal of nontheism is controversial reinforces this point. Americans still feel it's acceptable to discriminate against atheists in ways considered beyond the pale for other groups."[2]

In much the same way that the official prohibition of religious tests for office creates one standard for government but allows voters to impose such tests in actual practice, some aspects of contemporary American politics follow directly from the Constitution, while others stem more from tradition and public opinion. When thinking about the official role of religion in the formal structures of American government, we need to distinguish between impressions of how government works and what the Constitution actually says. In this chapter, we will examine the early history of church and state before analyzing the place of religion in the Constitution and Bill of Rights. Finally, the chapter will take a closer look at the First Amendment's religion clauses and how the courts tend to interpret them.

Religion and Government in the Colonies

A common rendering of American history teaches that the original colonists crossed the Atlantic in search of religious freedom.

Although this narrative is partially true, the motivations for early colonization were far more diverse. In the words of one author: "It was an eclectic cast of characters, some in search of God, others on the prowl for mammon—and even those for whom freedom of religion was a driving force soon found themselves doing unto others what had been done unto them."[3] Various motivations drove early colonists to the New World: some fled religious persecution, while many others came for commercial or financial reasons. Some who had previously suffered under repressive laws established equally intolerant regimes of their own.

None of the American colonies practiced religious freedom as we understand it today, but many practiced some form of toleration. The two phrases are not synonymous: "*Religious freedom* means that citizens are free to worship in any way or not at all—and that the state protects that freedom. *Religious toleration* means that the state allows a group to exist and to worship, but retains the right to withdraw or limit that permission at any time."[4]

The relationship between church and state varied widely in the original colonies, from early settlements that practically unified church and state to much more tolerant colonies founded later. The original laws in Anglican Virginia, for example, mandated attendance at prayer services twice a day, made a third-time violation of the Sabbath punishable by death, and penalized "those who took the name of God in vain or spoke 'impiously or maliciously against the holy and blessed trinity.'"[5] The Puritans in Massachusetts wrote a very strict legal code based on Old Testament law. Examples of capital crimes included worshiping another god, blasphemy, adultery, and murder. Church membership was a requirement for voting and holding public office.[6]

At the other extreme, two of the original colonies offered something close to religious freedom. Roger Williams, exiled from Massachusetts for his religious beliefs, founded Rhode Island, a colony that offered freedom of religion for most people. For a time, Roman Catholics were not welcome; eventually, Rhode Island accepted everyone but atheists. Pennsylvania, founded by Quaker William Penn, was designed as a haven for persecuted religious groups and practiced religious toleration.

Most of the other early colonies tolerated some religious differences but recognized official churches. At the time of America's founding, almost all of the colonies had established churches.

God and the Constitution, European Style

As representatives of the European Union (EU) met to write its first constitution in 2003, a bitter debate began. Should "God" or "religion" be included in the text, and if so, to what degree? Many advocates for acknowledging God or Christianity argued that European culture was founded upon religious principles and morals, and that Europe is "rooted in religious heritage."[7] Within the EU, Germany, Italy, Poland, and Slovakia were among those most passionately championing the inclusion of "Christian values," especially after the first fifteen Articles were released with no references to religion.

In opposition to this group stood the more secular nations of France, Spain, and the Netherlands. They contended that the inclusion of specific religious language in the text would create barriers within an extremely pluralistic EU, and that for Europe to truly be unified, it must be secular. Many also raised the concern that these references would constrain the EU's ability to expand, alienating Muslim countries such as Turkey.

In an effort to appease all sides of the argument, the convention of twenty-eight member and applicant states finally reached an attempted compromise that mentions all groups in the Preamble, specifically stating that the constitution "draws inspiration from the cultural, religious, and humanist inheritance of Europe."[8]

French and Dutch citizens voted against this version of the EU Constitution in national referenda in 2005, but their opposition was motivated by domestic political issues, not religious concerns. As Europeans discuss a new draft, debates over religious language have reemerged but are unlikely to play a crucial rule in negotiations.

Jonathan Flugstad

Establishment finally ended in 1833 when voters in Massachusetts agreed to sever ties with an official state church.[9]

Religion and the Constitution

Given the influence of religion in colonial America and references to the divine in early historical documents, many people think that the Constitution includes references to God. Others look at more recent American history and assume that the Constitution explicitly calls for the separation of church and state. In reality, neither of these assumptions is true.

The Constitution never mentions God, directly or indirectly. As historian Edwin Gaustad notes, "Unlike most state constitutions of the time, the national document did not mention God even in the vaguest terms of an 'overruling Providence' or 'Grand Architect' of the world or acknowledge the existence of any national creed."[10] The one mention of religion in the original text of the Constitution is the ban on religious tests for office in Article VI. The only other references to religion occur in the First Amendment.

The Origins of the "Wall of Separation"

Contrary to many popular assumptions, neither the original document nor the First Amendment includes the phrase "separation of church and state." As we will see in more detail in the next chapter, however, the language of separation dates back many centuries. The metaphor of a "wall of separation" is also nothing new. Historians date the phrase back to sixteenth-century Anglican theologian Richard Hooker. In his defense of the established church in Great Britain, Hooker derided his opponents, employing the phrase with an accusatory tone. Writing in the 1640s, Roger Williams used the metaphor as a positive description, defending separation of church and state as necessary to protect the church. He described the church as a garden surrounded by the worldly wilderness that needed a hedge of protection: "If He will ever please to restore His garden and paradise again, it must of necessity be walled in peculiarly unto Himself from the world; and that all that shall be saved out of the world are to be transplanted out of the wilderness of the world, and added unto His church or garden."[11] Scottish reformer James Burgh, writing in 1767, borrowed the metaphor in his writings in defense of religious toleration and freedom of conscience.

More than a decade after the passage of the First Amendment, Thomas Jefferson popularized the phrase "wall of separation between church and state" in a short letter written on January 1, 1802. Jefferson was in his first term as president, having survived campaign attacks claiming he was an atheist. The Baptists, a religious minority in Congregationalist Connecticut, had written a letter congratulating Jefferson on his election. Facing criticism for his unwillingness to declare official days of fasting and thanksgiving, Jefferson decided to use his short reply to the Danbury Baptist Association as an opportunity to defend his views. In a paragraph that begins, "Believing with you that religion is a matter that lies solely between Man & his God, that he owes account to none other for his faith or his worship," Jefferson describes the First Amendment as "building a wall of separation between Church & State."[12]

Over a century later, a Supreme Court justice would rediscover this letter and quote it in a landmark decision, permanently directing Jefferson's metaphor into American political discourse.

A Closer Look at the First Amendment

The First Amendment reads, "Congress shall make no law respecting an establishment of religion, or prohibiting the free exercise thereof; or abridging the freedom of speech, or of the press; or the right of the people peaceably to assemble, and to petition the Government for a redress of grievances." Taken together, this amendment guarantees different forms of freedom of expression.

The first sixteen words, divided between two clauses, provide the foundation for religious freedom in the United States. Most discussions shorten the first part, "Congress shall make no law respecting an establishment of religion," calling it the *establishment clause*. In much the same way, references to the second part, "or prohibiting the free exercise thereof," talk about the *free exercise clause*.

The establishment clause is designed to protect against government endorsement of a particular religion. At the time of the founding, most countries had an official "established" church that received taxpayer support, and many of the American colonies likewise recognized an official state church. The establishment clause breaks from this trend, clearly prohibiting the United States from creating an officially recognized, government-supported church. What else this clause prohibits or permits is a matter of much disagreement. Interpretations range widely, from those who say it forbids any government money in any form going to a religious organization or activity, to those who claim it allows almost any interaction short of establishing an official church.

The free exercise clause protects freedom of religious belief and worship. The government cannot require anyone to hold any particular religious beliefs, nor can it punish anyone solely for believing or not believing in religion. Interpretation of this clause gets more complicated, however, when laws or government activities sometimes interfere with or hinder religious practices. (The sidebar "Congress Shall Make No Law . . . Most of the Time" examines one Supreme Court case that highlights the tension between government interests and freedom of worship.)

Congress Shall Make No Law . . . Most of the Time

Does the free exercise clause literally prohibit the passage of any laws that restrict religion, or does it allow for the possibility of occasional limits to religious practice? Consider what happened in the landmark Supreme Court case *Lyng v. Northwest Indian Cemetery Protective Association*, decided on April 19, 1988.

For the Yurok Indians of northwest California, the sacred high country of the mountains and forest serve as the source of spiritual revelation and the training grounds for medicine men and Indian doctors. When the U.S. Forest Service proposed building a logging road (called the G-O Road) directly through their sacred space, for them it was comparable to building a "highway through the Vatican."[13] The Indians filed a lawsuit claiming that the construction would destroy the "solitude, privacy, and undisturbed natural setting necessary to Indian religious practices, thereby violating their First Amendment right to freely exercise their religion."[14]

In 1983 the Federal District Court held that building the G-O Road would unconstitutionally burden the Yuroks' exercise of sincerely held religious beliefs. The government appealed the decision to the Ninth Circuit Court of Appeals, and in July 1986, the lower court's decision was reaffirmed. While this case was pending, Congress passed a law designating the high country as a forest preserve, but it excluded a 1,200-foot corridor to allow for building the logging road. The government then appealed yet again to the Supreme Court, who accepted the case.

The Supreme Court reversed the lower court decisions. Unlike previous free exercise cases, the government action under review would not coerce the Yurok into any kind of action contrary to their religious beliefs. While admitting that the G-O Road could have "devastating effects on traditional Indian religious practices," the Court ruled in a 5–3 decision that unless the government is coercing individuals to act in a way that violates their religious beliefs, there is no need for the government to provide a compelling interest for its actions. In a scathing dissent, however, Justice Brennan argued that the ruling "[failed] utterly to accord with the dictates of the First Amendment."[15]

In 1990, two years after the Supreme Court ruling, the 101st Congress passed a law that designated the G-O Road corridor as a forest preserve, essentially protecting the land for the Yurok Indians. While they ultimately found a way to keep their sacred land preserved, the Yuroks' case broadened the government's ability to write laws that knowingly but noncoercively violate free exercise of religion.

Jonathan Flugstad

The debate over the application of these two clauses has created much controversy, especially in the latter half of the twentieth century. The wording of both clauses is sufficiently vague, leaving much room for interpretation, and the interpretation has changed

Absolute Rights? Absolutely Not!

The First Amendment guarantees freedom of speech, yet it is against the law to yell, "Fire!" in a crowded movie theater or threaten to harm the president. But doesn't the First Amendment guarantee citizens a limitless, absolute right to express themselves? More broadly, are there absolute rights, outside of free speech, that the government cannot touch? Contrary to popular belief, the answer to both questions is a resounding no. The government reserves the right to regulate citizen action when it has a compelling interest to do so. This balancing act stems from the inherent tensions of upholding legal rights. A multitude of Supreme Court cases attempt to draw the fine line between placing undue burdens on constitutional rights and maintaining order.

Consider the example of freedom of speech. While the First Amendment guarantees this right, in certain instances one person's free expression may inhibit the freedom of another, providing the government a warranted interest in holding rights in check. Other expressions are simply outside the bounds of our freedom. Here are a few examples of limitations imposed on the fundamental right of free speech:

- **Fighting Words**: Statements that would cause the average person to fight.

- **Hate Speech**: Speech or expression that specifically alienates a particular class in a hateful manner. Motivated by prejudice.

- **Obscenity**: Depicts or describes sexual conduct in a patently offensive way and, as a whole, lacks serious literary, artistic, political, or scientific value.

- **Libel**: Printed false statements that injure a person's reputation.

- **Slander**: Spoken false statements that injure a person's reputation.

As you can see from the examples above, it is sometimes necessary for the state to intervene and regulate even fundamental rights. Throughout its history, the Supreme Court has issued many rulings on these controversial topics, and it has developed legal tests that create a framework for judging the limits of individual rights while at the same time respecting fundamental freedoms.

Do Americans enjoy absolute rights? Absolutely not.

Jonathan Flugstad

over time. To complicate matters further, in certain instances the two clauses internally conflict. In the words of former chief justice Warren Burger, "The Court has struggled to find a neutral course between the two Religion Clauses, both of which are cast in absolute terms, and either of which, if expanded to a logical extreme, would tend to clash with the other."[16]

Consider an example. A public school student may want to freely exercise her religion by reciting a prayer in Jesus's name with her homeroom class, but this action would inhibit her Muslim classmate's ability to freely exercise his faith. At the same time, the state-funded school would violate the establishment clause if it officially sanctioned the Christian prayer.

In practice Americans are free to exercise their religion within certain limits. The government can interact with religious organizations, but it must respect certain boundaries. Like all political rights that appear absolute in theory, in practice government must place some limits on rights to maintain order. (See the sidebar "Absolute Rights? Absolutely Not!" for further explanation.)

The Supreme Court and the Religion Clauses

The history of legal decisions interpreting the religion clauses is far from consistent. Over time, judicial rulings have tended to alternate between cases that broadly interpret the clauses and cases that read the First Amendment more restrictively.

The First Amendment and the Incorporation Doctrine

Most of the foundational guarantees of civil liberties and civil rights are codified in the Bill of Rights, the first ten amendments that were added to the Constitution soon after ratification. The original text of the Constitution did not explicitly guarantee these rights. The Federalists did not see a need for such amendments because, in their view, the government already protected individual freedoms. Anything not explicitly prohibited by the Constitution was permitted. In contrast, the Anti-Federalists argued for the inclusion of a Bill of Rights similar to those included in many state constitutions at the time. From their perspective, the only way to guarantee that government would always protect citizens' rights and freedoms was to write these protections into the Constitution.

As originally understood, the Bill of Rights applied only to the federal government; the principle of federalism allowed state governments to do as they chose. The three amendments that passed in the wake of the Civil War, however, signaled change and a movement away from unchecked states' rights. In particular, the Fourteenth Amendment included the due process clause, which says that no *state* "may deprive citizens of life, liberty, or property, without due process of law." Beginning in the twentieth century, the Supreme Court began using the due process clause as legal justification for ruling that certain fundamental freedoms in the Bill of Rights applied to the states as well. Constitutional law experts typically refer to this process as *selective incorporation*— over time, the Court is incorporating, or including, provisions from some amendments into the due process clause. Once a provision has been incorporated, the Supreme Court gains jurisdiction over all state laws that might conflict with it.

This process is "selective" because the Supreme Court has not incorporated every provision included in the Bill of Rights, nor is it likely to do so. The Third Amendment, which forbids the government from quartering soldiers in private homes during peacetime, for example, seems almost irrelevant in an age of military bases and compounds, so it is no surprise that it has not been incorporated. On the other hand, the Court has not applied a few controversial amendments to the states. To this point in history, the Court has interpreted the Second Amendment's right to bear arms as applying only to federal laws.

Applying the Religion Clauses to the States

The Supreme Court began applying the First Amendment religion clauses to the states in a series of landmark decisions beginning in 1934. The case of *Hamilton v. Regents of the University of California* was the first to apply the general concept of freedom of religion to state actions. In 1940, the decision in *Cantwell v. Connecticut* specifically incorporated the free exercise clause. The court ruled unanimously to overturn the conviction of Jesse Cantwell, a Jehovah's Witness who was arrested for disturbing the peace and violating a Connecticut law requiring certification of anyone wanting to solicit on behalf of a religious cause. The 1947 case *Everson v. Board of Education of Ewing Township* challenged the use of state money to reimburse transportation expenses for children attending parochial schools. In a 5–4 decision, the Court upheld the New Jersey law, contending that the funding was a general program that helped all children get to school, irrespective of religion. In a move that had far-reaching consequences, Justice Black wrote the opinion of the Court, explicitly connecting the Fourteenth Amendment and the establishment clause—thus applying it to state laws for the first time.

Although *Everson* actually upheld a form of state funding that indirectly benefited religious schools, Justice Black's opinion redefined the relationship between church and state. Drawing inspiration from sources such as Thomas Jefferson's letter to the Danbury Baptists, Black wrote what would become the operative interpretation of the establishment clause for many years:

> The "establishment of religion" clause of the First Amendment means at least this: Neither a state nor the Federal Government can set up a church. Neither can pass laws which aid one religion, aid all religions, or prefer one religion over another. Neither can force nor influence a person to go to or to remain away from church against his will or force him to profess a belief or disbelief in any religion. No person can be punished for entertaining or professing religious beliefs or disbeliefs, for church attendance or non-attendance. No tax in any amount, large or small, can be levied to support any religious activities or institutions, whatever they may be called, or whatever form they may adopt to teach or practice religion. Neither a state nor the Federal Government can, openly or secretly, participate in the affairs of any religious organizations or groups and vice versa. In the words of Jefferson, the clause against establishment of religion by law was intended to erect "a wall of separation between Church and State."[17]

With the reading of this opinion, Jefferson's wall of separation reentered the American lexicon. For many judges and observers, the establishment clause became synonymous with separation of church and state.

Establishment Cases and the Lemon Test

As we saw in the previous chapter, Supreme Court decisions sometimes create legal tests that outline criteria for judges to follow in future cases. The most famous test for establishment cases, the *Lemon* test, gets its name from *Lemon v. Kurtzman* (1971), in which the Court agreed to decide three related cases at the same time. Plaintiffs in Pennsylvania and Rhode Island challenged laws that gave public funding to private religious schools. In Pennsylvania, for example, the state supplemented teachers' salaries and helped purchase books and materials for nonreligious courses in parochial schools. Chief Justice Burger wrote for the unanimous court, striking down the laws in both states for violating the establishment clause, and creating a new legal test. According to the *Lemon* test, laws that affect religious organizations must meet three criteria: (1) they must have a primarily secular purpose, (2) they should neither advance nor inhibit religion, and (3) they must avoid "excessive government entanglement with religion."[18] Using these criteria, the Court ruled state funding of nonreligious instruction in religious schools unconstitutional. The laws did have a secular purpose, but they failed the final two parts of the test, as they served to advance religion and created excessive entanglement between the government and the religious schools.

Although restrictive, the *Lemon* test leaves some room for formal interactions between government and religious organizations. For example, this test would allow a government program like Medicaid to pay for services rendered to a patient at a Catholic hospital.

Free Exercise Cases and the Sherbert Test

The 1963 case of *Sherbert v. Verner* considered the free exercise complaint of Adeil Sherbert, a Seventh-Day Adventist who was fired because she refused to work on Saturday, the day her church observed the Sabbath. The state of South Carolina did not accept her religious explanation and ruled her ineligible for unemployment insurance. In a 7–2 decision, the Supreme Court ruled in favor of Sherbert, arguing that the state violated her free exercise of religion and did not have a compelling interest in denying her unemployment insurance. Justice Brennan's decision created a two-pronged test for free exercise claims. According to the *Sherbert* test, state laws can interfere with religious practices only if (1) the state can show it has a compelling interest for creating the law, and (2) the state cannot achieve its goal any other way without hindering religious observance.

An example of a subsequent case that relied on the *Sherbert* test is *Wisconsin v. Yoder*, the 1972 ruling that Amish parents could opt out of state laws requiring children to attend school until age sixteen. Amish families educated their children through eighth grade, and the Court found that the added value to the government of assuring students received another year or two of schooling was not compelling enough to justify the strong violation of Amish religious practice.

For almost half a century, the Supreme Court has required that laws inhibiting free exercise of religion must pass the "compelling state interest" test. What does this phrase actually mean?

State and federal legislators cannot impose legal restrictions on a whim. Indeed, a primary role of the courts is to determine if and when government regulations are permissible. Judges use various legal tests to measure a law's constitutionality. The compelling state interest test is the most restrictive; very few laws survive legal challenges when this test applies.

Describing the origins of the standard, the First Amendment Center explains that the test first appeared in civil rights cases in the 1950s and 1960s. Justice Brennan described the application of the test, explaining that "the Court must give a 'heightened scrutiny' to cases in which fundamental rights were at stake and require the state to demonstrate that the law in question served only interests that were of paramount importance."[19] Such a test requires the government to meet a very high standard justifying the purpose of the law; national security and ensuring access to education are two examples of interests the Court finds compelling. A less rigorous test, the "rational basis" test, generally upholds laws as long as the state can show a good reason for creating the statute.

Changing Times? The Future of Religion Cases

In the decades since the landmark rulings in *Lemon* and *Sherbert*, the Supreme Court has decided several high-profile First Amendment religion cases by very close margins. The retirement of Justice Sandra Day O'Connor, often the deciding vote in religion cases, adds some uncertainty. For the future, much will depend on how the two newest members of the Court, Chief Justice John Roberts and Justice Samuel Alito, interpret the religion clauses.

Although the Supreme Court continues to apply the *Lemon* test in some establishment clause cases, several of the justices find the test too restrictive. Generally, the Court is more likely to uphold laws that provide indirect aid to religion than those that give funding directly to religious institutions. In the 5–4 decision in *Zelman v. Simmons-Harris* (2002), for example, the Court upheld a program that allowed parents to use tax-supported vouchers to pay for tuition at religious schools.

Interpretations of the free exercise clause have created the most controversy. In the 1990 case *Employment Division v. Smith*, the Court abandoned the *Sherbert* test. Two Oregon drug counselors had used peyote, a hallucinogenic drug, in an Indian religious ceremony. When they failed a drug test, they were fired and denied unemployment benefits. In a 6–3 decision, the Court ruled in favor of Oregon, abandoning the compelling interest test in *Sherbert* and applying different standards. The law did not specifically target religion, and the state has a reason for prohibiting drug use, so the law was constitutional. *Smith* thus gave states permission to pass and enforce laws that are generally applicable even if the unintended consequences harm free exercise of religion.

The outcry was immediate. Both conservative and liberal groups lobbied Congress for redress. In response, Congress passed the Religious Freedom Restoration Act of 1993 to reinstate the *Sherbert* test. The new law was short-lived; the Supreme Court overturned it in 1997, arguing that Congress did not have the power to tell the Supreme Court how to interpret the Constitution.

The issues the Supreme Court addresses are among the most controversial in American politics, so discussions of constitutional law are rife with controversy. One area about which experts on constitutional law readily agree, however, is the confusing status of cases interpreting the religion clauses. As one legal scholar summarized:

> Documenting the inconsistency of the Supreme Court's religion clause decisions is a virtual cliché in constitutional scholarship. The Court's decisions in this area have been described as "ad hoc," "eccentric," "misleading and distorting," "historically unjustified and textually incoherent," and—finally—"riven by contradictions and bogged down in slogans and metaphors." No one, it seems, much cares for the Court's work in this area.[20]

In this context of ever-changing court decisions, one can make only educated guesses as to how the Court will rule on future religion cases.

In the previous two chapters, we looked first at the two-party system in the United States and then discussed the structure and function of the different branches of government. It is time then to move to the final section of the book. The next five chapters will help you apply your faith to American politics. Let's begin by looking at some of the different ways Christian believers have approached political life.

PART 4

FINDING YOUR OWN PATH

APPLYING YOUR FAITH TO POLITICS

9

Applying Faith to Politics

Some Different Christian Approaches

Do not answer a fool according to his folly,
or you will be like him yourself.

Proverbs 26:4

Answer a fool according to his folly,
or he will be wise in his own eyes.

Proverbs 26:5

As God's Word, the Bible provides the foundation for Christian teaching, doctrine, and action. Christians across the centuries have found comfort, sustenance, and instruction in its pages. But the Bible is a complicated text, including books of various literary genres and styles, outlining the law and the gospel in different forms and voices.

Some biblical passages seem very straightforward, while others, like the parables, seem intentionally puzzling. Consider the two verses above from the book of Proverbs. Following one after the other, they appear to offer conflicting advice. According to these verses, is it wise to answer the fool or not? One Bible commentary considers these two verses together, concluding that the correct response to the fool depends on the situation: "Life is complex and the same easy answer is not applicable to every situation. The wise person is one who can see which piece of wisdom applies in each circumstance."[1] Wisdom helps us unravel the apparent paradox of Proverbs 26:4–5. As we will see in this chapter, we also need wisdom to apply biblical truth to complex political questions.

Christians need not struggle with the challenges of biblical interpretation all alone. Indeed, throughout the centuries God has given the gifts of pastors, teachers, and theologians to help Christians interpret God's Word and apply its truth to their daily lives. Through spoken words and written works, ministers of the gospel offer insights into the Bible and the God revealed in its pages.

When a pastor delivers a sermon that enriches our understanding of a favorite passage, we appreciate the Bible in a new light and learn more about God. In much the same way, theological traditions create frameworks that help us interpret and clarify biblical truth. In the first part of this chapter, we will explore four of the major streams of political theology that provide Christians tools for relating their faith to politics. The chapter then discusses different ways that Christians apply theory to practice, considering both the relationship between church and state and questions of faith and politics.

Political Theology: Frameworks and Perspectives

Four of the most significant Christian traditions of political theology offer a range of perspectives on the nature and scope of the interaction between Christian persons and congregations (the "church") and the government (the "state"). Political theology can be highly contested between and even within the various traditions; these frameworks cross denominational lines in their application and influence. With this in mind, consider each of these sketches as a brief and necessarily incomplete introduction to some of the basic themes and broad hallmarks of each approach. Some of you will see a version of your own faith tradition reflected here; others may find little that looks familiar. Whatever your vantage point, it is important to learn from the strengths and weaknesses of each theological perspective in order to grow in your own understanding of how faith applies to political life.

Members of different Christian communities share many core doctrines. To help you compare and contrast their different perspectives on government, however, the introductions below will highlight some of the variations in how each tradition interprets and applies biblical principles. Each brief overview will describe some of the distinctives of each theological tradition, its perspectives on the role of the church and the state, and its view of Christian political participation.

Catholic Political Theology

The history of interaction between the Catholic Church and the state dates back well over a millennium to the Roman emperor Constantine and the rise of Christendom. For centuries, church and state were integrated. In the context of this discussion, however, we will focus on the contemporary Catholic understanding of church and state since the reforms of the Second Vatican Council, or Vatican II (1962–1966).

The unity and mission of the Catholic Church are central to Catholic theology. Distinctives of the faith include the particular emphases on the incarnation, the sacraments, community, and concern for the poor. The model of Christ incarnate as fully God and fully man leads Catholics to place high value on humanity and the natural world, therefore striving for justice and the common good. Celebration of the sacraments connects Christians with Christ and is therefore the center of church life. Catholic teaching also emphasizes God's design for humans to live in community and our resulting responsibility toward one another. A fourth emphasis, special concern for the poor, "reflects the tension between the values of poverty and the relief of poverty."[2] The long-standing Catholic commitment to operate schools, hospitals, and charities is an example of the church living out its mission.

Catholic theology views government as part of God's creation. The state has important roles in maintaining order, punishing and deterring wrong behavior, and serving justice. The modern Catholic church is a "public church"; that is, the church necessarily has a role within political and social life to serve its purpose. Church and state need some separation to guarantee religious freedom, but the church can and should cooperate with government to achieve shared goals.

Following naturally from this perspective on church and state, the Catholic Church teaches that citizens can and should participate in government. The Catechism outlines three specific moral obligations of all Christian citizens: voting, defending one's country, and paying taxes.[3] But duty to country does not stop at national borders; engagement extends to the entire world community, especially the goal of promoting peace.

Most of the principles that govern the Catholic view of church and state come from Catholic Social Teaching (CST). This tradition officially dates from a particular formulation in 1891 and provides principles for preserving faith and living out the gospel when interacting with modern society. Seven key themes comprise the heart of CST: the dignity of all human life; the call to family, community, and participation; rights and responsibilities; preferential care for the poor and vulnerable; the dignity of work; solidarity; and care for God's creation.[4] Balancing these goals means that, in practice, "the political patterns for Catholic advocacy generally defy typical partisan divisions due to their 'progressive' stances on social welfare and labor and 'conservative' positions on abortion and education policy."[5]

Political scientist Clarke Cochran describes four aspects of the church's relationship with politics, culture, and society: cooperating with government to meet certain needs, challenging government policies Catholics believe are wrong, competing with government to provide similar services, and transcending government to further the gospel and follow the Great Commission. Depending on the circumstances and the issues at hand, the church can respond in different ways: "CST incorporates these four modes, recognizing a plurality of applications to particular social and political questions, which gives Catholic social doctrine unique power and flexibility."[6]

The principle of *subsidiarity* offers guidance to determine what problems government should address and what issues are better left to families, churches, or individuals. First introduced in 1931, subsidiarity is "the idea that government should not replace or absorb smaller forms of community, but should provide them with help (*subsidium*) when they are unable or unwilling to contribute to the common good on their own. The government directs and coordinates the activities of these smaller units or voluntary associations as needed."[7] Government is an important, necessary, and limited agent to provide for the common good, but it functions best in partnership with associations that are close to the people and best able to meet their particular needs.

Lutheran Political Theology

The modern-day Lutheran churches trace their roots to the writings of sixteenth-century Protestant Reformer Martin Luther. Hallmarks of Luther's teachings include the doctrine of justification by faith alone, an emphasis on human sinfulness, and the priority of the Word and sacraments as signs of the gospel. For the Christian, good works are not a means to salvation but a natural response to God's love expressed in love for neighbor: "A Christian lives not in himself but in Christ and his neighbor. Otherwise he is not a Christian. He lives in Christ through faith, in his neighbor through love. By faith he is caught up beyond himself in God. By love he descends beneath himself into his neighbor."[8]

At the heart of Luther's teachings are two principles: two kingdoms and two governments. As historian David Steinmetz summarizes:

> The two kingdoms refer primarily to the two overlapping spheres of Christian existence, the life of the Christian before God and the life of the Christian in society. The two governments refer to the two ways in which God governs the world. God governs the Church through the gospel, a government from which all forms of coercion are excluded; and he governs the world through law and coercion, a government which cannot achieve its ends through the persuasive preaching of love.[9]

The two kingdoms are distinct but intersecting. The spiritual lives of Christians are thus distinguished from their interactions as citizens, but their faith gives meaning and purpose for their service in the kingdom of the world.

The two governments of Lutheran theology establish very different roles and powers for the church and the state. Christians are subject to both civil and church authority. The church is ordained by God to preach the gospel, teach the Word, and administer the sacraments. Some form of church government is permissible as long as it is not coercive. The state, in contrast, is only necessary as a result of the fall. Because of sin, God created government both to restrain those who don't have God and therefore fall into wickedness, and to protect citizens and ensure justice for them. Governments can and will use force to restrain evil.

Traditional Lutheran teaching provides that Christian citizens can participate in government for two central reasons. First, the state is a part of God's established order and therefore a worthy place for Christians to serve. Second, the state provides a means for living out love for neighbor; Christians can and should serve in government because non-Christians need government to ensure justice and punish wickedness. If Christians lived according to the gospel, they would not need the state. Since they often live in disobedience to God, Christians also need government. The laws of God are higher than any laws of government, so Christians may choose to passively resist ungodly laws. Violent resistance is not an option.

The most common contemporary Lutheran application of the two-kingdoms doctrine emphasizes different roles for the church and the individual Christian. The church's primary focus is spreading the gospel through preaching the Word and administering the sacraments. The institutional church does not get directly involved in politics but teaches, challenges, and equips its members to love and serve their neighbors. Christians live out their faith as active citizens of both kingdoms: "It is the individual Christian, both as member of the church and citizen of the state, who is duty bound to become the primary 'speaker' of the church's many social concerns. . . . Therefore, individual Christians can, and must, learn to translate the concerns of God's Word into arguments appropriate for civil government."[10] This distinction between the role of the church and its members makes room for individual Christians to disagree on political matters and for Christians to partner in service with those outside the faith.

Anabaptist Political Theology

The term "Anabaptist" (from the Greek words for "again" and "baptize") emerged in the sixteenth century to describe a wide range of radical Reformers who rejected the practice of infant baptism and instead advocated baptism only for those who profess faith in Christ. Their teachings ran counter to those of the established churches of their time, so the early Anabaptists faced great persecution. Many were executed as heretics.

Although this umbrella term includes a wide range of thinkers, some general hallmarks of early Anabaptist thought include sharp distinctions between the church and the world, an emphasis on a church comprised only of professed believers, and a priority on New Testament writings, especially the life and teachings of Jesus. A commitment to pacifism or nonresistance became another distinctive of the movement, one that historian Werner O. Packull describes as "a unique contribution in a violent age."[11] In its earliest expression, nonresistance "means literally accepting powerlessness and abstaining from any use of force or coercion, even self-defence. For Anabaptists, non-resistance was not a calculated survival strategy but a principle for Christian life and conduct; an assumed non-political kingdom ethic revealed by Christ."[12]

The sixteenth-century Anabaptists developed a view of the state that accepted the basic structure of the Lutheran two-kingdoms doctrine: government is part of the kingdom of the world; the church is part of the kingdom of God. Government is ordained by God, so Christians must obey secular authorities unless their teachings violate God's commands.

Concerned about the corruption within the churches of their day, Anabaptist reformers sought to recover the true church: "The kingdom [of God] was to be made visible in the church, restored to its pristine apostolic purity. True followers of Christ gathered in closely knit, disciplined communities in which the rule and command of Christ prevailed."[13] The church thus stood in contrast to the world as God's witness and his community. These beliefs provided the foundation for the Anabaptist call for separation of church and state. To preserve the purity of the church, she must be set apart: "Arguing that the believing Christian community, not government, should govern the church, they rejected over 1,100 years of the union of church and state, demanding instead complete freedom from the state in all matters of religion."[14]

In stark contrast to the Lutheran view that Christians demonstrate love for neighbor through participation in government, most of the early Anabaptist writers "said that a Christian may not participate in government out of love for neighbor. A servant of Christ had no liberty to use coercion and vengeance or to kill because it was contrary to the commandments of Christ."[15] Governments rule by power and force, punishing those who violate the law; Christians, however, must renounce violence and take on love. Christ's command of love for neighbor therefore points the Christian to a different and better path than government: "Insofar as it were possible for a government to act in this way it could well be Christian in its office. Since however the world will not tolerate it, a friend of God should not be in the government but out of it, that is if he desires to keep Christ as Lord and Master."[16]

In contemporary practice, the Anabaptist tradition offers a distinctive model of Christian engagement that emphasizes Jesus's ethic of nonviolence and the church's role as the community of Christ. Jesus makes radical and countercultural demands, and Christians must seek to follow them. In keeping with their pacifist heritage, modern Anabaptists usually hold one of two views on government and the use of force. Some contend that government can use coercion when necessary, but Christians cannot participate in such actions. Others argue that violence is always outside God's will. Because this tradition promotes faithfulness to Christ's teaching by working as an active community of believers, Anabaptists are most likely to seek change through work and advocacy outside of government.

Reformed Political Theology

The Reformed tradition developed from the writings and teachings of noted sixteenth-century Protestants such as John Calvin, John Knox, and Ulrich Zwingli. Hallmarks of this tradition include an emphasis on the sovereignty of God and the use of the narrative of creation, fall, and redemption as a framework for understanding God's interaction with humanity.

Creation refers both to God's original creative acts and to the mandate for humans to fill the earth and subdue it. As such, institutions such as the family and the state were designed and established by God as part of the perfect created order.

Because of the fall, sin affects humans in all aspects of their lives. God's grace extends to the fallen world in two ways. *Particular grace* refers to the saving grace God extends to those whom he calls. *Common grace* "is experienced in the ordering of nature, the restraint of evil and the ability of unbelievers to reason and perform acts of civil good. The doctrine of common grace holds that God bestows on humanity a grace that, while not 'saving,' enables unbelievers to develop many virtues and express many truths."[17] The state is one agent of this common grace.

Redemption, the final piece of the gospel narrative, applies to all of creation. Just as individuals can receive personal redemption from their sins, so can institutions "become agents of redemption (not in terms of salvation but of transformation) in the society and world at large, fulfilling their original purpose by bringing about a right ordering of human interrelationships."[18] Although corrupted by the fall, government can thus serve a redemptive purpose. Complete redemption is impossible until Christ returns, but Christians must join in the work of renewal while they await the full restoration available only in Christ.

John Calvin wrote that God ordained government and holds its leaders accountable to him, so Christians must obey and respect the state. Contempt for government is not an option, for "to despise human government is to despise the providence which set that government in place. Rules must be obeyed, not on the grounds of human necessity, but on the grounds of obedience to God."[19] Furthermore, Christians can and should participate in government, as in all spheres of life, seeking to transform fallen institutions and structures.

One contemporary application of Reformed teaching is the concept of "principled pluralism," derived in large part from the work of Abraham Kuyper, Dutch Reformed theologian and former prime minister of the Netherlands. Kuyper focuses on the concept of *sphere sovereignty*, the view that society includes different and important institutions, or spheres, ordained by God, serving different roles. The state is one of these spheres that ensures justice in and between the different institutions of society. Constitutional law and representative government constrain the state's power.

Principled pluralism begins with recognition of the wide range of religious worldviews. It is not the role of the state to prescribe a particular religious perspective; instead, government should guarantee freedom of religion. The state is one of many structures in society designed by God, so its powers should be limited. The primary role of government is to secure justice—in the negative sense of protecting its citizens from harm, and in the positive sense of promoting the common good. Governments cannot and should not try to impose morality, for "the task of government is not to compel everything that is right or moral, nor to punish everything that is wrong or immoral, but to enforce that particular part of morality we call justice. . . . Because morality is a matter of the heart, no one can be forced to be moral."[20] Christians must discern

	Theological Distinctives	View of Government	View of Christian Political Participation
Catholic	Emphasis on incarnation gives high value to humanity and the natural world Sacraments are at the center of church life God designed humans to live in community; we are responsible for one another Special concern for the poor	Government is part of creation Some separation of church and state may be necessary for religious freedom Church can cooperate with government Principle of subsidiarity; government is a necessary but limited agent	Christians should participate Moral obligation to vote, defend their country, and pay taxes Promote peace around the world Notion of a "public church"
Lutheran	Doctrine of justification by faith alone Emphasis on human sinfulness and the Word and sacraments as signs of the gospel "Two-kingdoms" principle: life before God and life in society	"Two governments": one for the church, one for the state Government is a result of the fall Government will use force to restrain evil	Christians should participate; the state is a part of God's established order and provides a means for love of neighbor Permits passive resistance to ungodly laws Church should not be directly involved in politics
Anabaptist	Baptism for professing believers; the believers' church Sharp distinctions between church and world Priority of the New Testament, especially teachings of Jesus Nonresistance or pacifism	Government was ordained by God after the fall Advocate separation of church and state; the church must be set apart to preserve her purity	Love of neighbor compels Christians not to participate in government Obey secular laws unless they contradict God's commands Emphasis on Jesus's ethic of nonviolence
Reformed	Emphasis on the sovereignty of God Emphasis on narrative of creation, fall, and redemption	Government is part of God's created order The state is an agent of common grace Government is fallen but can serve redemptive purposes Primary role of government is to secure justice	Christians should participate in government as an agent of transformation Demands obedience to and respect of the state unless an act would contradict God's law Churches can act institutionally to organize political action

what tasks are best suited for different spheres of influence, not expecting too much or too little from government.

In contrast to the Lutheran and Anabaptist restrictions of the church's mission to evangelism, discipleship, and mercy, the Reformed tradition makes room for some corporate political activity by the church. While they do not envision the church ruling society as in Calvin's Geneva or Puritan New England, churches can act institutionally to advocate public policy or organize political action.

Learning from the Four Frameworks

The brief discussions above are intended as introductions, not definitive discussions, of these four streams of political theology. Each tradition brings new ideas and frameworks to the table to help shape our thinking about the role of the church, the purpose of the state, and the place for Christian participation in politics and government. As we have seen, it will not always be possible for Christians to find common ground on these questions. But it is possible to learn more about other traditions so we can grow in appreciation and respect for their approaches to such complicated matters.

We should bear in mind that each of these traditions arose in particular historical circumstances. The people in those times faced particular religious concerns that focused their attention as they approached the Bible. These original theological frameworks pre-date the rise of modern democracy, so none of them, at least in pure form, may be adequate for addressing the complexity of modern, globalized politics. At the same time, however, we need these centuries-old schools of thought to speak from history to inform our present-day understanding and application of Scripture.

Theory and Practice: Religion, the State, and the Christian

Every Christian citizen, regardless of theological or church background, must wrestle with questions about the relationship between religion, the state, and the individual Christian. Sometimes knowingly and sometimes inadvertently, the theoretical issues discussed so far in this chapter can and do converge with real-life experience. Every time you check on breaking news stories, head

An Alternative Political Vision: The Influence of Revivalism

In addition to the four major traditions of political theology described in this chapter, another tradition within Christianity informs the politics of many Americans. A conversionist approach—also known as *revivalism*—is common among Baptists, Methodists, Pentecostals, and those who worship in independent, or Bible, churches. This perspective emphasizes the centrality of personally experiencing transformation and devotion to God.

Revivalism has a long and rich heritage in the United States. It began with Jonathan Edwards, George Whitefield, and the Great Awakening of 1720 and continued through the nineteenth-century Holiness Movement, the preaching of D. L. Moody, and all the way to the evangelistic crusades of Billy Graham in the twentieth century. Revival movements often emphasize emotion as a crucial dimension of faith and include public calls for people to repent from their sins and accept Jesus Christ as their personal Savior.

Although Christians can and should engage in good deeds that meet the needs of those around them, the ultimate expression of love for neighbor is evangelism, sharing the good news of Christ with a lost and broken world. The solution to political problems thus comes from Jesus Christ changing people's hearts one by one, not primarily by changing social structures or through political processes. Many of the leaders in the contemporary Religious Right who come from this perspective now advocate political involvement on certain issues of personal morality.

Many revivalists have been affected as well by popular versions (often even misunderstandings) of "dispensationalism." This approach finds distinct time periods within the Bible regarding how God administers his plan for the world. Often focused on the nation of Israel distinct from the church, dispensationalist views on biblical prophecy and the Rapture frequently led Christians away from social and political engagement. Recently, though, dispensationalists have been debating among themselves about their future identity. Moreover, popular uses (or misuses) of their views such as in the Left Behind series reflect new forms of political concern. A tendency toward negative or even paranoid views of culture often has them fitting into the agenda of the Religious Right.

to the polling place, or talk about politics with friends, you are making connections between your faith and your political views. This final section will help you bridge theory and practice.

In common conversation about religion and American politics, most people talk in terms of "church and state." At the extremes, one camp raises the alarm that the United States is in danger of becoming a theocracy, while the other worries that God has been entirely removed from public life. Too much of the popular discussion sets up a false choice, as if American government must either be thoroughly Christian or else scrubbed clean of all connections to religious ideas and practices. In reality, the balance between church and state has fluctuated over the course of American history as interpretations and applications of the Constitution change and new issues arise.

One important reason that discussions of religion and politics grow confusing is that many people confuse church and state questions with their views on how personal faith should inform politics. In its formal usage, the phrase *church and state* is generally accepted as shorthand for the connection (or lack of connection) between formal religious organizations and formal governing institutions. In contrast, questions of what I will call *faith and politics* ask how personal faith convictions should or should not inform citizens' politics. The two types of questions are interrelated but distinct, and both raise issues that Christians need to consider. Yet when we mix up personal concerns with legal and constitutional questions, confusion often reigns.

Moving Beyond Simple Categories: A Church-State Spectrum

What is the proper Christian understanding of the relationship between church and state? What may appear to be a simple question is quite complex in practice. Far too many discussions of church and state issues begin with assumptions that everyone's views can fit neatly and easily into discrete categories. Each person either supports separation or else wants everything to mix. In practice, views on these questions are rarely so sharp and defined, so it makes much more sense to think about notions of separation and integration as points on a spectrum of beliefs rather than discrete, mutually exclusive categories. Let's sketch three general positions on the relationship between church and state that span a range of possibilities.

On one end of the spectrum are those who call for *separation of the state from the church* out of concern that religion could wield too much influence. Borrowing from the ideals of the Enlightenment and an emphasis on moral reason, advocates of this view are most concerned about protecting the autonomy of government. They want to separate religion and government into distinct spheres for at least two fundamental reasons: to ensure freedom of religious expression and to guard against theocracy. If the state sanctions an official religion, all others are in jeopardy. Without safeguards in place, churches might impose their religious views through government policy. Organizations like Americans United for Separation of Church and State reflect this vantage point.

At the opposite end of the scale are those who support *separation of the church from the state*, sometimes called pietistic separationists. They also advocate formal separation of church and state, but their fears are in the reverse order. Their concern is to maintain the church's purity and authenticity. If churches are too dependent on government, they risk assimilating and losing their prophetic role. The church thus needs distance from the state so it can speak against government failures and injustice. Proponents of this perspective also stress that authentic religion must be voluntary. The state can try to force people to believe, but such coercion does not create true religion. Members of Anabaptist denominations such as Mennonites and Brethren are likely to hold some version of this view.

If we envision the two forms of separation placed at each end of a spectrum of perspectives, in the center of the two would be a third perspective, *interaction*. Proponents of this view advocate some blending of church and state. They maintain that organized religion enhances the state because it is the foundation for moral and civic life. The church teaches virtues that make better citizens and improve government. Furthermore, many advocates of this view argue that you cannot completely strip religious views from public life; religion provides a strong motivation and rationale for many people who pursue political activities. Moreover, even nonreligious views are not truly neutral, for they too are based on presuppositions. It is unreasonable and unrealistic to expect people to ignore their religious beliefs when serving in government. Members of Reformed denominations such as Presbyterians and the Christian Reformed Church tend to advocate some version of this perspective.

These three categories anchor a spectrum of views on church and state. Figure 9.1 presents one way to visualize this. When developing your own view of how you believe religious and governmental institutions should interrelate, consider your theological convictions and personal experiences, weighing the strengths and weaknesses of each perspective. These tools can help you decide where your view best fits on the scale. A Mennonite who respects the separationist tradition of her church but sees slightly more room for Christians to participate in government, for example, might place herself between full interaction and the complete separation of church from state. Alternatively, a lifelong member of the Christian Reformed Church and career politician who serves in the U.S. Senate might place himself at or very near the midpoint of the diagram.

Figure 9.1: A Spectrum of Views on Church and State

Separate State from Church	Interaction	Separate Church from State

Many factors influence opinions on religion and government— for example, one's understanding of faith, personal experience with different levels of government, the ever-changing political landscape, or new seasons of life. In much the same way that views about the relationship between church and state may not easily fit into discrete categories, they may also change with time and reflection.

The Personal Is Political: Faith, Politics, and Individuals

Although church-and-state debates can grow quite heated, many of the contemporary controversies about the role of religion in public life are actually faith-and-politics questions. This distinct category, related to yet still different from church-and-state questions, reflects citizens' convictions about how their personal religious beliefs should inform their politics. In conversations about religion and politics, people too often talk past one another instead of with each other because they confuse legal and constitutional questions with matters of personal opinion and judgment. Once you learn to distinguish church-and-state issues from dilemmas of faith and politics, conversation becomes easier and more productive.

If you ask American Christians if their faith influences their politics, most will answer a resounding yes. But if you ask them to explain the particular ways their religious views affect them, you are likely to get a wide variety of answers.

Now that you understand more about why people hold differing views of religion and politics and church and state, you can see how Christians can in good faith reach different conclusions about political questions. Christians from different theological traditions will have different assumptions about what government can and should do, just as they may find very different ways to address political dilemmas. As we seek to apply our faith to politics, we need to be aware of our theological and ideological assumptions and be willing to engage with others about theirs.

Many Christians face challenges applying their faith to politics when they encounter tensions between their theological or ideological goals and the reality of what is pragmatically possible. Government cannot solve every problem, nor should we expect it to do so. We each must weigh our personally held beliefs to determine which of our concerns are likely to be issues of public policy and which are best left to individuals. More mundanely, we may not have enough votes, time, or money to champion a particular policy. The practical realities of politics often require us to scale back our expectations, recognizing that government may not be ready or may not have the resources to tackle every aspect of a problem. Even if we don't achieve our ultimate goals, we can make progress.

This chapter has introduced various theological perspectives and conceptions of the role of church and state to help you better characterize your own views. Unfortunately, it is not as easy to create discrete categories for approaching faith-and-politics questions, for such dilemmas refer more to the day-to-day decisions that individuals make as they interact with politics.

The full practical value of the distinction between dilemmas of faith and politics and perspectives on church and state will likely become clearer in the remaining chapters of this book. Each chapter includes background information and some pointers to help you apply your faith to a different realm of politics. The next chapter explains why political dialogue can be so complex and frustrating and offers suggestions for how to engage in meaningful conversations about politics. We will then explore the complexity of public policy, examining different ways that people might approach a political issue. The final two chapters will help you apply your faith to voting and to other forms of political participation.

10

My Way or the Highway?

Toward Constructive Political Dialogue

Most of us are conditioned for many years to have a political viewpoint—Republican or Democratic, liberal, conservative, or moderate.
The fact of the matter is that most of the problems . . . that we now
face are technical problems, are administrative problems. They are
very sophisticated judgments, which do not lend themselves to the
great sort of passionate movements which have stirred this country
so often in the past. [They] deal with questions which are now beyond
the comprehension of most men.

John F. Kennedy (1917–1963),
thirty-fifth president of the United States

I have never found, in a long experience of politics, that criticism is
ever inhibited by ignorance.

Harold Macmillan (1894–1986),
British prime minister

As part of his 1992 campaign for the presidency, Bill Clinton promised to "end welfare as we know it." Reflecting the widely shared
belief that the existing system of cash assistance for single mothers
was deeply flawed, the Democratic nominee promised change.
Four years and two vetoes later, President Bill Clinton signed the
Personal Responsibility and Work Opportunity Reconciliation

Act, a welfare reform bill that had passed in both the House and the Senate with the support of most congressional Republicans and some Democrats.

The debate over welfare reform had been intense. The legislation planned to replace the old system, Aid to Families with Dependent Children (AFDC), with a new program, the aptly named Temporary Assistance for Needy Families (TANF). TANF offered states blocks of money, giving them more freedom to design the specifics of their welfare programs while at the same time adding work requirements for recipients and placing lifetime caps on receipt of benefits.

Supporters of the new program clashed with those who feared that such changes would worsen the lives of the many Americans living in poverty and put millions of children at risk. The Children's Defense Fund warned the bill would "leave a moral blot on [Clinton's] presidency and on our nation that will never be forgotten."[1] Patricia Ireland of the National Organization for Women derided Congress and the president for "pulling a shift and shaft on poor women and their children."[2] The *New York Times* editorial page described the bill as "draconian welfare reform" that would "[throw] perhaps a million children into poverty."[3] Senator Daniel Patrick Moynihan (D-NY) warned, "Those involved will take this disgrace to their graves."[4] Explaining her "no" vote during floor debate in the House of Representatives, Congresswoman Lynn Woolsey (D-CA) explained, "This bill says to poor children, do not get hungry, do not get sick, and, for Pete's sake, do not get cold, because your time is up, and we do not think you are important enough to provide you with the basics that you need to survive."[5]

Supporters of the bill offered a very different perspective. Congressman Bill Archer lauded the bill as "the biggest, most helpful change to social policy in America since the 1930s. This vote recognizes that America is a caring country, that Americans are a giving people, and that welfare recipients are capable of success if we would only let them try."[6] President Clinton captured the front page of the *New York Times* when he signed the bill and heralded "a new day that offers hope, honors responsibility, rewards work and changes the terms of the debate so that no one in America ever feels again the need to criticize people who are poor or on welfare."[7]

The inflated rhetoric from interest groups, editorial boards, and elected officials masked much of the genuine agreement between the opponents in the welfare debate. Almost all of the politicians and activists on both sides shared similar goals: keeping people, especially children, from poverty and hunger; promoting work and responsibility; and helping parents find meaningful work to support their children. They fundamentally disagreed, however, about what particular policies would best achieve these goals.

The story of the welfare battle mirrors that of many policy debates in American politics. Elected officials and activists often share similar policy goals but disagree about the best ways to achieve them. In the midst of often heated battles, temptations increase to lash out at opponents and mischaracterize their motives. This chapter explores some of the ways in which confusion over the ends and means of public policy creates stumbling blocks for honest and open public debate. In particular, we will consider two broad categories of political issues—so-called easy issues and hard issues—and the specific challenges that each set of policies creates.

Talking about Public Policy: The Roles of Ends and Means

Have you ever wondered why politicians always seem to be fighting with each other? Does it seem like the government takes too long to address a problem or cannot fix it? If you have pondered these or similar questions, you are not alone. One of the reasons policy debates can seem so hopeless is that most of the work of government involves trying to solve problems that have no easy solutions. If a problem is simple to fix, government acts quickly and solves it. Everything else—the complex, seemingly intractable issues—is left for public debate.

"Easy" and "Hard" Issues

One way political scientists divide political issues is to talk about them as "easy" or "hard" issues, differentiating between those that seem easy to understand and others that seem more complicated. When asked if government should allow gay marriage, for example, most people can answer quite quickly either yes or no. This is an "easy" issue. On the other hand, if you ask someone whether the government should try to stop terrorism, almost everyone (except perhaps terrorists and their sponsors) would immediately say yes; but when you ask the necessary follow-up question—what should we do?—the early consensus quickly disintegrates. Terrorism is a perfect example of a "hard" issue—almost everyone agrees on the end goal but disagrees on the means of achieving it. Policy debates over terrorism are not about *if* we should stop terrorism but *how* we can stop it.

The term *easy issues*—a misnomer for sure—gets its name from the notion that people can quickly and easily decide their views on certain subjects. People think they understand them and know their position instinctively. Typically, easy issues are presented as if they have only two sides: someone is either for something or against it; there is a right side and a wrong one with little room for middle ground. The categories seem simple; the focus is sharply and intently on the end goal. Most so-called moral issues fall into this category: abortion, gay marriage, and criminalization of narcotics, for example.

Unlike easy issues that appear to be black-and-white, *hard issues* are by definition complex. The debate over hard issues is rarely about ends and almost always about means. The center of controversy on these subjects is not the desired policy goal—almost everyone agrees on the desired result. Disagreements emerge and multiply as people debate the best way to accomplish a goal and struggle to weigh the relative importance of a problem compared with all the other matters government might address. Classic examples of hard issues include ending poverty, maintaining peace, or combating pollution. Voters rarely dispute that such goals are laudable; the problem is reaching consensus on how to achieve them and when to act.

When We Disagree on Ends and Fail to Talk about Means

Because the locus of debate on easy issues is typically over ends, not means, activists often frame the debate in absolutist terms, cueing voters that compromise is not only impossible but may even be immoral. Thus, political debates over moral issues use the language of black-and-white, us versus them, right and wrong. Such stark contrast offers little space for shades of gray.

And herein lies the problem. As discussed in chapter 2, the heart of politics is bargaining and compromise. To an outside observer, an easy issue appears to have two distinct sides, but in reality government may have multiple options for addressing all or part of the issue. As soon as people take sides, staking claims as either for or against a particular end goal, the likelihood of cooperating to find solutions dwindles. Such issue framing leaves us with two options: either an issue is truly dichotomous and requires taking one side or the other, or the subject matter is instead multifaceted and thus a more likely candidate for seeking partial resolution in the political process.

Activists often have strong incentives for using divisive rhetoric to keep the debate raging and fill their bank accounts. Potential donors are much more likely to contribute to a cause if the stakes are high and the situation appears dire. Consider the following warning from a recent email message from MoveOn.org: "This week, Bush proposed a new budget with devastating cuts to public broadcasting. 'Sesame Street' and other ad-free kids' shows are under the knife. So is the independent journalism our country needs."[8] In reality, the budget outline proposed cutting government funding for public broadcasting by about 25 percent, a significant cut but hardly a move that would automatically eliminate *Sesame*

Street. However, a more realistic description of the proposal would likely not generate 37,000 phone calls to Congress in thirty-six hours, as writers of the above message claimed.

Most of the debate over easy issues is highly charged and intentionally polarizing, but it need not be that way. Demonstrating a different approach to the discussion of abortion, Senator Hillary Clinton made national headlines after delivering a speech to a pro-choice audience, the New York State Family Planning Providers. Beginning with the principle that "every child born in this country (should) be wanted, cherished and loved," she charged the audience to find common ground on the abortion issue. "We can all recognize that abortion in many ways represents a sad, even tragic choice to many, many women."[9] Some observers applauded these remarks, while others scoffed. But the speech made a simple point that was politically distinctive because it touched on an issue usually discussed in all-or-nothing terms. Clearly, those on both ends of the abortion debate have many areas of disagreement, but, as the senator noted, they do share some similar goals. They will likely hold opposing views on more comprehensive policy proposals, but they can find some common ground by seeking incremental yet notable change on areas of shared concern.

When We Agree on Ends and Disagree on Means

What about the other category of issues, those so-called hard issues? How do politicians, activists, and voters approach these kinds of policy problems? Ironically, it is usually easier to debate hard issues and find room for political compromise. When people recognize instinctively that an issue is complex, they are more open to considering various policy alternatives. At the same time, they are also more willing to accept partial solutions as beginning steps toward solving larger problems. Debate over hard issues can grow intense, but most of the key players enter the discussion fully aware that bargaining will be necessary.

Although successful public policy will very likely come through compromise, much of the sloganeering on hard issues ignores this political reality. In the same way that divisive language usually rallies the troops on easy issues, politicians often find that they can capture voter attention by demeaning their opponents' positions on hard issues and thus elicit fear. Even when opposing sides agree on policy goals, many of the political arguments tossed back and

Rhetoric that reframes debates in moral terms can harness great political power. Even though the political debate over hard issues is technically about *how* to solve a problem, activists and politicians often rally their troops as if in a moral battle between right and wrong.

Consider the debate over raising the federal minimum wage, a complex and multifaceted issue. Substantial evidence demonstrates that raising the minimum wage decreases jobs; equally compelling data show that a full-time minimum-wage worker earns less income than necessary to support a family above the poverty level. But commentators and activists find that moralizing strikes a more responsive chord than wrestling with the complexities of competing evidence for and against wage increases. Some condemn the minimum wage itself as immoral while others describe it as an essential moral value:

> First, the minimum wage is immoral. That's right—it is objectively wrong. By instituting and enforcing a minimum wage, government does what government should never do—that is to regulate the simplest economic transactions between you and your neighbor, between consenting adults.
>
> *WorldNetDaily*
> columnist Joseph Farah

> The minimum wage is a bedrock moral value. The minimum wage is where society draws the line: This low and no lower. Our bottom line is this: A job should keep you out of poverty, not keep you in it.
>
> Holly Sklar and Rev. Paul Sherry, summarizing the message of the Let Justice Roll Living Wage Campaign

forth distort the truth and magnify disagreements. Honest differences in opinion about what policy is best can quickly turn into accusations, distortions, and lies.

Although it is indeed possible to find and claim common ground while also advocating divergent policy proposals, such civility is uncommon in today's politically charged climate. In media appearances, press releases, and constituent communications, activists and politicians choose how they frame their support of and opposition to policy proposals. Shrill sound bites are easy to create but lack substance; most enduring political arguments engage the complexity of policy problems.

The day after the Iraq Study Group issued its report to Congress, Senator Chuck Hagel delivered a policy speech at the School for Advanced International Studies (SAIS) of Johns Hopkins University. Hagel opened his speech with this call for discussion:

Too often in Washington, the most deadly serious issues become fodder for the 24-hour news cycle. Thoughtful discussion is welcome as long as you can compress it into a 10 second sound bite or scroll it at the bottom of a television screen. I want to take this opportunity to talk in a little more detail about some of the most urgent and dangerous challenges facing our country and the world.[10]

Hagel then proceeded to deliver a detailed speech that assessed the situation in Iraq and in the larger region, offering substantive reflections on the study group's recommendations. Some observers agreed with Hagel's assessments; others disagreed. But the senator responded to a heated debate with careful, reasoned arguments that opened a path for meaningful dialogue.

From Theory to Practice: The Case of Welfare Reform

Having considered some of the challenges of debating easy and hard issues, let's return to the case study introduced at the beginning of this chapter. It has been more than a decade since Bill Clinton signed welfare reform into law. Who was right? Did the landmark legislation usher in a new era of rewarding work and responsibility, or did millions more children end up in poverty? Obviously, any issue as complex as determining the best way to help poor mothers and their children has no quick fix, and no public policy will completely eliminate the problem. On balance, however, most assessments view the 1996 welfare reform as a success. The number of families on welfare has declined 57 percent, and the number of individuals receiving cash assistance has dropped 64 percent. Many people have left the welfare rolls to find permanent employment. One policy expert summarized the results in congressional testimony:

> Compared to any major change in social policy in the last several decades, I think it is fair to conclude that welfare reform stands out as federal legislation that actually met its goals. . . . There's something here for everybody to like: both more work and government support—except now the bulk of government support is for those working, not those avoiding work. The results of major changes in public policy rarely work out this well.[11]

In large part, welfare reform accomplished what its supporters said it would.

It is unlikely that so many observers would view welfare reform as a success without significant policy changes that occurred in other related areas. At the same time government rewrote and tightened the rules for providing cash assistance to poor families, other legislation and programs expanded and added services such as child-care assistance, medical insurance, and tax credits that helped many of the working poor. Moving from welfare to work would have been almost impossible for most Americans without additional legislation and policy changes that addressed some of the other difficulties associated with poverty.

As is the case for almost all attempts to solve public problems, the solutions are imperfect. The champions of the bill in 1996 cannot claim complete victory because struggles remain. Many people are still trapped in poverty; more than half of current welfare recipients have not found and likely will not find work for a host of reasons. Those who have moved off the welfare rolls have difficulty finding jobs that pay enough to support their families. Some people who are currently eligible for assistance don't seek the help available to them.

At least with this example, the critics who warned of gloom and doom wildly overstated their case. The scary scenarios they predicted did not come to pass. On the other hand, a single welfare reform bill was not sufficient to meet all the reformers' policy goals. Other legislation was necessary to work toward solutions, and still the underlying problems of persistent poverty are only partially solved. When embroiled in a raging political debate, it is difficult to step back from the battle lines and make reasoned assessments of what a proposed policy is likely to achieve. But if we want our faith to inform our political actions and offer a positive Christian witness, such a measured approach is necessary.

Toward Faithful Political Engagement

Given the complexities of seeking solutions to seemingly impossible problems, what can Christians realistically do? Is it even feasible to model our faith in the combative political arena?

Is Any Issue Really Easy? Admitting Complexity

The first step toward more faithful political engagement begins with awareness of the particular tensions created in policy debates over so-called easy and hard issues. We must recognize that many issues that seem simple at first glance look much more complex once you dig deeper; compromise may be not only possible but wise or even necessary. Likewise, we may be able to tackle those hard issues and large-scale problems that seem insurmountable if we accept that we cannot fix everything at once.

Many policymakers and citizens talk and act as if they can solve most public policy problems in one easy step. A strong declarative sound bite—"We will win this battle overnight!"—captures more attention and praise than an outline of a multipronged, and likely more accurate, path in the right direction. Who wants to hear an elected official admit that a problem is so challenging that perhaps the best government can do is address pieces of it over time and hope to stop the bleeding? American voters are much more likely to respond to optimism than pragmatism, so politicians love to promise quick fixes. In reality, few can deliver them. As long as voters respond so enthusiastically to pledges of easy solutions, few candidates will have the courage to speak frankly about the dilemmas government needs to confront.

We can serve those in public office by doing our homework and giving them the benefit of the doubt. When we perpetuate the illusion that policymaking is quick and simple or blindly follow those who try to incite us by acting as if it is easy, we make it much harder for government officials to do their very demanding jobs. Instead of immediately jumping to conclusions when someone sends an alarming email or letter, investigate the claims and do a little research. Their claims may indeed be valid, but often you may discover that they used exaggeration to capture your attention. If a story seems too outlandish to be true, it probably is. If advocates claim a policy proposal will fix a major problem overnight, their pronouncements are likely overblown.

Playing Fair in the War of Words

An additional and crucial step for Christians in politics is to stand firm against mean-spirited, false, and misleading political talk. So much contemporary political debate shows few signs of nuance and creates a harmful Christian witness. The polarizing rhetoric exacerbates us-versus-them thinking and perpetuates the stereotypes of bomb-throwing religious activists. Moreover, as we have seen, such discourse disassociates rhetoric from reality, creating false perceptions of what political choices are possible.

Many Christians enter public debate assuming that they know God's truth on a particular issue. Such an approach may indeed be warranted, but it is also potentially quite dangerous.

When someone begins a conversation with the assumption that the truth is clear and his or her side is right, meaningful dialogue and mutual respect can seem almost impossible. If indeed one side of an argument perfectly captures the truth, then those who disagree are either ignorant and need to be educated or they are willfully malevolent and knowingly seek to mislead others from seeing the truth.

If we assume that our opponents are intentionally misleading others, we grow angry and mistrustful. In such a context, it seems difficult, if not impossible, to extend love to our adversaries. On the other hand, if we enter political debates with the assumption that our opponents are sincere and acting in good conscience but are nonetheless wrong, this opens a path for extending charity and respect.

The Bible contains God's truth, and we can seek to know that truth. But we must interpret the Bible in order to understand it, and human interpretations can and do fail. Knowing these limitations, we must be careful to avoid the trap of assuming God is on our side simply because our human interpretation suggests it.

Before speaking about political opponents or characterizing their positions, apply the simple test of the golden rule. Would you want someone speaking of you and your policy positions in the same way that you speak of them? It may seem impractical to use such criteria, but practicality is not the end goal for the Christian. In political dialogue, as in all other interactions, we must first and foremost honor God. It is possible to model an alternative path, avoiding polarizing and uncharitable characterizations of those who hold different views.

Instead of playing by the typical rules of the game, Christians can "play fair," choosing rhetoric that shows respect for their opponents while advocating different political means to achieve their goals. In the same way, policymakers can encourage cooperation and model a different form of political engagement, explaining what policy they believe offers the best means for achieving a goal without demeaning those who disagree.

Facing the Hard Issues

Christians also need courage to enter the much more complex political waters of the hard issues. Many Christians focus almost all of their attention on the so-called easy issues that raise cultural concerns. Issues of personal morality are important and need to be a part of public debate; some people are called in particular to raise awareness of these issues and challenge the church to respond. But such issues are not the only ones on the political agenda. In fact, they represent a tiny fraction of the policies and proposals facing elected officials each year. If Christians focus almost all of their political attention on these issues, they lose the opportunity to contribute to the public debate on other policies that consume the lion's share of the political agenda and our federal budget.

Political dialogue about hard issues is often complex, and disagreement is common within the church. It can be uncomfortable when others do not share our policy views, especially when we disagree with other Christians. But concerns about disagreeing with one another should not keep us from seeking ways to address the wide range of problems affecting us and our world.

In the next chapter, we will look more carefully at why Christians disagree about how to achieve their political goals. After giving you some tools for applying biblical truth to public policy, we will walk through a concrete example, considering different approaches Christians might advocate.

11

Can Christians Honestly Disagree?

Tackling Tough Issues

Even if you believe there's only one way to get to heaven, you can still believe there is probably more than one way to balance the budget.

Ralph Reed, first executive director,
Christian Coalition

Politics is the art of looking for trouble, finding it everywhere, diagnosing it incorrectly and applying the wrong remedies.

Groucho Marx (1890–1977), actor and comedian

Prominent evangelical scholar Randall Balmer complains about the activism of politically conservative Christians: "Deeply complicated subjects have become mere political cudgels in the hands of the Religious Right, issues calculated to rally the faithful for political ends. . . . They have distorted the faith, the 'good news' of the New Testament, into something ugly and punitive."[1] At the same time, Rev. Louis Sheldon, an evangelical minister and interest group leader, decries Democrats who reference God and religion on the campaign trail, contending that "liberal thinking is the antithesis of true Christianity. Americans need to understand that these pseudo-evangelicals are nothing more than shills for the Democrat Party and trying to use whatever credibility they think they have to draw Christians away from the Republican Party and a truly Biblical worldview."[2] Which story should we believe? Are conservatives distorting the gospel? Are liberals drawing Christians away from biblical truth?

To hear some of the harshest accusations hurled back and forth, it looks as if Christians in politics are at war with one another. Organizations and politicians from the left and the right routinely claim that God is on their side, spouting Bible verses to buttress their points. Often by implication (and occasionally in direct attacks), Christians accuse their political opponents of godlessness.

Such combative rhetoric captures headlines and garners attention. But it oversimplifies complex political issues and distorts honest differences between Christians. In reality, people often disagree on public policy matters for legitimate reasons. Christians can in good faith hold to biblical truth yet reach different conclusions about how to apply it in politics.

As we saw in the last chapter, policy problems that we often describe as "hard issues" test the limits of political systems. Because most observers share end goals but disagree on the best means to achieve them, disagreements are inevitable. Through a case study of a classic hard issue, poverty, this chapter examines how and why Christians can honestly disagree about politics. We will begin with suggestions for interpreting the Bible and then look at what the Bible says about the poor. Next, we will consider some of the possible approaches for combating poverty. The chapter concludes with some thoughts about searching for common ground in policy debates and for interacting charitably with others when disagreement appears inevitable.

Approaching the Bible in Context

The Scriptures are an invaluable resource for Christians seeking to apply their faith to their daily lives. Yet, although the Bible reveals God's truth, our human interpretations of it often fall short. One need only look to the mixed record on biblical interpretation in American politics for a reminder that well-meaning Christians can misapply "biblical" truth with disastrous consequences.

The classic, and likely most disturbing, example of such misinterpretation in American history was the debate over the Bible and slavery, which led to what historian Mark Noll calls "a theological crisis of the first order."[3] Common-sense literalism, the predominant American approach to reading the Bible in the early 1800s, led many Christians to believe that because the Bible contained slavery, it condoned it, creating the appearance of a false choice: "In theological terms, what was in fact a wide-ranging debate looked like it could be reduced to a forced dichotomy—either orthodoxy and slavery, or heresy and antislavery."[4] Only after the bloodshed of the Civil War did many American Christians see the need for broader theological awareness to help them understand and apply biblical truth regarding slavery.

Context versus Proof Text

In contemporary American politics, one can still find Christians misusing biblical texts to justify their political positions on both sides of major policy debates. How can Christians avoid misusing Scripture when seeking biblical truth? Equally important, how can we faithfully apply biblical truth to political questions?

A first step is avoiding oversimplistic proof texts. In its negative connotation, proof-texting refers to the practice of misusing a single Bible verse, or fragments of several verses strung together, to claim biblical justification for an idea or practice. Christians should be cautious not to twist the meaning of a Bible verse for personal ends. At the same time, theologian Daniel Treier reminds us, "For all its deserved derision, however, some concept of 'proof text' seems essential to Christian theology. . . . If God says what the Bible says, we logically pursue the development and defense of theological claims on such a basis."[5] The key often lies in avoiding taking single verses out of context and instead finding several verses or longer passages that fit into a larger biblical pattern.

Many tools can help you read the Bible theologically and apply its truth to political questions. Biblical scholars and theologians have written an array of resources, study Bibles, and reference guides that offer guidance.

Another way to avoid misleading proof-texting is to approach the Bible with attention to context, literary style, and use of language. Often without thinking about it, we read the Bible with an eye for literary style. For example, when Jesus tells his disciples,

"I am the vine; you are the branches" (John 15:5), most readers immediately recognize the use of metaphor. Jesus is not saying that he is an actual grapevine; he uses the image of the vine and branches as a concrete example to help the disciples understand their true relationship with him. In the same way that readers can recognize literary devices like metaphor, so can we distinguish between history, law, poetry, prophecy, and pastoral teaching, recognizing the particular purpose of each genre.

Although there are many ways to read the Bible theologically, one helpful method is to begin with a passage and move outward. If you want to understand what the Bible teaches about a particular subject, start first by finding a few relevant passages and reading them in their context. Second, follow the verses and see where they lead. Does the passage quote other Scripture? Many Bibles footnote internal cross-references to make it easy to find the other verses directly quoted; reading these references in their original context often adds clarity. For further insight, look for additional Old and New Testament passages that also relate to the theme. The comparison of related sections from different books of the Bible reveals important patterns and consistent emphases.

Consider a simple example. In John 12:8, Jesus tells his disciples, "You will always have the poor among you, but you will not always have me." What does this verse tell us about Jesus's view of the poor? Should we ignore the poor and focus on serving Jesus? By itself, the verse seems rather puzzling. But once it is placed in its larger context, its meaning becomes clearer.

The narrative of John 12 begins in Bethany a week before the crucifixion. After hosting a banquet honoring Jesus, Mary anoints Jesus's feet with expensive perfume. Verses 5 and 6 record Judas Iscariot's questioning response: "'Why wasn't this perfume sold and the money given to the poor? It was worth a year's wages.' He did not say this because he cared about the poor but because he was a thief; as keeper of the money bag, he used to help himself to what was put into it." In these verses, John reveals Judas's corrupt motives for asking the question in the first place—information that sheds new light on Jesus's response. In addition, the narrative continues as Jesus chastises Judas and affirms Mary: "'Leave her alone,' Jesus replied. 'It was intended that she should save this perfume for the day of my burial. You will always have the poor among you, but you will not always have me.'" By considering

John 12:8 in the context in which it appears, the verse already begins to make more sense.

If we follow the next step, seeing where the verses lead, we learn even more. A listing of internal cross-references shows that Jesus quoted from Deuteronomy 15:11 in his reply to Judas. Part of a longer section of laws concerning cancellation of debts and caring for the poor, that particular verse reads: "There will always be poor people in the land. Therefore I command you to be openhanded toward your brothers and toward the poor and needy in your land." Jesus references the Mosaic law in his reply to Judas, pointing him (and us) to God's command of generosity to the poor.

As this simple example demonstrates, a single Bible verse in isolation may at times confuse more than it clarifies. What could at first glance be read as downplaying the need to care for the poor reveals quite the opposite when viewed in context. Reading the passage surrounding a verse and finding cross-referenced Scriptures are two tools that can improve our understanding of Scripture. In much the same way, reading and comparing multiple texts on similar subjects adds richness and meaning.

Addressing Poverty in the United States: A Case Study

With some tools for biblical interpretation in mind, let's apply these steps to a public policy concern. How do we determine the best way for Christians to approach a political issue? What steps should we follow? As with any other issue or concern, the first step in seeking God's direction is looking to the Bible to see what, if anything, it says about the issue. If the Bible does not speak directly about a particular issue, look for biblical insights on related principles that may help guide your decision making.

The Biblical Mandate to Serve the Poor

The Bible describes God's active concern for defending the fatherless and widows, hearing the cries of the poor, rescuing them, and giving them refuge. From Genesis through Revelation, the Bible includes more than two thousand verses that talk about the poor and needy. A comprehensive analysis of so many texts would require books in and of themselves, so for the purpose of this short case study, we'll look at just a few biblical themes concerning the poor.[6]

The Bible describes several reasons for poverty. Some verses in Proverbs and in some of Jesus's parables say that laziness can lead to poverty, yet many other verses blame the wealthy who get rich by exploiting the poor. The travails of the Israelites reveal how God sometimes allows poverty as judgment for sin, yet God often selects the poor for special roles in redemption. Many other biblical references reveal systemic and institutional causes of poverty.

Although the causes of poverty are complex, the response God commands is clear. Reflected in the history of the Israelites, the wisdom books, the words of the prophets, and the New Testament, the Bible's condemnation of oppression is clear. It is evil to exploit the poor and deprive them of justice. Consider part of a passage from the prophecy of Amos:

> You trample on the poor
>　　and force him to give you grain.
> Therefore, though you have built stone mansions,
>　　you will not live in them;
> though you have planted lush vineyards,
>　　you will not drink their wine.
> For I know how many are your offenses
>　　and how great your sins.
> You oppress the righteous and take bribes
>　　and you deprive the poor of justice in the courts.
>
>　　　　　　　　　　　　　　　　　Amos 5:11–12

This passage and many others like it call attention to structural sins and political actions that deliberately prey on the poor. To gain at the expense of the poor is sin.

The Bible also makes it clear that God commands us to care for the poor and meet their needs. In the Gospel of Matthew, Jesus warns his disciples about the final judgment, making sharp distinctions between the righteous and the unrighteous. In the famous passage we often call "the sheep and the goats," Jesus divides the two groups by how they had responded to the hungry, strangers, prisoners, and others in need. The story ends with sobering words directed at those who failed to respond: "[The King] will reply, 'I tell you the truth, whatever you did not do for one of the least of these, you did not do for me. Then they will go away to eternal punishment, but the righteous to eternal life'" (Matt. 25:45–46). Passages throughout the Old and New Testaments remind us to care for the most vulnerable in society as part of our love for God and neighbor.

Biblical texts also emphasize the value of poverty—both physical and spiritual. Riches can offer a false sense of security that keeps people from seeing their desperate need for God. The poor, however, are much more aware of their physical needs and are thus more likely to seek the security that only God can provide. Poverty finds its ultimate expression in the incarnation: "For you know the grace of our Lord Jesus Christ, that though he was rich, yet for your sakes he became poor, so that you through his poverty might become rich" (2 Cor. 8:9). By leaving the riches of heaven for life on earth, Christ took the greatest vow of poverty possible, submitting to sacrificial death.

Concern for the poor is woven throughout the history of Christianity. From the work of the early churches recorded in the book of Acts to the present day, Christians live out their faith by caring for those in need. As the National Council of Churches summarized in a recent report: "One thing surely unites the many and varied traditions of the Christian faith: the common tradition of love for those who are poor. . . . Love for the poor has formed a major part of the witness of the Church universal throughout all times and places."[7]

Addressing Poverty: The Search for Solutions

As we have seen, biblical teaching about poverty is quite clear. God cares for the poor and commands his children to care for them as well. The Bible condemns those who exploit others for personal gain. Concern for the poor and the oppressed is one of the marks of true discipleship. Given this teaching, it seems natural that Christians will embrace poverty reduction as a biblical goal.

Agreeing that Christians should care about the problem, however, is the easy part. The remaining questions are far more complicated: What means are best to achieve the end goal? What is the best way to address the problem of poverty? What should Christians do to live out the biblical mandate? As is the case with any hard issue, trying to answer these questions can quickly create conflict. Well-meaning Christians can honestly arrive at different conclusions. Poverty is a multifaceted problem with no simple solutions. Political debates over the best means to combat poverty will always be complex and often contentious.

Although poverty is a global issue, for the purpose of this discussion, let's narrow our focus to domestic poverty. Consider three possible means to reduce the number of Americans living in poverty: cutting taxes to stimulate economic growth, increasing government spending on safety-net programs, and relying more on religious and community organizations to meet the needs of the poor.

Poverty in the United States: A Brief Overview

In the United States, we attempt to measure poverty with a formula designed to calculate the money required to provide for basic human needs such as food, shelter, and clothing. Official government poverty statistics calculate how many households and people live on incomes below the estimated poverty threshold (also called the poverty line).[8] An estimated thirty-seven million Americans, or 12.6 percent of the population, lived in poverty in 2005. Since 1966, poverty rates have ranged from a low of 11.1 percent in 1973 to a high of 15.1 percent in 1993.[9]

From the time of the nation's founding until the Great Depression, the federal government provided very little direct help for society's poor. Churches and other charities did their best to meet the needs, while government largely stayed away. In the wake of the devastating poverty, hunger, and job losses during the Depression, President Franklin D. Roosevelt promoted widespread reforms that shifted the burden of care significantly (but not entirely) from private organizations to the federal government, ushering in the era of the so-called welfare state.

As the scope of government has expanded, so have programs to care for the poor and needy. Workers and their employers contribute to Social Security and unemployment insurance, which in turn provide benefits to retirees, the disabled, and the unemployed. Other assistance programs supplement the income of the poorest Americans by helping them purchase food and by providing low-cost housing or rent subsidies. Medicare and Medicaid provide health insurance to the elderly and the poor. By any measure, these and other related government programs reduce poverty and help meet basic human needs. The combined effects of safety-net programs kept an estimated twenty-seven million Americans out of poverty in 2003.[10]

Although one hears the occasional call for abandoning these and other programs that provide a safety net for the poor, everyone in the mainstream policy community and in government accepts that they are now a permanent part of the American economy. Thus, the debates about how to best care for the poor are not about *if* the government should provide assistance but instead about *how much* and *in what form*. Conservatives typically advocate scaling back large programs and adding more requirements to receive government assistance; liberals usually promote expanding the reach and scope of public aid. The heart of current debates over poverty policy is thus about where and how best to spend government money.

Cutting Taxes to Stimulate the Economy

Many factors contribute to poverty, but one factor in particular provides a direct way to increase household income. In the words of a researcher at the Goldwater Institute, a free-market think tank: "The best antipoverty program is a four-letter word: jobs."[11] When people find work, they can support their families and likely move out of poverty. Although there is widespread agreement that job creation is a good way to reduce the number of poor Americans, people disagree about what factors contribute most to job growth.

Advocates of free-market economics support tax reduction as a way to stimulate the economy and create new jobs. The explanation goes something like this: high taxes and government regulations increase the costs of doing business. As costs go up, business owners look for ways to save money anywhere they can—often starting with eliminating jobs. Similarly, when the government cuts individual income taxes, people have more money they can spend or invest. Increased investment and increased consumer spending can lead to economic growth and more jobs.

At the signing ceremony for a 2005 tax bill, President Bush praised the impact of earlier cuts in taxes on capital gains and dividends: "When these cuts were passed in 2003, business investment had been dropping for several years. Since then, business investment has been growing at more than 9 percent a year. . . . And businesses have hired millions of new workers to fill the jobs that this investment creates."[12]

A Goldwater Institute study analyzed Census Bureau poverty statistics from 1990 to 2000 and found a link between low taxes and poverty reduction: "The 10 states with the lowest tax burdens saw a 13.7 percent decline in poverty during the 1990s (more than double the national average), according to the study. Meanwhile, the 10 states with the highest tax burdens suffered an average poverty rate increase of 3 percent."[13] Although many factors besides taxation affect poverty rates, the Goldwater study does provide support for proponents of tax cuts.

Yet not everyone agrees that tax cuts create economic growth. A report by United for a Fair Economy, a progressive think tank, suggests that the record on job creation is mixed: "Tax cuts have sometimes been followed by periods of increased unemployment; at other times, tax cuts have been followed by sharp declines in unemployment. By the same token, tax increases have not always been followed by the doomsday predicted by conservatives."[14] Do tax cuts have an independent effect on economic growth and job creation? Most (but not all) economists think so, but such direct cause-and-effect relationships are difficult, if not impossible, to measure.

Expanding Public Assistance Programs

Another possible method for combating poverty is expanding existing government programs that serve low-income Americans. Congress decides how much to spend on these and all other programs through what we call the *budget process.*

Most federal dollars are spent automatically as determined by permanent law, but hundreds of billions of dollars remain to be divided among a wide scope of government agencies and activities. (See the sidebar "An Overview of the Federal Budget Process" for more details.) Congress allocates this money in two steps. First, legislators pass bills that authorize spending, creating ceilings on how much money particular programs can receive. Next, they pass bills that appropriate funds; that is, they determine the exact amount of money for each line item. To complicate matters, lawmakers routinely pass legislation authorizing far more funding than they are actually able to spend, so appropriations almost always involve allocating less money than what was originally promised. For example, imagine if your boss offered you up to two hundred dollars to buy a retirement gift for a colleague.

The Statistics War: Whom Should You Believe?

When evaluating policy options and trying to discern which seems best, it makes sense to do a bit of research and find out what the "experts" say about particular programs or proposals. But what do you do when different studies seem to reach opposite conclusions? When competing studies report results that appear contradictory, how do you know whom to believe?

As with any discernment process, there are no foolproof methods to identify what source is best. However, you can do some things to help you evaluate the relative strengths and weaknesses of published reports and the organizations that release them.

- *Always read the fine print.* Look for disclaimers and other clues about the limitations and weaknesses of a study. What, if anything, seems to be missing from the analysis? What questions didn't they ask? What findings and data do they minimize or downplay?

- *Realize you may be reading just one side of the story.* Advocacy groups in particular are famous for reporting incomplete data. Most organizations tell the truth; their reputations, and even their survival, are at risk if they are caught misleading the public. But they are likely to tell only one side of the story and overexaggerate the effects of policy change. Ask yourself: Does this analysis make room for differing viewpoints, or does it represent only one side of a policy debate? Are any of the findings negative? Do they make claims that seem particularly outlandish?

- *Evaluate the source of the information.* Who is reporting this information? Do they appear to represent a particular perspective or set of interests? Who benefits from what they report? Who loses? Who paid for the study?

- *Rely on multiple sources.* Compare what different people and groups say about a particular proposal.

After you spent time researching options and finding the perfect gift, your boss then gave you only fifty dollars to make the actual purchase. Your boss authorized spending at one level but appropriated far less.

Every year during the budget battle and the appropriations process, organizations descend upon Congress, lobbying legislators to allocate money for the programs they care about. Advocates for the poor vie for time with representatives from businesses, unions, trade associations, and other interest groups. Those who seek to reduce poverty by expanding public assistance

Early each calendar year, the president submits a budget proposal to Congress, outlining a plan for allocating government spending in the coming year. This detailed proposal includes estimates of how much tax revenue the government will receive, how much money the government should spend, and the difference between the two. Congress considers the president's budget plan and then writes a budget resolution, a broad outline for federal spending that does not require the president's signature. Over the coming months, Congress then works on appropriations bills that determine the specific amounts to spend on government programs.

In the years that spending exceeds revenue, the government borrows money to make up the difference—what we call the *annual deficit*. Lawmakers face difficult choices: they want to support a wide range of programs, but they also try to balance the budget. In recent years, the combination of tax cuts and increased spending has resulted in annual deficits.

About 60 percent of annual spending automatically goes to permanent programs established by law—the so-called entitlement programs like Social Security and Medicare—and to pay interest on the accumulated national debt. About 20 percent of the budget pays for national defense, leaving slightly less than 20 percent for "discretionary programs" that expire every year. Nonentitlement public assistance programs such as cash assistance to the poor and Head Start are part of this discretionary spending.

programs must compete with everyone else for scarce government resources.

Because the goal of public assistance programs is helping those with the greatest financial need, many are "means-tested"; that is, participants must demonstrate financial need to qualify for receiving benefits. The National School Lunch Program (NSLP) is an example of means-tested assistance that provides meals for schoolchildren living in low-income households. The guidelines for the 2007–2008 school year, for example, set eligibility for free lunches for children in households with incomes at or below 130 percent of the poverty guidelines (less than $26,845 for a family of four). Children whose families earn between 130 percent and 185 percent of the poverty guidelines (less than $38,203 for a family of four) and have few other assets typically qualify for reduced-price meals.[15] By setting eligibility criteria, the program ensures that school lunch funding gets to the children who need it the most.

Government can expand or contract the size of means-tested programs by adjusting eligibility requirements, thus making sure that the programs serve the very poorest households. When Congress cuts funding or keeps it the same as the previous year, programs often respond by tightening income limits. Low-income families who previously qualified may find that they now make too much money to continue receiving a particular benefit.

Activists who emphasize the need for public assistance programs often begin their advocacy by responding to the president's annual budget request, combing through the hundreds of pages to see how programs targeting the poor have fared. In recent years, leaders of the Religious Left have begun referring to budgets as "moral documents," contending that fiscal priorities reflect the government's values. As Jim Wallis, convener of the Christian Left organization Call to Renewal, explains:

> Examining budget priorities is a moral and religious concern. . . . Poverty reduction should be a moral imperative in politics. A budget that scapegoats the poor, fattens the rich, and asks for sacrifice mostly from those who can least afford it is a moral outrage. These budget priorities would cause the prophets to rise up in righteous indignation, as should we. Our nation deserves better vision.[16]

From this vantage point, tax cuts are not a means for reducing poverty but instead redistribute money to the rich that would be better spent in direct government aid to the poor.

Given the unwritten rules of budgetary politics, it is difficult to reduce taxes and increase spending on public assistance at the same time. To a large extent, therefore, the debate reflects ideological differences over the roles of government and the private sector. Those who support expanding assistance programs typically believe in a strong role for government, a hallmark of liberal ideology. On the other hand, those who advocate tax cuts are usually ideological conservatives who prefer more limited government. When Tony Perkins, president of the Christian Right organization Family Research Council, was asked why he wasn't joining religious protests against President Bush's budget proposal, he responded, "There is a [biblical] mandate to take care of the poor. There is no dispute of that fact. . . . But it does not say government should do it. That's a shifting of responsibility."[17]

Reinvigorating Religious and Community Groups
That Serve the Poor

At the same time liberals and conservatives are likely to disagree over the relative merits of tax policy and public assistance, another approach looks to religious and community organizations for help. Private charities undoubtedly play a significant role in meeting the needs of the poor.

In addition to the thousands of independent and congregation-based organizations across the country, large faith-based networks provide social services to millions of Americans each year. The Salvation Army serves thirty-three million people annually, providing help such as emergency food and shelter, substance abuse treatment, and disaster relief. Catholic Charities, a network of social service agencies, spends over $3.3 billion each year to assist about 7.5 million people. In 2005, for example, their affiliates provided food for 5.6 million Americans. Lutheran Services in America helps about six million people annually, providing a range of services including health care, housing, mental health programs, and emergency and disaster relief.

Some charities offer assistance to the poor, replacing services government might otherwise provide or helping the poor in ways that the government does not. In many instances, however, charities and government work together in partnership. Government agencies rarely provide services themselves; typically they contract with private and nonprofit organizations that do the actual work. For example, the Department of Housing and Urban Development's Continuum of Care program provided $1.2 billion in 2007 to meet the needs of the homeless and those at risk of becoming homeless.[18] HUD does not operate its own homeless programs; instead, it gives grants to local organizations in communities across the nation that have track records addressing these issues.

President George W. Bush's faith-based initiative is an example of a policy proposal that sought to meet the needs of the poor by expanding partnerships between religious or community groups and the federal government. Starting with the supposition that religious organizations often provide the most effective and efficient social services, the initiative included three parts. The first goal was changing government practices that excluded certain groups from partnering with the government because they were "too religious." The Bush administration viewed these written and unwritten rules as perpetuating discrimination against religion. A second part of the plan helped smaller organizations learn the rules of the game in order to increase their success at applying for grants and partnering with government agencies to provide services. The third element of the initiative, tax reform, sought to assist all charities through new tax incentives. Although the original idea received bipartisan support, the initiative grew controversial and lost much of its momentum. The administration accomplished some of the first two parts of the initiative, but most of the tax incentives proved too costly.[19]

Whether partnering with government or working independently, local charitable organizations contribute greatly to serving the poor. Churches, nonprofits, and other groups in every community feed the hungry, shelter the homeless, train people for employment, teach English, and provide other tangible assistance that meets human needs.

Then again, some observers note that charitable work is rarely enough to deal with the underlying problems of poverty. Distinguishing between the concepts of "charity" and "justice," one commentator explained, "It's the difference between running a soup kitchen to feed the hungry and working in the political system to change the policies that allow people to go hungry."[20] Meeting immediate needs may be necessary, but it will never be sufficient for solving poverty.

All or Nothing?

The examples described above are brief snapshots of some of the issues raised when comparing different ways to reduce poverty. They are not necessarily mutually exclusive, for it is possible to pursue some or all of these policies at the same time. The highest-profile debates in American politics appear to be between those who advocate change through government programs and spending and those who give preference to private sector solutions. The rhetoric often suggests that either the government *or* private organizations hold the key to solving poverty. In reality, almost all social policy in the United States reflects a combination of government action and private assistance. Almost everyone agrees that the government should provide some basic safety net for the poorest and most vulnerable members of society, just as there is widespread agreement that religious and charitable organizations play a significant role in meeting human needs. The real arguments are at the margins over how much the government should do and in what ways private organizations should contribute. Christians with different ideological views will likely disagree about the answers.

Search for Common Ground, Then Agree to Disagree

All too often, people who disagree about policy proposals criticize their opponents as if they are against the end goal. A strong proponent of government antipoverty programs might accuse someone who advocates tax cuts of ignoring or even hating the poor. But, as we have seen, such attacks are dishonest or at least misleading. Well-meaning people can and do champion either policy alternative as an attempt to reduce poverty. On debates over hard issues, we must avoid accusing those who disagree about the means of not caring about the end goal.

Christians are by no means immune from using such tactics to mischaracterize their opponents' motivations. All too often, we confuse our values with our political views. As Donald R. Eastman III, president of Eckerd College, noted: "'Christian values' do not amount to specific political positions, and they are simply manipulated when such claims are made. Christian values are much less political and much more specific and difficult than 'Christian' politics."[21]

Returning yet again to the command to love God and neighbor, how might Christians respond to fellow believers who hold different political positions? How can we advocate our particular policy views in ways that honor those with whom we disagree?

A good place to start is searching for areas of agreement and acknowledging common ground. Evaluate policies from a perspective of means and ends, carefully distinguishing between the two. So many political disagreements center upon differences in perspective about the best way to achieve a shared goal, yet most political dialogue ignores or distorts this reality. When beginning a political discussion, affirm one another's shared goals first and then talk about the disagreements over which policy—or policies— will work best.

When discussing policy alternatives with those who disagree, ask them questions to help you understand their perspective and to learn more about their proposed solution. At the same time you ask probing questions, be prepared to answer similar questions about your positions and why you think they make sense. Consider some questions you might use to begin this conversation:

- Why do you believe that this particular solution is best?
- When did you first learn about this policy? What in particular captured your attention?
- What are the strengths and weaknesses of going this route?
- Has this solution been tried before? If so, what happened?
- What biblical principles inform your support for this policy alternative? What biblical principles potentially conflict with it?

By asking each other questions with a willingness to listen to other perspectives, we demonstrate love and respect.

Entering conversations with genuine humility can help us gain new insights into the many complexities of public policy. Talking with those who hold different political views may seem risky, for such discussions require that we challenge presuppositions and ask questions of ourselves. But the rewards clearly outweigh the risks, for in facing tough conversations, we learn from one another and learn about ourselves, gaining a richer understanding of multiple political perspectives and the reasons behind them.

Finally, and most importantly, we should make sure that our political differences do not hinder our fellowship with brothers and sisters in Christ. As Peter wrote to the early church: "The end of all things is near. Therefore be clear minded and self-controlled so that you can pray. Above all, love each other deeply, because love covers over a multitude of sins. Offer hospitality to one another without grumbling" (1 Peter 4:7–9). The unity of believers is of far greater scope and consequence than disagreements over policies for realizing political goals.

Having made it this far in this book, it is now time for us to look at applying our faith as political action. The next chapter offers practical steps to prepare you for the next Election Day. After explaining why the roles and duties of political office matter for voting, the chapter offers tips to help you order policy priorities, research and evaluate political candidates, and ultimately make an informed voting decision.

12

Behind the Curtain at the Voting Booth

A Decision-Making Guide

The average man votes below himself; he votes with half a mind or a hundredth part of one. A man ought to vote with the whole of himself, as he worships or gets married. A man ought to vote with his head and heart, his soul and stomach, his eye for faces and his ear for music. . . . The question is not so much whether only a minority of the electorate votes. The point is that only a minority of the voter votes.

G. K. Chesterton (1874–1936), British author

On October 7, 2003, California voters went to the polls for a special election. At the end of a seventy-five-day campaign that cost more than eighty million dollars, Californians faced a daunting task. Voters were first asked if their governor, Gray Davis, should complete his term in office or if he should be recalled, removing him from power. Next, they had to choose a replacement in the event the recall succeeded. For this step, a voter could choose only one name from a list of 135 candidates on the ballot, each identified by name, party affiliation, and "ballot designation," a short descriptor chosen by the candidate. With options that included Mike McCarthy/ Independent/Used Car Dealer, Joel Britton/Independent/Retired

Meat Packer, Cruz Bustamante/Democrat/Lieutenant Governor, as well as a smattering of attorneys and students, Californians made their choice. At the end of the day, the vote to remove the sitting governor passed, and Arnold Schwarzenegger, a Republican with the ballot designation Actor/Businessman, garnered 48 percent of the votes and won the governorship.

Although most elections in the United States are simpler than the 135–candidate California recall, even selecting a choice from a field of two or three candidates can be quite complicated. With more than half a million elected officials, the United States has far more elections than any other country in the world. We also spend more money on campaigns than any other nation. In the 2006 election cycle, for example, candidates and parties raised and spent a record-breaking 2.6 billion dollars to communicate with citizens and try to convince them how to vote. When television and radio stations blast what seems like an endless barrage of competing messages, mailboxes are cluttered with frightening flyers warning of impending doom, and multiple-page ballots list candidates for a vast range of positions, it is no wonder that so many prospective voters find election time confusing and exhausting.

This chapter will help you apply ideas and themes from the rest of this book, offering pointers to guide your decision making at election time. It will not tell you *how* to vote. Rather, the goal is to provide tools so you can make an informed decision. First, we will consider how some of the different ways that people view representation may affect their assessments of candidates and elected officials. Next, the chapter presents a two-part framework for approaching political elections, first discussing the significance of qualifications for political office and then suggesting different resources that can help you learn more about candidates running for office.

The Expectations Game: Theories of Representation

Before deciding how to vote, it helps to begin with some simple but essential questions: What is the purpose of voting? Why is political representation important? Derived from the Latin verb that means "to show," *representation* refers to showing again, or standing in the place of something or someone else. Thus, we vote to elect people to office who we believe will stand for us in government, making wise decisions for all those they claim to serve. In practice, representation means different things to different people; that is, voters (and most politicians) operate with different expectations about the proper role of an elected official, even if they are unaware of the technical terms for these views. Before assessing candidates for political office, it therefore makes sense to learn about the underlying models of representation that, knowingly or unknowingly, influence our evaluations of politicians.

Delegates and Trustees

Political theorists describe two common models of representation: delegate and trustee. According to the *delegate model*, elected officials represent their constituents by directly reflecting their desires and opinions. If a majority of voters holds a different position on an important issue of the day than their legislator, the legislator should set aside personal convictions and vote for the policy approved by the majority. As delegates for the people, the primary job of elected officials is to discern the popular will of their constituents and translate that into public policy.

An alternative view of representation, the *trustee model*, expects elected officials to draw on their knowledge and experience to make decisions that are in the best interests of their constituents. Voters are not likely to have enough information to weigh the complexities of all the political issues of the day, so they are wise to place their trust in someone with specific skills and expertise to act on their behalf. A variant of this second model, *descriptive representation*, rests on the premise that elected officials who mirror the racial, gender, and religious diversity of the people are more likely to add a healthy breadth of perspectives to political discussions.

Although these two models of representation appear to be opposites, in practice voters seem to expect candidates to somehow serve as both delegates and trustees. Each election season, communications from political campaigns typically alternate between personal and policy appeals. Particularly in early advertisements, candidates stress their background and character, describing themselves to voters to earn their trust. Other advertisements typically appeal to voters with more of a focus on the delegate role, as candidates stake out positions on issues and often contrast their views with those of their opponents. Data from postelection polls suggest that voters base their decisions

Theory Meets Practice: Appeals in Campaign Ads

In the beginning weeks and months of a campaign, candidates need to introduce themselves to voters, presenting their biographies in ways that will earn voters' trust. Consider the following biographical ad, "Journey," that introduced Bill Clinton to voters in the 1992 campaign:

> BILL CLINTON NARRATING: I was born in a little town called Hope, Arkansas, three months after my father died. I remember that old two-story house where I lived with my grandparents. They had very limited incomes. It was in 1963 that I went to Washington and met President Kennedy at the Boys' Nation program. And I remember just, uh, thinking what an incredible country this was, that somebody like me, you know, who had no money or anything, would be given the opportunity to meet the president. That's when I decided I could really do public service because I cared so much about people. I worked my way through law school with part-time jobs—anything I could find. After I graduated I really didn't care about making a lot of money. I just wanted to go home and see if I could make a difference. We've

worked hard in education and health care to create jobs and we've made real progress. Now it's exhilarating to me to think that as president I could help to change all our people's lives for the better and bring hope back to the American dream.[1]

Other ads build their appeals with the delegate model of representation in mind. Such commercials contrast candidates' positions on policy issues or criticize the opponent for holding unpopular views. The "Windsurfing" ad from the Bush/Cheney 2004 campaign attacks John Kerry for inconsistency:

> [Open with two shots of George W. Bush with his arm around his wife as they stand on a porch. TEXT appears in the bottom left.]
> GEORGE BUSH (narrating): I'm George W. Bush and I approved this message.
> TEXT: www.GeorgeWBush.com
>
> [Cut to image of John Kerry windsurfing. TEXT appears and fades as the NARRATOR talks, Kerry switching direction again and again. Popular classical tune plays in the background.]

both on their perception of candidates' character and on the policy issues they advocate.

Once in office, elected officials seem to serve as delegates on some issues and as trustees on others. As one popular textbook explains, "Most legislators shift back and forth between the delegate and trustee roles, depending on their perception of the public interest, their standing in the last and next elections, and the pressures of the moment."[2] Recent research on the House of Representatives

NARRATOR: In which direction would John Kerry lead? Kerry voted for the Iraq war, opposed it, supported it, and now opposes it again.
TEXT: Iraq War; Supported; Opposed

NARRATOR: He bragged about voting for the eighty-seven billion to support our troops before he voted against it.
TEXT: $87 Billion for Our Troops; Supported; Opposed

NARRATOR: He voted for education reform and now opposes it.
TEXT: Education Reform; Supported; Opposed

NARRATOR: He claims he's against increasing Medicare premiums but voted five times to do so.
TEXT: Increasing Medicare Premiums; Supported; Opposed

NARRATOR: John Kerry: whichever way the wind blows.
TEXT (accompanied by small image of George W. Bush): APPROVED BY PRESIDENT BUSH AND PAID FOR BY BUSH-CHENEY '04, INC.[3]

suggests that members are more likely to think of themselves as delegates on economic and domestic policy but feel more freedom to vote their conscience and serve as trustees on so-called moral issues such as abortion or gay rights.[4]

When making a voting decision, it therefore makes sense to evaluate candidates with your preferred model of representation in mind. If you generally follow the delegate model and believe that an elected official should primarily make decisions that reflect the majority opinion, you should choose the candidate who seems most responsive to voter concerns and most likely to vote with the constituents regardless of the issue. In contrast, if you are most concerned that an officeholder is trustworthy to make decisions on your behalf, you should primarily evaluate candidates based on their background and preparation for the office as well as their perceived character and competence.

Deciding How to Cast a Ballot, Part 1: Duties, Powers, and Priorities

Once you have an expectation of what makes a good representative, the next step toward making an informed voting decision is determining criteria for selecting the best candidate. Two preliminary factors to consider are qualifications that would best prepare a person for office and the powers inherent in each position. With these factors in mind, voters can then prioritize which issues will be of greatest concern when selecting a candidate.

Duties of Office

Given the diversity of jobs filled through elections in the United States, it makes sense to consider the duties of each political position to help select the best candidate. Although few states or localities require that candidates have a particular background to run for office, specific training or qualifications seem especially beneficial for certain positions. In much the same way that an employer screens résumés, looking for applicants who have experience and skills relevant to a particular job opening, voters should evaluate the background and experience of political candidates to see if they are qualified for the job. All things being equal, a voter will prefer that candidates for sheriff have law enforcement experience, that coroners have medical degrees, and that judges have legal training. Thus, a useful first step in choosing how to vote is considering the roles and duties of each political office to determine what particular qualifications and background seem most relevant.

Powers of Office

Just as it is wise to consider the duties of office, it is also important to consider the powers of each office. It makes little sense to make a voting decision based on an issue or policy over which an elected official has no decision-making power. Thus, a next step in evaluating candidates is thinking realistically about the scope of a political office—asking what a candidate can and cannot do and where he or she is likely to have the most direct influence.

To see how this might work, consider the difference in the powers and influence of the president and a state legislator. The areas of greatest potential presidential influence are those in which the president has the most unilateral power. First, as the head of the executive branch, the president can make independent decisions that affect only its members, issuing directives that those working in the federal bureaucracy must follow. Second, the president has significant power over foreign policy and the use of military force, setting the tone for diplomacy and making initial decisions about when and if to commit American troops to combat. Although Congress funds the military, in practice if a president initiates military engagement, it is very difficult, if not impossible, for Congress to stop the action quickly. Third, only the president can make judicial appointments. Although the Senate participates in the process by voting to confirm or reject a nominee, the president, and only the president, initiates the process by selecting the specific candidates. Federal judges serve for a term of "good behavior," which in practice means they generally serve lifetime appointments. In a single four-year term, enough judges will retire that a president will likely replace about a quarter of the judiciary, an act with consequences that may endure for decades.

When voting for president, therefore, it makes sense to weigh most heavily the candidates' positions on foreign policy, judicial politics, and the executive branch, those issues over which the president has the most influence.

A different set of issues will likely take priority in elections for the state legislature because a state legislator has different powers of office. Criminal law, family law, health regulations, and sales and property taxes are primarily state issues. Although the federal government provides some funding and regulations for certain domestic policies such as education and assistance for the poor, states make most of the decisions about the provision of these services. At the same time, state legislatures have no power over foreign policy or federal income taxes. When choosing how to vote for a state legislator, a discerning voter will compare candidates by weighing their views on state issues.

Priorities of Office

Once you have a general understanding of the duties and powers of a political office, the next step toward selecting a candidate is deciding which issues matter the most to you. Given the diversity of issues raised in a political campaign and the even wider range of topics elected officials are likely to consider over the course of a term in office, it seems impossible to find any candidate with whom you will agree completely. Given this likely incongruity, how do you decide which issues are most important?

Some voters answer this question by choosing the one issue they believe is most important and evaluating candidates based on it. We call this *single-issue voting*. If you are so passionate about a particular issue that its importance genuinely eclipses all other potential policies an elected official might deal with, single-issue voting may be a wise method for deciding how to vote.

However, single-issue voting rarely works. Sometimes political opponents agree on the issue. If a voter is most concerned about low taxes and both candidates take a pledge that they will not increase taxes, voting based on the tax issue makes little sense. In other cases, the roles and duties of office may have little or nothing to do with the identified issue. Single-issue voters who favor the provision of universal health care, for example, will likely be able to find a preferred candidate in a race for the Senate, but their voting philosophy will be of little help for a school board election.

In practice most people evaluate candidates on the basis of several issues at the same time. In such situations, therefore, voters must find ways to prioritize issues to help them make an informed decision. One method is to list *nonnegotiable issues*, determining which policy positions (if any) are so important that a candidate must share these views to earn your vote. In those races in which neither candidate agrees on truly nonnegotiable issues, you should abstain from voting. Another approach is to create a set of *priority issues*, selecting the candidate whose positions are closest to yours on a set of issues that you believe most important for each elected office.

Much like the nature of politics itself, weighing the importance of issues and selecting a candidate among imperfect choices requires a delicate balancing act and will likely require compromise. There is no perfect formula for choosing a candidate. Even as a professional political scientist, I have found an occasional voting decision so difficult that I have skipped voting in that particular race. If you enter the voting booth and don't feel comfortable making a choice between a certain set of candidates, leave that race blank and cast your vote in the other races on the ballot.

Deciding How to Cast a Ballot, Part 2: Educating Yourself

Voter education is at the same time one of the easiest and one of the hardest aspects of making a voting decision. As an election nears, the news media run frequent stories about the election, and political campaigns flood the airwaves, mailboxes, and phone lines with their appeals. Such an environment makes it all but impossible to ignore political communication. Even though the typical voter will hear more than enough messages about candidates during an election season, the barrage of campaign-related communication may actually confuse voters more than it educates them.

Is it possible to learn anything useful in the midst of such chaos? Although campaigns are often tiring and frustrating, with a bit of persistence, you can indeed educate yourself about candidates for office through careful analysis of news media reports, campaign advertisements, and educational resources.

Campaign Communications: Voter Education That Is Hard to Ignore

In the era of modern campaigning, it is all but impossible to avoid seeing some form of campaign communications during a hotly contested election. Political scientists distinguish between two broad categories of media found in almost all campaigns: paid media and free media. *Paid media* includes all campaign communication created for and distributed by the candidate—in other words, advertising. In contrast, *free media* refers to coverage of the candidate in print and broadcast news. The communications strategy for almost all political campaigns is the same: try to maximize free media coverage while simultaneously targeting voters with paid media.

Although every candidate hopes to receive significant and positive media attention, competitors are all but guaranteed media coverage on only four occasions. First, local news outlets almost always cover a candidate's announcement—when he or she formally enters a political race. Second, the media reports the results of the primary election. Third, most newspapers and some broadcast stations will devote one story to each of the winners of the primaries, introducing each candidate in a profile piece. Finally, every major party candidate will receive some media coverage as journalists report the results on Election Day.

To be taken seriously as a true contender for an election, candidates need to garner more media coverage than just the "magic four" stories described above. Thus, candidates and their campaign staff work with the news media to draw attention to their campaigns and encourage news stories. One of the best ways to encourage media coverage is by sending *press releases*, prefabricated news stories distributed to local news organizations for their use. Press releases alert the media to events and issues of concern to the campaign and provide ready-made news stories that journalists can quote freely. Another common tactic for attracting free media is scheduling events with high-profile guests. When the president of the United States or a well-known rock star campaigns for a candidate, the local media are sure to follow.

Candidates always hope to receive positive media coverage and work very hard to achieve that goal, but an interesting irony of campaigning is that bad news is almost always better than no news at all. Many voters, often unknowingly, measure a candidate's chance of winning in part from the amount of media coverage the campaign receives. If the news media never mention a particular candidate, voters assume he has no chance. If stories about a candidate appear with regularity, voters believe she can win. Since the volume of media coverage can signal voters in this way, campaigns typically prefer negative news coverage to none at all. Obviously, a candidate is more likely to lose if every story reports bad news, but a mixture of negative and positive media coverage is typically good news for a candidate.

Although it can be dangerous to rely exclusively on media cues, following the patterns of campaign coverage will provide a rough estimate of a candidate's realistic chances of winning. Consider the following scenario. Your neighbor is running for mayor. Her candidacy is the talk of your block; you and your friends are very excited. As the election nears, however, you notice that the local media provide little or no coverage of her race. Two other mayoral candidates are sharing the media spotlight instead. In all likelihood your neighbor's chances of winning are slim, so it makes sense to learn more about the views of the other two candidates, as one of them is very likely to win the election.

News media reports are an important source of information useful for comparing candidates. Stories about campaign events are often the least informative; candidate profiles and broadcast debates usually offer the most details. The evening network news programs always cover presidential races and occasionally run a short story on a particularly competitive congressional or guber-natorial race, but for the most part, local news stations will be the primary broadcast sources for regular updates on state and local races. Because newspapers have much more space to tell a news story than the typical short television or radio broadcast piece, they are likely to offer the most frequent and most detailed coverage of state and local elections. In the weeks and days preceding an election, newspaper editorial boards often offer candidate endorse-ments. Although the political slant of the editorial page is usually well known (the *Chicago Tribune*, for example, last endorsed a Democratic presidential candidate in 1872), endorsements can provide new information to help voters make a final decision.

Family Photos and Red, White, and Blue: Paid Media in Campaigns

While campaigns devote significant time and effort to court free media coverage, they allocate most of their budgets for paid media. Candidates want to control the content of much of their communication, crafting messages to appeal both to broad and narrow groups of voters.

Candidates need to build their name recognition with the voters, so basic advertising is at the core of any campaign. Most campaigns begin with a simple logo, commonly some combination of patriotic red, white, and blue with the name of the candidate and the office sought. This logo will appear in many forms—in signs dotting neighborhood lawns, in banner ads on the side of city buses or pasted across billboards, as stickers affixed to car bumpers and windows, and on T-shirts of college students. Simple logos communicate very little about the candidate, but the combined effect of thousands of stickers, signs, and billboards viewed for many months creates a lasting impression.

Other forms of general campaign communication include brochures and door knockers—threefold or single-page ads briefly describing the candidate's background and issue positions. Usually full color and often including a cheerful family photo, brochures are typically printed in mass quantities for general distribution at events and for candidates and campaign workers to leave on doors when walking through neighborhoods. These ads rarely highlight controversial issues but instead list uncontroversial accomplishments and include promises designed to have broad appeal. As such, general campaign literature tells little about candidates beyond their political party and background experience, so this material is not likely to add considerable details that will help you make a voting decision.

In a time of declining newspaper readership, campaigns are devoting less money to print ads. Most candidates will run occasional advertisements in local newspapers if for nothing other than to try to curry favor by buying the ad space, but such ads rarely include specifics. In Pennsylvania an unsuccessful congressional candidate with a very small budget spent most of his advertising money running small ads on the bottom of the obituary page. Although many newspaper readers jump first to the death notices, it may not be the best place to garner positive support.

The most pointed and focused campaign messages appear in targeted communications, ads designed to connect with a particular segment of the voting public. In *direct mail pieces*, campaigns send large postcards, often with sinister photographs and dire warnings, to selected groups deemed likely to resonate with the message. A candidate who favors gun control, for example, might target direct mailings to mothers of young children, using pictures of automatic rifles and small children on a playground to warn against his opponent's lax policies on assault weapons. Direct mail pieces often rely on emotional appeals and exaggeration; rarely will such ads offer enough information to educate voters.

Campaigns also target voters in radio ads. Because radio stations offer a wide variety of formats, candidates can tailor ads to the likely concerns of the listeners. A candidate reaching out for the Latino vote might run an ad on a Spanish language station; a candidate hoping to appeal to younger voters may advertise on a rock station. Although limited to fifteen, thirty, or sixty seconds, these advertisements can provide some useful information about a candidate's background or issue stances.

One of the most visible forms of paid media, television advertisements, is typically a factor in only a small number of political contests. Only the highest-profile campaigns—president, governor, Congress, and some statewide offices—are likely to have the budget and geographical reach to make television spots feasible. The nation is divided into 210 designated market areas (DMAs), the broadcast reach of television stations. DMAs range in size from the behemoth New York market, which reaches 7.4 million viewers, to the five-thousand-person media market in Glendive, Montana. The largest DMAs command the highest advertising rates and include several congressional districts; a few media markets even cross state borders. Candidates running for governor of Missouri may choose to run ads in the Paducah-Cape Girardeau-Harrisburg DMA, but their commercials will also reach ineligible voters in Illinois and Kentucky.[5]

In the weeks immediately before the election, political commercials seem to dominate the airwaves, but in reality, they are likely sponsored by only a handful of the candidates who will be on the ballot. Candidates for state legislature, mayor, or city council rarely have the budget or the media market overlap to make television ads feasible.

Television commercials can help inform voters, but they are also likely to create distorted views of the candidates. Although there is no perfect formula for evaluating the content of broadcast commercials, tools such as ad watches—media stories that evaluate the truthfulness of campaign advertising claims—can help voters separate truth from distortion. The political communications watchdog organization Annenberg Political Fact Check monitors the accuracy of political speeches and advertisements, posting regular analyses of campaign rhetoric on their website, http://www.factcheck.org.

Even if media critics do not evaluate a particular ad, voters can make reasonable judgments about commercials on their own. Clever media consultants can cull voting records to make the most reasoned and careful legislator appear sinister or bizarre. As Senator Barack Obama explained, "What every senator understands is that while it's easy to make a vote on a complicated piece of legislation look evil and depraved in a thirty-second commercial, it's very hard to explain the wisdom of that same vote in less than twenty minutes."[7] If you think an ad makes a claim that sounds preposterous or overly exaggerated, your instincts are likely correct. Instead of accepting an ad's message at face value, do further research to make sure the information is truthful.

And Now for a Word from Outside the District . . .

To add further confusion to the communications blitz common in campaign season, political parties and outside groups are likely to inject their own forms of paid media into high-profile, high-stakes political contests. Groups that have an interest in the outcome of an election can advertise openly—as long as they do not coordinate their efforts with any candidate's campaign; they comply with campaign finance laws, including disclosing who funded the advertising; and they never directly tell voters to vote for or against a candidate. Although it is very difficult to find legal ways of bypassing the first two rules, the third is easy to circumvent. Advertising can easily criticize or praise a candidate without ever saying directly how to vote. Consider, for example, a direct mailing sponsored by the outside group Emily's List, designed to support Tammy Duckworth's 2006 congressional bid. The piece never *told* voters to vote for her, but it demonized her opponent with the claim, "Peter Roskam puts partisan politics ahead of our kids."

The rules, regulations, and terminology affecting outside groups and political campaigns are complex and constantly changing. From the vantage point of a prospective voter, perhaps it is most important to be aware that organizations beyond the individual candidates and their campaigns can and do seek to sway election results. When evaluating information from campaign advertising, check the source of the material. Because candidates are directly accountable for the claims they make in their campaign communications, as a general rule, official campaign sources are more likely than those created by outside groups to provide constructive information that will help you learn about a candidate's views.

Resources for Conducting Your Own Candidate Research

All of the resources we've discussed so far are useful tools to help you learn about candidates for office, but what are ways you can do your own research and dig a bit deeper into the issues to prepare for an election? In the Internet age, an excellent place to begin is at each candidate's campaign website, which you can locate using a search engine. If you don't know the names of all of the candidates, most county political parties provide links from their official sites. Of course, campaign websites will be one-sided and will portray candidates as positively as possible, but this does not mean they are unhelpful. Most candidates list their priority issues on their websites, allowing for direct comparisons of your policy priorities and views with theirs.

In addition, interest groups often provide voter education with focused attention to their issues of special concern. The two most common forms of information are *ratings* and *voter guides*. An organization that calculates ratings typically evaluates candidates currently in office, listing the most important votes related to issues the organization advocates and rating the percentage of times the legislator votes with its members. The U.S. Chamber of Commerce, for example, compiles ratings based on pro-business votes, ranging from a score of one hundred (indicating voting with the Chamber every time), to a score of zero (for those who never voted with the Chamber). Interest group ratings are biased by design; that is, they indicate how closely a legislator votes with the organization's policy agenda. If you are a member of an interest group or simply find yourself supportive of their views, checking to see if they rate voting records may help you evaluate the performance of candidates running for reelection or who currently hold legislative office.

Before each election, many interest groups create voter guides, which are side-by-side comparisons of major party candidates on selected issues. Although groups typically describe these as non-partisan, the organizations choose issues that fit with their mission and values. As such, most voter guides favor candidates of the party most closely aligned with the organization's mission. One of the most famous organizations to issue voter guides, the Christian Coalition, offers this typical disclaimer: "This voter guide is provided for educational purposes only and is not to be construed as an endorsement of any candidate or party." The fifteen issues selected for their 2004 presidential election guide, however, read much like the platform of the Republican Party.[8]

Other resources are available that provide more balanced information on political candidates. Several nonpartisan organizations compile information to help voters make side-by-side candidate comparisons on a broader range of issues. One of the oldest and most respected of these groups, the League of Women Voters, provides local voter education through projects such as newspaper inserts with candidate information and the sponsorship of candidate debates. The organization's website (http://www.vote411.org) provides information on voter registration, polling times and places, and candidates and ballot issues. The League sends questionnaires to candidates and compiles the responses.

Another reliable voter education group, Project Vote Smart (http://www.vote-smart.org; 1-888-868-3762) asks candidates to complete a survey they call the "National Political Awareness Test," noting the policies with which they agree. In addition to compiling results from this survey, Project Vote Smart also provides a wealth of data on each candidate, including biographical information, campaign finance reports, voting records, interest group ratings, and public speeches.

When All Else Fails, Vote with Your Party

The first election after I turned eighteen, I went to vote with great excitement but was soon overcome by the sheer number of races listed on the ballot. When I didn't know whom to choose, my default was to vote for the female candidate or pick the name I liked best.

Have you ever entered the voting booth and felt overwhelmed? With so many elections on a typical ballot, it can be almost impossible to learn enough about every race to feel prepared to vote. This chapter has highlighted some of the tools available to help you make educated choices, but there is one reasonably simple way to cast an educated vote. When all else fails, vote for candidates from the political party that most closely aligns with your views. All Democrats do not think alike, nor do all Republicans. But a candidate who runs under a party label will likely share that party's views on many, if not most, issues. Voting based solely on party identification is not the most informed vote possible, but it is an educated one.

Although outside resources can be quite useful to raise voter awareness, one of the most important (and often overlooked) sources of voter education is conversation with friends and family. From casual conversations about an outlandish commercial to discussions about who won or lost a candidate debate, some people you know are likely to talk about upcoming elections. Those who follow politics most closely are apt to initiate conversations about candidates and public policy; those who have the least knowledge of the system may want to ask family and friends to explain how they are planning to vote and why. Such conversations, particularly with people you trust who are willing to dialogue, offer a low-pressure environment for asking questions and formulating opinions.

Although the idea of voting sounds simple enough, the actual practice of deciding how to vote can be quite complicated. Hopefully the tools in this chapter will be helpful to you, so the next time you walk into a voting booth, you will be more comfortable and equipped to cast your ballot.

Christians can and should exercise their right to vote. Free elections are the bedrock of any democracy. But voting is just one of many options for participating in government. In the next chapter, we will explore some additional ways your faith can inform politics, offering practical suggestions for how to get involved in the political process.

13

Beyond the Ballot Box

Other Ways Faith Can Inform Politics

with Jennifer L. Aycock

The people reign in the American political world as the Deity does in the universe. They are the cause and the aim of all things; everything comes from them, and everything is absorbed in them.

Alexis de Tocqueville (1805–1859),
Democracy in America

I have come to the conclusion that politics are too serious a matter to be left to the politicians.

Charles de Gaulle (1890–1970), president of France

At the end of the day on November 7, 2006, cities and municipalities across the United States faced a daunting problem: the election was over, but millions of campaign signs remained, littering lawns, street corners, and public thoroughfares. Candidates and supporters of ballot initiatives had purchased a staggering twenty million campaign signs to advertise everything from measures opposing gay marriage, abortion, and legalized marijuana to candidates running for offices as varied as Eden Prairie councilperson at-large and the U.S. Senate. Burdened with tons of brightly colored litter, some states began imposing fines on campaign organizations that had not removed their signs fast enough after Election Day. Steve Grubbs, whose business VictoryStore supplied over five million of the twenty million signs, claimed, "It's a lot of signs to deal with, but they're [the campaign organizations] slackers if they can't get them down within a week of the election."[1] Finding enough energetic volunteers to erect signs is quite a challenge; gathering more troops to remove them, especially in the wake of an election loss, is even more difficult.

These millions of abandoned yard signs remind us that participation in American politics stretches far beyond simply voting. As we saw in the last chapter, casting a ballot is a significant way we can participate in government. But other opportunities to contribute to public dialogue abound, and there are many other ways we can affect political change.

How to Make a Difference without Running for Office

Have you ever left the voting booth a little dissatisfied, not knowing if your favorite candidates would win and wondering what else you could do? Would you like to have more voice in politics than just your vote? Political participation extends far beyond the ballot box, including a range of activities such as attending local meetings, volunteering for political campaigns, or communicating with elected officials. This chapter will explore these and other avenues for participation in which you might invest your time, money, and energy.

So what exactly is political participation? Textbooks usually describe it as any activity that has the intent or effect of influencing government action. In particular, participation "affords citizens in a democracy an opportunity to communicate information to government officials about their concerns and preferences and to put pressure on them to respond."[2] As such, political participation encompasses a vast range of activities, from discussing politics with some friends over dinner to planting a political sign in your yard or stuffing envelopes at a campaign headquarters. Some political scientists like to narrow the definition a bit further by distinguishing between *formal* participation (the work of paid professionals hired to contribute to the political process) and *informal* participation (engaging in political activity for personal reasons on one's own time).

This chapter focuses on informal participation, considering different ways that you can apply your faith to politics. In particular, we will look at three general areas of political engagement: civic education, electoral activities, and interacting with government. The chapter then considers how the church prepares and connects Christians to meet community needs. Finally, we examine prayer as the ultimate form of political participation.

Back to the Basics: Civic Education

The first category of political participation, civic education, provides the foundation for all other political activity. People need some understanding of political issues and current events before they can meaningfully participate in politics and government.

Studies of American political behavior find that political knowledge—what a person knows about current political issues, needs, and concerns—affects how and to what extent a person will be involved with politics and government. Those who know the most about politics are more likely to vote regularly and to contribute to political causes than those who know less. If you decide to purchase a new car, for example, you will likely conduct some research before making the purchase. Perhaps you talk with friends, read consumer magazines, and go for a test drive before signing on the dotted line. In much the same way, people are unlikely to vote, to volunteer at a local homeless shelter, or to place a candidate's sign in their yard without first asking some questions.

Most Americans find that news outlets are the best place to start when seeking information on political candidates, current legislation, and local civic issues. Even in today's constantly changing media environment, the best source for political news remains the newspaper. Although the paper's perspective on a candidate, political issue, or policy debate may not highlight your particular concerns, print and Internet versions of newspapers offer some of the broadest and most detailed information available to the public. Whether you are interested in program funding for local after-school tutoring or proposed changes to Medicare, newspapers provide current information on a range of political topics.

All the News That's Fit to Post: Media Websites

A wide range of news media sources provide access to background information and breaking news that will greatly enhance your civic education. While local newspapers are likely the best starting place for coverage of local politics, they rarely have the budget to hire reporters to cover the national and international scene. National newspapers and media organizations are thus the best sources to help the "politically savvy" citizen learn more about most political issues and current events. Here are a few examples of media websites that may be helpful:

- **The *New York Times* (http://www.nytimes.com):** Perhaps the most trusted news source on international issues, the *New York Times* is the newspaper of record in the United States. Most world leaders begin their day reading the *Times.* The front page presents the day's top stories, and the site offers a free subscription that will deliver the headlines to your email inbox daily. It lives up to its motto, providing "all the news that's fit to print."

- **The *Washington Post* (http://www.washingtonpost.com):** The *Post* is generally regarded as the nation's leading media source on domestic issues, particularly the federal government. It also provides a straightforward front page that offers thumbnails to specific topics, including politics, that you may wish to read about.

- **Reuters (http://www.reuters.com):** Reuters is a comprehensive source of articles on a wide range of topics. One of the nation's leading "wire services," Reuters distributes national and international stories to media outlets across the country. Like the other newspapers, it has lead stories on the front page and a layout that is easy to navigate. In addition, it offers a free subscription that delivers the top ten news stories of the day to your inbox.

- **WatchingAmerica.com (http://www.watchingamerica.com):** If you're looking for a different perspective on American politics, this site provides English translations of articles from newspapers around the globe. It may not be the most credible source for the political details, but it can help put our politics in an international framework.

Jonathan Flugstad

Their online editions often update content during the day, providing almost instant access to the latest developments. Most local television news broadcasts reach several cities and towns, so they rarely focus attention on issues in one locality. Local newspapers are therefore likely to provide the only significant coverage of local politics and campaigns.

We also learn about politics through formal and informal conversations. Friends, family, and acquaintances are often important sources of information and opinions. Simply raising questions about a current event seen in the paper may trigger significant feedback. Although conversations with friends and co-workers are a normal part of our daily routine, such discussion can contribute greatly to political education. Learning in a group can introduce new ways to think about public policy or community needs and action, as well as offer insight into one another's political commitments. If you want to foster more political discussion, consider hosting a political reading group to discuss a new book or the cover story from a weekly newsmagazine. Inviting friends to a dinner party for the purpose of discussing and sharing information might broaden the circle as well.

Just as we can learn from interactions with other people, we can also learn from the resources available at libraries, online, or in bookstores. Before you form an opinion or take political action, researching the background of a policy, organization, or issue can be helpful. Reference librarians can direct you to excellent resources. Magazines, online journals, and recent books will offer a range of perspectives on political issues.

Those seeking more formal and structured political education might take a class. Community colleges, four-year colleges, universities, and local organizations sometimes provide continuing-education courses or allow area residents to audit classes on topics like foreign policy, congressional politics, or political philosophy. Many will offer options on community service and volunteerism or a survey course on current foreign policy issues. One aspect of formal education that appeals to many students is the access to instructors with specialized professional or academic training. Professors and teachers can also offer good suggestions of resources for further education and action.

A Few Good Men and Women: Helping with Elections

Schools, civic centers, and church fellowship halls open early on Election Day, and eager voters line up to cast their ballots before heading to work. Before the polls open and voting begins, however, volunteers have already logged hours of work, convincing voters to show up and persuading them to select particular candidates. This behind-the-scenes work is part of a second category of political participation, electoral activities. Examples of this type of participation include volunteering for a campaign or "get out the vote" efforts, donating money to candidates or interest groups, or working at a polling center.

Volunteering for Campaigns

In the process of researching different candidates and their positions, people may find some so appealing that they decide to volunteer for their campaigns. Indeed, candidates' strongest and most influential allies are volunteers who will not only vote for them but also commit their time to the campaign effort. Most political campaigns are managed by a handful of paid, formal staff, while volunteers provide the backbone of any strong effort. Political candidates rely on locals who help with a range of tasks, such as knocking on doors, distributing flyers, stuffing envelopes, and calling registered voters on the day of the election to make sure they vote. If you discover a candidate whom you want to help, call or email the campaign office and let them know your availability. In all likelihood, they will put you to work quickly. Those who don't have much time to volunteer can still attend a candidate's rallies, dinners, or meetings to demonstrate support and to learn more about the candidate's issue positions.

Two other important electoral activities are voter registration and Get Out the Vote (GOTV) drives. Voter turnout in the United States is the lowest of all modern democracies.[3] Because most states require people to register to vote days or weeks before the election, political parties and interest groups organize registration drives that encourage people to complete the necessary forms. If you aren't interested in helping with a particular candidate's campaign, you can still participate by distributing voter registration cards and increasing voter awareness of all the candidates and platforms.

Voter registration is only the first step. Campaigns devote significant time and resources to encouraging people to vote and maximizing turnout. Some volunteers call likely supporters to remind them of their polling location; others provide transportation or child care for those who otherwise could not make it to the polls.

In recent decades, nonprofit organizations have devoted more resources to GOTV efforts. Groups like the League of Women

Voters, an organization dedicated to voter education for almost a century, and Rock the Vote, a newer group targeting younger voters, organize nonpartisan voter mobilization efforts to educate people and encourage them to vote. Volunteering for a voter education group as well as encouraging members of your family, co-workers, and friends to vote helps the electoral effort. Increasing general voter turnout ensures that a widely representative voice guides democratic procedures.

Why Donating Money Matters

When we think of political participation, donating money to campaigns may not immediately come to mind. However, campaign contributions are necessary for electing candidates at every level of office, from the local school board to president of the United States.

The amount of money candidates raise and spend is one of the best predictors of their electoral success; those who outspend their competitors usually win. Any time a challenger is able to spend as much or almost as much as an incumbent, the person defending the seat usually loses. Consider the example of the 2004 race between the then senate minority leader Tom Daschle (D-SD) and former Republican congressman John Thune. Even though he was the highest-ranked Democrat in the U.S. Senate, Daschle's race was highly contested. Senate Majority Leader Bill Frist (R-TN) was one of many high-profile politicians who visited South Dakota to support Thune. Daschle spent $21 million on his campaign, and Thune spent almost $15 million on his, setting a record for the most expensive congressional race of 2004.[4] Thune won by a 2 percent margin.

As total campaign spending has increased exponentially in recent decades, so have the calls for campaign finance reform. In 2002, Congress passed the Bipartisan Campaign Reform Act (BCRA), which tightens campaign giving and spending regulations. BCRA changed the limits on how much individual donors can give to congressional and presidential candidates, allowing each person to give up to $2,000 per candidate, per election, for a combined total of no more than $95,000 over a two-year election cycle. The law was indexed to inflation, which means that each year the limits increase slightly.

Federal law prohibits corporations and unions from contributing directly to political campaigns, but they can form political action committees (PACs), tightly regulated groups that collect and distribute money to political candidates and parties. Other interest groups face strict legal limits on what they can donate to campaigns, but they can spend as much as they please on advertisements created independently of campaigns, as long as they do not directly advocate voting for or against a candidate. If you want to contribute financially, you can donate directly to campaigns or to interest groups that raise awareness of issues relevant to your concerns.

Lifting Every Voice: Interacting with Government

A third and final broad category of activity includes those actions that foster citizen interaction with government. All citizens have an interest in what government does and does not accomplish; laws and regulations affect almost every part of our lives. In most cases, the best way to have some influence over governmental decisions is to follow the activities of elected representatives and communicate with them when needed.

Can just one person really make a difference in local, state, or federal policy making? How do you make your voice heard? Although many forms of civic participation require a significant commitment of time and effort, it is indeed possible to get the attention of elected officials and directly influence their decision making.

Watching Elected Officials at Work

One avenue for civic participation is attending government meetings. In most cases, elected officials hold public meetings at which they discuss issues, debate alternatives, and vote. If you turn to cable channels C-SPAN or C-SPAN 2 on weekdays, you are likely to see the House of Representatives or the Senate in action. These channels broadcast open committee sessions in which members gather to discuss and revise legislative proposals, and they show activity on the floor of each chamber. Although legislative business rarely makes for riveting television, anyone with access to cable

Politics 101: Some Helpful Websites

Many people want to learn more about politics and get more involved, but these tasks can seem quite daunting. As it turns out, political research and participation may not be as difficult as you think. The rise of the Internet has brought many helpful political websites that not only provide access to useful research and data but also show citizens easy ways to get involved. Here are a few examples of websites that may be worth visiting:

Sites for Political Involvement

Congress.org (http://www.con gress.org/congressorg/home): Don't let the name fool you; this website is a phenomenal resource that provides an easy way to connect citizens and government. On the front page of the site, simply type in your zip code to link to contact information for your state and federal elected officials. The site also includes legislative voting records, information about key legislation facing Congress, and a forum for debate.

Project Vote Smart (http://www .votesmart.org/index.htm): Project Vote Smart provides information about elected officials and candidates for office, compiling biographical information, voting records, interest group ratings, and other data that may help you make a voting decision. If you would like to register to vote, the site lists registration information for each state.

Rock the Vote (http://www.rock thevote.com): While this site is designed for younger generations in an effort to encourage participation, it offers an easy way for all citizens to register to vote.

Research Sites

The Heritage Foundation (http:// www.heritage.org): Regarded as one of the top think tanks in Washington DC, this site offers in-depth scholarly analysis of a number of issues from a conservative point of view.

Progressive Policy Institute (http:// www.ppionline.org): Also a well-respected think tank, PPI offers scholarly research on a range of political issues from a liberal point of view.

OpenSecrets.org (http://www .opensecrets.org): Run by the Center for Responsive Politics, this is the best resource for campaign finance data. Visitors can follow the money trail for political candidates. The thumbnails at the top of the site provide easy navigation tools for information on campaign finance law, specific election cycles, who gives money, and who receives it.

Jonathan Flugstad

television or the Internet can watch lawmakers at work. Likewise, visitors to Washington DC can watch the proceedings live.

Local governing boards also hold public meetings, and some are televised on local access channels. Anyone interested in the issues affecting a city can attend city council meetings. A parent concerned about public school policies can attend school board meetings. Although the format varies somewhat across the country, almost all local boards and commissions hold regularly scheduled meetings. In addition to watching the elected officials at work, citizens in attendance have the opportunity to ask questions, make statements, and raise particular concerns.

If you want to watch local government at work, visit your city or town website to find out when and where different boards and commissions meet and if they are broadcast on a local access channel. While boards and councils may call special meetings or hearings for emergency concerns, they seldom deviate from the published calendar. As the date draws near, websites will generally announce the agenda. If you hear that the local schools are considering changing the curriculum or that the state transportation board is thinking about widening the road behind your house, you may want to attend the proceedings and share your perspective on the proposals. Speaking at a meeting does not guarantee that your representatives will ultimately decide as you would like, but it does offer you the chance to give your input.

The Power of the Pen: Communicating with Elected Officials

Yet another way to interact with government is contacting legislators and other policy makers. Faxes, letters sent via email or traditional mail, and phone calls link elected officials with their constituents. Such communications link voters and citizens to the democratic process.

Many people contact elected officials to share their views on issues that concern them. As we saw in chapter 12, models of representation may vary, but the need to respond to constituents almost always remains a priority. Members of Congress, for example, are always preparing for the next election; lessons from history suggest that those who fail to listen and respond to constituent needs are among the most vulnerable to losing office.

When constituents contact the president, their governor, or a legislator, designated staff members sort through the information

Capturing the Attention of Elected Officials: Myths and Realities

Contrary to popular belief, when it comes to constituent communications, not all contact is created equal. Government officials are likely to pay at least some attention to all of their mail and phone calls, but certain modes of contact are more effective than others. Consider a few pointers to maximize your influence and minimize your frustration.

Whenever possible, compose your own letter. Especially in the electronic age, nothing compares to a personal letter. Depending on the elected official, an office may receive dozens to tens of thousands of communications each day. Letters clearly written by individuals expressing their personal opinions matter most. Almost every elected official makes sure the office replies to individual letters.

Elected officials may or may not pay attention to mass mailings. Some people receive preprinted postcards from interest groups, which they then sign and send to their legislators. Some offices will enter the information from such contacts; others will not. To maximize the potential influence of your voice, use such form letters and postcards as templates to write letters in your own words.

If you email, you may or may not get a response, and the elected official may or may not record your concern. Email is one of the quickest and easiest forms of contact, which means that offices get flooded with emails. Some legislators track all emails and reply to them, while others send only automated responses. If you write the president, for example, you're guaranteed only an automatic response that begins with generic thanks but does not reply to the specific question: "On behalf of President Bush, thank you for your correspondence. We appreciate hearing your views and welcome your suggestions. Due to the large volume of email received, the White House cannot respond to every message."

Most legislators do not answer mail from or keep records of calls from nonconstituents. Given the flood of communications to most offices, the staff members focus their time and attention on responding to their own constituents.

When contacting an elected official for help with a government agency, call his or her local office. Most elected officials have designated staff who help constituents with a range of problems. Call and talk directly with a caseworker; you're likely to get a more immediate response to a phone call than a letter.

and respond to their concerns. Because most elected officials do not have the time to read and reply to correspondence directly, most rely on staff to report how many people have contacted the office and what the nature of their concerns is. On especially contentious issues when an upcoming vote looks like it will be close, some legislators actually count the "pro" and "con" letters to determine how to vote. Such communication gives policy makers an opportunity to hear from multiple vantage points and possibly take action in response.

In many ways, individual voters' opinions count the most, but group communication efforts can also speak to elected officials. Interest groups, unified by a common bond to influence policy in their favor, may organize members to write letters, sign petitions, send postcards, or flood legislators' offices with phone calls and emails when a bill particular to their cause is under debate. If you and others you know share a policy concern, contact your elected officials individually as part of a timed and organized effort.

Constituents also communicate with elected officials when they have problems with government agencies or policies. Much of the work in the local offices of federal and state legislators involves responding to such requests. Caseworkers for U.S. senators and representatives can help people with problems such as navigating the immigration process, receiving their veterans' benefits, or finding a missing Social Security payment. When a member of a congressional staff requests help for a constituent, government agencies often respond quickly. In the same way, state legislators assist constituents with state benefits and programs.

Although it requires time and energy to interact with government, such contact is essential for the healthy functioning of representative democracy. Voting allows each person a voice in selecting public officials, but other forms of participation before and after Election Day provide additional opportunities for interacting with government and with one another.

Participation in and through the Church

Although we may not think of it in such terms, participation in a local church prepares members for civic participation and connects them with many opportunities to care for others in need. Even those who have little to no interest in the political process

The Power of Many: Political Rallies

During a year charged with political partisanship on every issue from privatizing Social Security to the war in Iraq, a hopeful collaboration across parties, agendas, and faiths emerged on April 30, 2006. As reported in the *Washington Post*, more than ten thousand individuals who gathered on the National Mall in Washington DC were joined by thousands more in fifteen cities across the United States, demanding action in the Darfur region of Sudan.[5] Concerned with the killing of at least four hundred thousand Sudanese and the displacement of an estimated two million, members from Amnesty International, the National Association of Evangelicals, and Jewish synagogues joined with Sudanese refugees and many others to set aside their differences and raise awareness of the violence in Darfur. Both Democratic and Republican representatives and senators addressed the crowd, calling on the United States to use its global power to move toward a lasting peace process. The star power of actor George Clooney sparked energy in the attendees.

Rallying or protesting in a public venue is another way to communicate with political leaders and raise public awareness of political issues. The history of the United States is peppered with examples of citizens taking to the streets. Sometimes successful rallies and protests lead to immediate policy shifts; at other times, they raise general awareness of a problem. Although the atrocities and fighting continue in Darfur, international pressure seems to be working. In the fall of 2006, the United Nations approved a resolution to deploy peace-keeping forces to Darfur. That October, the president signed the Darfur Peace and Accountability Act. The legislation describes the violence in Darfur as "genocide," asks for expansion of the African Union peacekeeping effort, and supports pursuing in the International Criminal Court those guilty of committing war crimes.

can live out the command to love God and neighbor through the local church and the organizations it supports.

Individual congregations equip their members with knowledge and skills that likely apply to political participation. Consider some of the many ways within the church that participation routinely occurs. Volunteers commit each week to teach Sunday school. Others prepare and deliver meals to the sick and homebound. Still others write, modify, and implement an annual budget. Even this short list of examples demonstrates ways that members of the church routinely organize activities and contribute to the health of the congregation. Regular participation in congregational activities helps people develop communication and organizational skills, training them to work with others to complete tasks. While not all Christians will be called to political participation, those who are will find that many skills they develop in church activities will help them in their political endeavors.

Churches also connect their members to outreach organizations and opportunities. As described in some detail in chapter 11, faith-based and community organizations play a crucial role in meeting needs within their communities. Some congregations serve the poor and needy through on-site programs; many others partner with nearby churches or local organizations that provide various outreach services.

Church and community-based programs provide what is likely the best way to meet the specific needs in a local area. Anyone can partner with these programs by donating time, money, goods, and services. Job-training programs, food banks, and classes teaching English as a second language are just a few examples of the types of organizations and services that depend on volunteers. After-school youth outreach programs always need mentors to tutor and encourage children and teens. Crisis pregnancy centers rely on donations of maternity and baby clothes, cribs, car seats, diapers, formula, and other infant items to meet the needs of the families they serve. Most soup kitchens depend on groups of volunteers to prepare and serve meals.

It's surprisingly easy to connect with community and faith-based organizations that need volunteers. Church bulletins and newsletters often include announcements of service opportunities; pastors and priests can easily connect you with church programs and local organizations that provide a wide range of services. Although almost all organizations need regular volunteers, most also offer one-time or short-term opportunities to help, providing an outlet for people with packed schedules as well as offering prospective volunteers the chance to participate before making a longer commitment. Volunteer work is rarely an individual effort; many projects provide opportunities for families, small groups, or groups of friends and co-workers to volunteer together.

Adult education classes and topical small groups provide other ways to raise political awareness within your congregation. Consider teaching or organizing an election-year class or group that encourages scriptural reflections, prayer for political leaders, and analysis of current events from a Christian perspective. If you don't feel equipped to facilitate such a class or group, attend one and participate in the discussion.

Each of the options described above offers tangible ways to serve God and neighbor. Whether volunteering at a community organization, sharing a meal with the homeless, or attending an adult education class at church, Christians can connect with community needs and concerns that might otherwise go unnoticed in their daily lives.

A Matter of Prayer

As we have seen, we have many possible ways to engage with American politics beyond voting. Individual circumstances, abilities, and experiences all influence how and whether people choose to participate. For the follower of Christ, however, one form of political participation is not optional: we are all called to prayer. In 1 Timothy 2:1–2, Paul charges us to intercede, especially for political leaders: "I urge, then, first of all, that requests, prayers, intercession and thanksgiving be made for everyone—for kings and all those in authority, that we may live peaceful and quiet lives in all godliness and holiness." Although the other more visible forms of political participation are important, nothing can replace the centrality of prayer.

Most people are quick to criticize political leaders who hold positions they do not support. Followers of Christ are called to a higher standard. Instead of complaining about government and bemoaning election results, we should be lifting governmental officials and their decisions to God in prayer. Even though it may be more difficult to pray for leaders with whom we disagree, we are not given an option.

As we have seen throughout this book, government addresses problems that have no simple solutions, and political leaders face daunting tasks in their daily work. Although we should not discount the role of individual and corporate activities designed to bring about change, we must not lose sight of the fact that prayer makes a tangible difference. C. S. Lewis describes the role of petitionary prayer, commenting that "[God] allows soils and weather and animals and muscles, minds, and wills of men to co-operate in the execution of His will. . . . It is not really stranger, nor less strange, that my prayers should affect the course of events than that my other actions should do so."[6] Although the political agendas and concerns facing those inside and outside the church are often the same, the gift of prayer provides Christians another way to make a difference.

Though it can be exciting and even fun to participate in politics, our individual actions are only a small piece of a much larger picture. While Christians wait, hope, and pray for God's restorative work, we can bring the needs of our communities and our world to him in prayer.

In this final section, we have explored many different ways that Christians can apply their faith to politics. Now it is time to take a final step back and look at the larger picture, thinking more broadly about politics as a means for loving God and neighbor.

14

Can We All Get Along?

Politics and the Great Commandments

The Christian ideal has not been tried and found wanting. It has been found difficult; and left untried.

G. K. Chesterton (1874–1936), author

When I arrived in a new city to begin my first teaching position after graduate school, I knew no one and hoped to make friends quickly. A colleague with an office down the hall from mine befriended me and began introducing me to other members of the college community. One evening she invited me to a local restaurant with one of her close friends, another professor in her department. The evening was a disaster. Conversation was stilted and uncomfortable. I wasn't sure why things seemed so terrible, but I knew I just wanted to get home.

The next day at the office, my colleague from down the hall came to see me. She was very embarrassed, apologized for her friend's rudeness the previous evening, and tried to explain what had happened. Her friend was Jewish and a lesbian. When she saw the cross necklace I always wear, she assumed I was a Christian and therefore determined she wanted nothing to do with me. She was still stinging from negative past experiences with Christians; she assumed that I would be hateful, judgmental, and rude. Not wanting to relive her painful past, she had no interest in getting to know me or in extending kindness toward me. Although I had often interacted with colleagues and friends who did not share my religious views, this was the first time someone had made it clear they wanted nothing to do with me because of assumptions about my beliefs.

I never did get to know this particular colleague on a personal level, and I regret that I never heard her story to find out what had happened to create such animosity toward Christians. Perhaps someone offended her; perhaps she drew her own conclusions from unfair cultural stereotypes. Whatever the reasons, she thought she knew enough about Christianity to make an immediate judgment to avoid me.

As Christian believers, we should expect that some people will react to us unfairly and with undue harshness. Although the immediate temptation is to respond in kind, the best alternative is to respond according to the gospel, conducting ourselves in a way that helps dispel unfairly negative reactions toward Christianity. At the same time, we must also recognize that we too face the temptation to stereotype others. Instead of writing people off immediately without listening to what they have to say, we should invite conversation and encourage dialogue when possible.

The political arena may be one of the few places where many people outside of the church interact with Christian believers. Our words, our actions, and our demeanor when advocating for political issues and candidates are an important part of our public witness for or against following Christ. This concluding chapter offers some final reflections on politics as a means for demonstrating love for God and neighbor, including some exhortations to those who are called more directly to political engagement.

Christian Witness in Word and Deed

The central assumption of this book is that those involved in politics should work together in humility and with respect. From a legislator explaining her most recent vote to a concerned parent writing a letter to the editor of his local newspaper, everyone makes choices about how to communicate. Instead of speaking with an air of entitlement and superiority, we can foster respect for one another with honest, straightforward communication. Far too much contemporary political rhetoric raises alarm and captures attention by demonizing opponents and criticizing them unfairly. Christians interacting in politics should avoid speaking with hate and hyperbole, committing instead to model Christ's love.

And so we return once again to Paul's words in 1 Corinthians 12 and 13 and his reminder of the centrality of love as a guiding principle for life in community. Knowing that we see as in a mirror dimly, we can find comfort in the recognition that we won't have all of the answers to life's vexing questions, nor do we need to pretend that we do. Instead, we can place our trust in the triune God, the source of all truth, and undertake lives of humility and service. We can also look toward the day when we are in God's presence, when we will have the clarity promised to us.

Likewise, the 1 Corinthians passage and many others remind us that love is the guiding principle for all aspects of the Christian life. We extend God's love to others through political activities as one part of the larger call to imitate Christ. Thus, political engagement becomes a means of demonstrating God's love and responding in obedience.

Many well-meaning people are engaged in politics. Some are motivated by faith in Christ, others by different religions, and still others by a general sense of duty or concern not connected to spirituality. As Christians, we have three options in the public square: blending in with the crowd and the standards of other well-meaning people who may imitate Jesus without knowing it; standing apart from others for negative behavior that fosters damaging stereotypes of Christians; or standing apart for positive reasons, modeling genuine Christlike behavior and the fruit of the Spirit. At a minimum, it often makes sense to adopt the standards of others in the public square who seek to do good. Particular cases may require blending one or more of these options. But those of us who publicly profess Christianity or who explicitly credit our faith for motivating our actions are called to the higher standard of seeking distinctively Christian ways of extending love to God and neighbor.

The political arena can be terrifying; observers have many reasons for using battle metaphors to describe it. Although the temptations are just as great for Christians to engage in politics as warfare, in Christian charity we can work to demonstrate that a different kind of politics is possible, one that invites conversation and transformation, not condemnation of the other side. It is indeed possible to create a political strategy based on the premises of presenting each side's political positions fairly and clearly, raising honest differences where they exist, and fostering open dialogue about different means to achieve policy goals. Such an approach undoubtedly runs counter to almost all of the norms of contemporary political behavior; then again, following in the path of Jesus Christ is by definition countercultural.

Entering the Political Arena: Some Final Thoughts

As we have seen in this book, Christians can interact with and seek to influence government in many different ways. Because government has such a profound influence on society, many Christians will choose politics as one means of demonstrating love for God and neighbor. If you follow this path, here are a few things to keep in mind that may promote respectful and fruitful political engagement.

- **Accept that politics is complex.** Government has already solved those problems that are easy to fix. Almost all of the issues that remain for public debate are complex and multifaceted. Accept the complexity of the process. Ask hard questions of anyone who proposes a quick fix or simple solution. Sometimes creative people find new and simple ways to address policy issues, but most options that seem to offer an easy way out are really too good to be true.
- **Expect compromise.** Representatives bring a diversity of views, interests, and concerns to the table, so the political arena rarely, if ever, brings people to consensus. By design,

government depends on compromise and bargaining. Enter the process aware that you are more likely to achieve your goals through a series of small steps than with one sweeping change. On those issues where you cannot compromise, seek nonpolitical solutions first.

- **Prepare yourself before entering public policy debates.** Distinguishing between means and ends is a tried-and-true method for avoiding unnecessary frustration. Separate the goals you hope to achieve from the many different potential methods of achieving them. Seek agreement where possible, and determine the areas where disagreement will be inevitable. When debating means of achieving shared goals, be prepared to discuss many sides of the issue. Do your homework so you can advocate your position with clarity, detail, and precision. Seek opportunities to learn from and engage in conversation with people representing other viewpoints.

- **Set reasonable expectations for what government can (and cannot) achieve.** Since government is in the business of addressing problems that are difficult (if not impossible) to solve, political solutions often only scratch the surface of a complex issue and leave many aspects unsolved. Representative government is only one of many institutions that pursue the common good. Churches, families, schools, faith-based and community organizations, and other institutions play important roles in meeting people's needs and addressing problems.

- **Respect and honor your elected officials.** Although the lives of politicians may look glamorous from a distance, the reality is far more complex. Elected officials face many pressures, often work grueling schedules, and make significant sacrifices to enter public life. Although some politicians abuse their power, most are dedicated public servants trying to do their best to make a difference. Share your views with your political leaders. Let them know when you respectfully disagree, and commend those whose actions you support. If you don't like what someone is doing in office, get involved in the next campaign to work for change. Above all, pray for political leaders with sincerity.

In addition to noting the practical steps summarized above, Christians in politics should take care not to lose sight of the larger goals and purposes motivating their work and actions. Although public office and advocacy groups provide people of faith access to power that can be transformative, Christian politicians and activists should keep their priorities carefully ordered. Power is incredibly seductive—it may transform us rather than society. Once we are in the spotlight and in the corridors of power, it is very easy to lose sight of the principles and values that originally motivated our actions. If doing what is right costs the next election or all but assures a policy defeat, so be it. The desire to serve God must be higher than the desire to serve the public.

Although many Christians will find ways to serve in politics and government, it is important to remember that interaction with government is not the only form of public service. The political arena is a significant forum for addressing the major issues of the day, but it is not the only area of influence in a democratic nation. Society benefits from the work of dedicated servants in a wide range of professions and from all walks of life. Some are called to political office and some are called to serve in other ways, but we are all called to love God and neighbor.

A Call to Perseverance

As we have seen throughout this book, the structure and functions of American government are quite complicated, and political change is far from quick and easy. Work in the political arena requires determination, focus, and much perseverance. At times, the temptation to give up will be very strong, but don't lose heart. Despite the many challenges facing Christians who want to serve God in their political participation, the task is vital. Václav Havel, playwright and former president of Czechoslovakia and the Czech Republic, offered this advice: "If your heart is in the right place and you have good taste, not only will you pass muster in politics, you are destined for it. If you are modest and do not lust after power, not only are you suited to politics, you absolutely belong there."[1] Our nation and our world need more committed Christians willing and able to see beyond left and right to participate in politics as a means of demonstrating God's love and mercy.

Discussion Questions for Small Groups

You may want to begin each discussion with some general questions: What new insight did you gain from reading this chapter? Where did you find yourself disagreeing with the author? Why?

A good way to end the discussion: What do you most want to remember from this chapter?

Chapter 1: Who Speaks for God in Politics?

1. What are some of your central assumptions about the role of religion in politics? Where did you develop these views? Have any of your assumptions changed over time?
2. What do you think about the trends that reveal increasing religious diversity in the United States? What problems might religious diversity create? In what ways is it beneficial?
3. In what ways do your religious views directly influence your thoughts on politics? What might be some of the indirect effects?
4. What are some common ways that we tend to misuse God's name? What are some practical ways that we can honor God's name in politics? In other areas of our lives?

5. Have you ever considered 1 Corinthians 13 a helpful text for thinking about politics? What are some specific ways you could apply this passage to your political life?

6. Think of times in the past when you have talked about politics with friends, family, or co-workers. What was one of the most satisfying conversations? What made it so positive? What was one of the most upsetting discussions? Why was it so troubling?

7. What are some practical ways that politics can be a means for demonstrating love in action and building the body of Christ?

Chapter 2: When It's No Sin to Compromise

1. What words and phrases come to mind when you hear the word *compromise*? Can you think of examples of ways that you need to compromise in your daily life?

2. Do you think of religion as black-and-white? Why or why not? Do you think of politics as shades of gray? Why or why not?

3. The author suggests that "many politicians and political activists intentionally frame issues with sharp contrasts as a technique to rally their supporters and gain credibility" (p. 33). Can you think of any examples?

4. What are some problems that government probably cannot solve? What are some things that government can probably do better than any other institution?

5. Suggest some ways that compromise in politics could be a "tool for good." Think of other ways that compromise might be a "pathway to temptation and sin" (p. 39).

6. In what ways, if any, has reading this chapter changed your thoughts about compromise?

Chapter 3: Is *Liberal* a Bad Word?

1. What kinds of things do you typically associate with the term *conservative*? With the term *liberal*?

2. In what ways did the descriptions of conservative and liberal ideologies in this chapter confirm your previous

understanding of them? Did anything catch you by surprise or challenge your previous assumptions?

3. Are you more likely to connect your own political views with a party (Democrat, Republican, etc.) or with an ideology (conservative, liberal, etc.)? Why?

4. What are some examples of using ideological labels in an insulting or demeaning manner? What are some examples of constructive ways to use such labels?

5. What are some practical ways to look beyond ideological labels for ourselves and in our interactions with others?

Chapter 4: Is the United States a Christian Nation?

1. Are you surprised by the reaction of Pastor Boyd's congregation that was described in the opening of this chapter? Why or why not?

2. In what ways does it make sense to describe the United States as a Christian nation? In what ways might this description be inaccurate?

3. If historians from the twenty-third century were looking for evidence to confirm your religious beliefs and practices, what would they find?

4. What do you think are the most significant Christian influences on American government?

5. In what ways might civil religion enhance American politics? In what ways might it be problematic?

6. How do you respond when presidents use religious language in their public speeches? What factors affect your response?

Chapter 5: Are All Christians Republican?

1. How has this chapter influenced the way you think about opinion polls?

2. Would a survey categorize you as Mainline Protestant, Evangelical, Black Protestant, Roman Catholic, Jewish, or Secular? Do you think the profiles described in the chapter adequately reflect your political views?

3. From what you have seen and heard in the media, how do the Democratic and Republican parties appear to reach out to religious voters? Are these efforts convincing? Why or why not?

4. In what ways are politicians' personal religious views important to you politically?

5. Political scientist John DiIulio contends that "political talk, whether on the campaign trail or inside government, is not only very cheap, but also not always highly predictive regarding what people actually believe" (p. 84). How can we be discerning in our evaluations of what politicians say and do?

Chapter 6: Good Guys and Bad Guys?

1. Do you identify yourself as a Republican or Democrat? Why or why not?

2. How would presidential and congressional elections be different if we didn't identify candidates by political party?

3. In what ways do political parties seem to improve government? In what ways might parties complicate or hinder government's work?

4. Can you think of examples of partisanship and bipartisan cooperation demonstrated in any recent news events?

5. What are some practical steps you can take to make sure that your party loyalty does not cloud your judgment?

6. In the partisan environment of contemporary American politics, how can we be agents of reconciliation and not divisiveness?

Chapter 7: Who Does What?

1. What are some potential dangers of government wielding too much power? What are some potential dangers of a government that is too weak?

2. What government policies are best handled at the state level? At the national level?

3. This chapter describes the president as having limited powers. From what you see and read on the news, what seems to

limit the president's powers? In what ways does the president seem to have command and control?

4. How do you interact with government bureaucracy in your daily life? What has been positive or negative about these interactions?

5. Given the long and uncertain road to the Supreme Court, why do you think people pursue policy goals through the courts? What might they hope to achieve? What risks are involved?

6. Would you prefer that the Supreme Court or state legislatures have the power to write and enforce abortion regulations? Explain.

Chapter 8: Does the Church Have Any Business in Politics?

1. Did any of the descriptions of religion and government in the early colonies surprise you?

2. Do you find the metaphor *wall of separation* helpful for discussing the relationship between church and state? Why or why not?

3. What legal test would you suggest to guide judges interpreting the establishment clause? In your opinion, what interactions, if any, between the government and religious organizations are permissible?

4. What legal test would you suggest to guide judges interpreting the free exercise clause? In your opinion, what limits, if any, should government place on religious worship and belief?

5. What factors do you think contribute to the confusion and controversies surrounding judicial interpretation of the First Amendment religion clauses?

Chapter 9: Applying Faith to Politics

1. Consider the example of Proverbs 26:4–5 that begins this chapter. Can you think of other verses or biblical passages that appear to create tensions? What resources help you with challenges of biblical interpretation?

2. Which aspects of each of the traditions of political theology described in this chapter appeal to you? Which aspects trouble you or raise questions in your mind? Why?

3. Do you think government is part of God's creation, or did it become necessary because of the fall of humankind? How does your answer to this question affect your views about Christians and political participation?

4. Is it possible to distinguish between questions of "church and state" and "religion and politics"? Why or why not?

5. Where would you place your personal views on the church-state spectrum shown in Figure 9.1? Explain why you chose that position.

6. The author suggests that "as we seek to apply our faith to politics, we need to be aware of our theological and ideological assumptions and be willing to engage with others about theirs" (p. 154). What are your theological and ideological assumptions? What are some ways you can encourage constructive engagement with others who hold different views?

Chapter 10: My Way or the Highway?

1. In what ways is the term *easy issues* useful and descriptive? What are some of the potential problems with this phrase?

2. In what ways is the term *hard issues* useful and descriptive? What are some of the potential problems with this phrase?

3. As you think about current events in the news right now, which ones would you classify as easy issues, and which ones as hard issues? Explain your reasoning.

4. How has the welfare reform example helped you see some of the challenges that arise in public debates over policy issues?

5. Offer a few examples of ways you can "play fair" when discussing and debating political differences.

6. Are there any issues that do not seem to be on the political agenda that you believe deserve more discussion? If so, which ones? Why should Christians care about these issues?

Chapter 11: Can Christians Honestly Disagree?

1. How do you respond to claims that a particular political position is *the* Christian view?
2. What tools do you use to help you apply biblical truth to political questions? What resources help you in this process?
3. What are some of the strengths and weaknesses of the different means of reducing poverty in the United States, as discussed in this chapter?
4. Which, if any, of the three proposals for reducing poverty appeals to you the most? Why?
5. How would you respond if you discovered that a Christian friend held a different political position than you?
6. What can you do to foster constructive dialogue with those who do not share your political views?

Chapter 12: Behind the Curtain at the Voting Booth

1. In the quote that opens this chapter, G. K. Chesterton contends that we "ought to vote with the whole of [ourselves]" including head, heart, soul, and stomach. What does it mean to you to vote with your whole self?
2. Do you prefer your elected representatives to serve more as delegates or more as trustees? Why?
3. How do you determine which political issues are most important to you?
4. What do you like about political advertisements? What do you dislike?
5. What resources are most helpful to you as you decide if and how to vote?

Chapter 13: Beyond the Ballot Box

1. What is your first political memory? How and when did you first learn about government and politics?
2. Have you ever volunteered or worked for a political campaign? If yes, what did you learn from the experience? If no, why not?

3. What would you most like to tell or ask the president? A member of Congress? A local government official?

4. Which of the examples of political participation discussed in this chapter are most interesting to you? Which ones are least interesting? Why?

5. In what ways has your involvement in a local church helped you live out the command to love God and neighbor?

6. It may seem easier to criticize political leaders than to pray for them. How can you pray specifically for your political leaders?

Chapter 14: Can We All Get Along?

1. Can you think of times when people reacted against you harshly or unfairly because of your faith? How should Christians respond to such situations?

2. The author argues that political engagement is a "means of demonstrating God's love and responding in obedience" (p. 223). What are some specific ways to do this?

3. Look over the list of things to keep in mind, presented near the end of the chapter. Which of these seems easiest to follow? Which do you think would be most difficult?

4. Could you ever see yourself running for political office? Why or why not?

5. In what ways has this book helped you make sense of American politics? What new questions has it raised?

Notes

Chapter 1 Who Speaks for God in Politics?

1. The Graduate Center, "American Religious Identification Survey," December 19, 2001, http://www.gc.cuny.edu/faculty/research_briefs/aris/key_findings.htm.

2. Lyndon Baines Johnson, "Special Message to the Congress: The American Promise," Lyndon Baines Johnson Library and Museum, March 16, 1965, http://www.lbjlib.utexas.edu/johnson/archives.hom/speeches.hom/650315.asp.

3. Ronald Reagan, "Address to the Nation on the Challenger Disaster," The Ronald Reagan Presidential Library and Foundation, January 28, 1986, http://www.reaganfoundation.org/reagan/speeches/challenger.asp.

4. Bill Clinton, "Oklahoma City Speech," PresidentialRhetoric.com, April 23, 1995, http://www.presidentialrhetoric.com/historicspeeches/clinton/oklahomacity.html.

5. George W. Bush, "Address to the Nation," PresidentialRhetoric.com, September 20, 2001, http://www.presidentialrhetoric.com/speeches/09.20.01.html.

6. Colin Smith, *The Ten Greatest Struggles of Your Life* (Chicago: Moody, 2006), 49.

7. David E. Garland, "1 Corinthians," in *Dictionary for Theological Interpretation of the Bible*, ed. Kevin J. Vanhoozer (Grand Rapids: Baker Academic, 2005), 133.

8. Gary Fineart, "Crist Cancels Inaugural Ball," *Miami Herald*, December 10, 2006.

9. C. S. Lewis, *God in the Dock* (Grand Rapids: Eerdmans, 1970), 198.

Chapter 2 When It's No Sin to Compromise

1. For more details about the Safe Havens Support Act, see Amy E. Black, *From Inspiration to Legislation: How an Idea Becomes a Bill* (Upper Saddle River, NJ: Prentice Hall, 2007).

2. Elizabeth Anne Oldmixon, *Uncompromising Positions: God, Sex, and the U.S. House of Representatives* (Washington DC: Georgetown University Press, 2005), 43–44.

3. Paul Weyrich, quoted in William Martin, *With God on Our Side: The Rise of the Religious Right in America* (New York: Broadway, 2005), 171–72.

4. Paul Henry, quoted in Douglas L. Koopman, ed., *Serving the Claims of Justice: The Thoughts of Paul B. Henry* (Grand Rapids: Paul B. Henry Institute, 2001), 261.

5. Stephen Monsma and Mark Rodgers, "In the Arena: Practical Issues in Concrete Political Engagement," in *Toward an Evangelical Public Policy: Political Strategies for the Health of the Nation*, eds. Ronald J. Sider and Diane Knippers (Grand Rapids: Baker Books, 2005), 335.

6. U.S. Department of State, *Action Today, a Foundation for Tomorrow: The President's Emergency Plan for AIDS Relief*, Second Annual Report to Congress, 17, February 8, 2006, http://www.state.gov/documents/organization/60950.pdf.

7. These statistics are widely reported. For example, see U.S. Department of State, *Action Today*, 21.

Chapter 3 Is *Liberal* a Bad Word?

1. James W. Skillen, *The Scattered Voice: Christians at Odds in the Public Square* (Grand Rapids: Zondervan, 1990), 97.

2. For a brief introduction to neoconservatism, see Irving Kristol, "The Neoconservative Persuasion: What It Was, and What It Is," *The Weekly Standard* 8, no. 47 (2003).

3. I computed these numbers from ANES data available at http://www.umich.edu/~nes/nesguide/toptable/tab3_1.htm (accessed October 24, 2006).

4. The ANES data on party identification are available online at http://www.umich.edu/~nes/nesguide/toptable/tab2a_1.htm (accessed October 24, 2006).

5. John Danforth, *Faith and Politics* (New York: Viking, 2006), 10.

Chapter 4 Is the United States a Christian Nation?

1. Gregory Boyd, *The Myth of a Christian Nation* (Grand Rapids: Zondervan, 2006), 9.

2. D. James Kennedy, *Character and Destiny: A Nation in Search of Its Soul* (Grand Rapids: Zondervan, 1995), 90.

3. Americans United for Separation of Church and State, "Is America a 'Christian Nation'?" http://www.au.org/site/PageServer?pagename=resources_brochure_christian nation (accessed July 30, 2007).

4. Isaac Kramnick and R. Laurence Moore, *The Godless Constitution: The Case Against Religious Correctness* (New York: W. W. Norton, 1997), 27.

5. Ibid., 28.

6. David L. Holmes, *The Faiths of the Founding Fathers* (New York: Oxford University Press, 2006), 134–41.

7. Ibid., 46.

8. Clinton Rossiter, ed., *The Federalist Papers* (New York: New American Library, 1961), 322.

9. Law Center ITS, "A Chronology of US Historical Documents," University of Oklahoma College of Law, March 10, 2006, http://www.law.ou.edu/ushistory/mayflow.shtml.

10. Kenneth D. Wald and Allison Calhoun-Brown, *Religion and Politics in the United States*, 5th ed. (Lanham, MD: Rowman and Littlefield, 2007), 48–49.

11. Robert Bellah, "Civil Religion in America," *Daedalus* 96, no. 11 (1967), http://www.robertbellah.com/articles_5.htm.

12. Jean Jacques Rousseau, *The Social Contract*, book 4, chapter 8, http://www.constitution.org/jjr/socon_04.htm#008.

13. Ibid.

14. Religion News Service Survey, "Majority of Americans OK with Ten Commandments, Pledge in Public," Beliefnet, August 2003, http://www.beliefnet.com/story/130/story13066.html.

15. Wald and Calhoun-Brown, *Religion and Politics*, 54.

16. Frank Bruni, "Bush Insists to Voters His Blood Is Red, Not Blue," *New York Times*, April 24, 2000.

17. Michael Gerson, "Religion, Rhetoric, and the Presidency" (Ethics and Public Policy Center Forum, Key West, FL, December 6, 2004).

18. John Woolley and Gerhard Peters, "Statement by the President upon Signing Bill to Include the Words 'Under God' in the Pledge to the Flag," The American Presidency Project, http://www.presidency.ucsb.edu/ws/?pid=9920 (accessed July 30, 2007).

19. Pew Research Center/Pew Forum on Religion and Public Life Survey, August 2004, 5–10, http://www.pollingreport.com/religion.html.

20. Roderick P. Hart, *Campaign Talk: Why Elections Are Good for Us* (Princeton, NJ: Princeton University Press, 2000), 48–49.

21. See, for example, Roderick Hart, *The Political Pulpit* (West Lafayette, IN: Purdue University Press, 1977); Cynthia Toolin, "American Civil Religion from 1789–1981: A Content Analysis of Presidential Inaugural Addresses," *Review of Religious Research* 25 (1983): 39–48; and Michael Waldman, *POTUS Speaks: Finding the Words That Defined the Clinton Presidency* (New York: Simon & Schuster, 2000).

22. Carl Cannon, "Response" (Ethics and Public Policy Center Forum).

23. The Pew Forum on Religion and Public Life, "Religion and Politics: Contention and Consensus (Part II)," July 24, 2003, http://pewforum.org/docs/index.php?DocID=28.

24. Dwight D. Eisenhower, "First Inaugural Address," January 20, 1953, http://www.eisenhower.archives.gov/speeches/1953_inaugural_address.html (accessed July 30, 2007).

Chapter 5 Are All Christians Republican?

1. Susan Page, "Churchgoing Closely Tied to Voting Patterns," *USA Today*, June 3, 2004.

2. All data reported here accessed at http://www.pollingreport.com/abortion.htm.

3. The 2000 exit poll did not include a question to distinguish evangelical and mainline Protestants. The estimated numbers in this paragraph and those immediately following come from calculations of the Pew Research Center for the

People and the Press, "Religion and the Presidential Vote," December 6, 2004, http://people-press.org/commentary/pdf/103.pdf.

4. Andrew Greeley and Michael Hout, *The Truth about Conservative Christians: What They Think and What They Believe* (Chicago: University of Chicago Press, 2006), 75.

5. John J. DiIulio Jr., *The American Catholic Voter*, Program for Research on Religion and Urban Civil Society, Report 06-2, 2.

6. 2000 National Exit Poll, MSNBC.com, http://www.msnbc.com/m/d2k/g/polls.asp?office=P&state=N1; 2004 National Exit Poll, CNN.com, http://www.cnn.com/ELECTION/2004/pages/results/states/US/P/00/epolls.0.html.

7. Senator Barack Obama (D-IL), "Call to Renewal" (keynote address, June 28, 2006), http://www.barackobama.com/2006/06/28/call_to_renewal.php.

8. Senator Sam Brownback (R-KS), "Remarks on World AIDS Day," CQ Transcriptions, December 1, 2006.

9. DiIulio, *The American Catholic Voter*, 10.

Chapter 6 Good Guys and Bad Guys?

1. David Maraniss, "Edwards Soundly Defeats Duke for Louisiana Governor," *Washington Post*, November 17, 1991.

2. Daniel Magleby, et al., *Government by the People: National, State, and Local Version*, 21st ed. (Upper Saddle River, NJ: Pearson Education, 2006), 162.

3. Speaker Nancy Pelosi, "Pelosi Calls for a New America, Built on the Values That Made Our Country Great," http://speaker.gov/newsroom/speeches?id=0006 (accessed January 4, 2007).

4. George Washington, "Washington's Farewell Address 1796," The Avalon Project at Yale Law School, http://www.yale.edu/lawweb/avalon/washing.htm (accessed July 30, 2007).

5. The role of elector is almost entirely symbolic: election results determine the outcome of the presidential race; the electors merely make it official. The political parties typically choose activists, state and local officeholders, and other party loyalists to serve as electors. For more details on this process, and the Electoral College in general, see John C. Fortier, ed., *After the People Vote: A Guide to the Electoral College*, 3rd ed. (Washington DC: AEI Press, 2004).

6. Two states, Maine and Nebraska, do not allocate electoral votes by the winner-take-all method.

7. Gail Chaddock, in "The Polarization of American Politics: Myth or Reality?" Princeton Transcript, December 3, 2004, 4, http://www.princeton.edu/~csdp/events/pdfs/Panel2.pdf.

8. Barbara Sinclair, "Hostile Partners: The President, Congress, and Lawmaking in the Partisan 1990s," in *Polarized Politics: Congress and the President in a Partisan Era*, eds. Jon R. Bond and Richard Fleisher (Washington DC: Congressional Quarterly Press, 2000), 137–40.

9. AEI *Political Report* 3, no. 1 (January 2007): 3.

10. See, for example, the trends in party identification from the recurring American National Election Studies: http://www.electionstudies.org/nesguide/toptable/tab2a_1.htm (accessed July 30, 2007).

11. Posting on http://www.firedoglake.com, December 23, 2006.

12. Michael Cutter, http://www.counterterrorismblog.org, January 3, 2007.

13. Posting on http://www.malkinwatch.blogsome.com, July 6, 2006.

14. Posting on http://www.malkinwatch.blogsome.com, July 8, 2006.

15. Vin Weber, "Panel III—Reports from the Hill," in "The Polarization of American Politics," 2.

16. Larry Bartels, "Panel I—Trends in Polarization: Public Opinion," in "The Polarization of American Politics," 6.

17. David Broder, "The Polarization Express," *Washington Post*, December 12, 2004.

18. Paul Goren, "Party Identification and Core Political Values," *American Journal of Political Science* 49 (2005): 882–97.

19. Danforth, *Faith and Politics*, 16.

Chapter 7 Who Does What?

1. Philip B. Kurland and Ralph Lerner, "George Washington to James Warren," *The Founders' Constitution* (Chicago: The University of Chicago Press, 1987), http://press-pubs.uchicago.edu/founders/documents/v1ch5s9.html.

2. The Seventeenth Amendment changed this; we now choose senators directly by popular elections in each state.

3. George C. Edwards III, Martin P. Wattenberg, and Robert L. Lineberry, *Government in America: People, Politics, and Policy*, 11th ed. (New York: Pearson Longman, 2004), 66.

4. For an insider look at the legislative process, see Amy E. Black, *From Inspiration to Legislation*.

5. U.S. Constitution, art. 1, sec. 8.

6. Richard E. Neustadt, *Presidential Power and the Modern Presidents* (New York: Free Press, 1990), 10.

7. Scholars of the judiciary debate the extent to which judges act independently of politics. For an example of an argument that rejects the notion of judicial independence, see Gerald Rosenberg, "Judicial Independence and the Reality of Political Power," *Review of Politics* 54 (Summer 1992): 369–98.

8. Martin, *With God*, 384.

Chapter 8 Does the Church Have Any Business in Politics?

1. American Humanist Association, "Humanists Praise Pete Stark for 'Coming Out' as a Nontheist," March 12, 2007, http://www.americanhumanist.org/press/petestark.php.

2. Ibid.

3. Jon Meacham, *American Gospel: God, the Founding Fathers, and the Making of a Nation* (New York: Random House, 2006), 41.

4. Holmes, *Faiths of the Founding Fathers*, 21.

5. Edwin S. Gaustad, *Proclaim Liberty Throughout All the Land: A History of Church and State in America* (New York: Oxford University Press, 2003), 3.

6. Mark A. Noll, Nathan O. Hatch, and George M. Marsden, *The Search for Christian America* (Colorado Springs: Helmers and Howard, 1989), 35–36.

7. B. A. Robinson, "Do 'God' and 'Christianity' Have a Place in the European Union Constitution?" Religious Tolerance, http://www.religioustolerance.org/const_eu.htm (accessed July 30, 2007).

8. Conference of the Representatives of the Governments of the Member States, "Treaty Establishing a Constitution for Europe," October 29, 2004, http://ue.eu.int/igcpdf/en/04/cg00/cg00087-re02.en04.pdf (accessed July 30, 2007).

9. Gaustad, *Proclaim Liberty*, 40.

10. Ibid., 26.

11. Roger Williams, quoted in Daniel L. Dreisbach, *Thomas Jefferson and the Wall of Separation Between Church and State* (New York: New York University Press, 2002), 77.

12. Thomas Jefferson, "Jefferson's Letter to the Danbury Baptists," January 1, 1802, http://www.loc.gov/loc/lcib/9806/danpost.html.

13. Ellen Alderman and Caroline Kennedy, *In Our Defense: The Bill of Rights in Action* (New York: Avon Books, 1991), 58.

14. Ibid., 61.

15. *Lyng v. Northwest Indian Cemetery Protective Association*, 485 U.S. 439 (1988).

16. *Walz v. Tax Commission of the City of New York*, 397 U.S. 664 (1970).

17. *Everson v. Board of Education of Ewing Township*, 330 U.S. 1 (1947).

18. *Lemon v. Kurtzman*, 411 U.S. 192 (1973).

19. Claire Mullally, "Free Exercise Clause," First Amendment Center, http://www.firstamendmentcenter.org/rel_liberty/free_exercise/index.aspx (accessed July 30, 2007).

20. Frederick Mark Gedicks, *The Rhetoric of Church and State: A Critical Analysis of Religion Clause Jurisprudence* (Durham, NC: Duke University Press, 1995), 1.

Chapter 9 Applying Faith to Politics

1. G. J. Wenham, J. A. Motyer, D. A. Carson, and R. T. France, eds., *New Bible Commentary*, 21st-century ed. (Downers Grove, IL: InterVarsity Press, 1994), 604.

2. Clarke Cochran, "Life on the Border," in *Church, State, and Public Justice: Five Views*, ed. P. C. Kemeny (Downers Grove, IL: IVP Academic, 2007), 45.

3. *Catechism of the Catholic Church*, 2nd ed. (Washington DC: U.S. Catholic Conference, 1997), 540.

4. U.S. Conference of Catholic Bishops, "Faithful Citizenship: A Catholic Call to Political Responsibility," 2003, http://www.usccb.org/faithfulcitizenship/faithfulcitizenship03.pdf (accessed August 1, 2007).

5. Kristin E. Heyer, "Insights from Catholic Social Ethics and Political Participation," in *Toward an Evangelical Public Policy*, 105.

6. Cochran, "Life on the Border," 42.

7. Heyer, "Insights," 104.

8. Martin Luther, quoted in David C. Steinmetz, *Luther in Context* (Bloomington, IN: Indiana University Press, 1986), 121.

9. Steinmetz, *Luther in Context*, 115.

10. "Render unto Caesar . . . and unto God: A Lutheran View of Church and State," *Report of the Commission on Theology and Church Relations of the Lutheran Church* (Missouri Synod, September 1995), 67.

11. Werner O. Packull, "An Introduction to Anabaptist Theology," in *The Cambridge Companion to Reformation Theology*, eds. David Bagchi and David C. Steinmetz (Cambridge: Cambridge University Press, 2004), 214–15.

12. Ibid.

13. Ibid., 209.

14. Ronald J. Sider, "An Anabaptist Perspective on Church, Government, Violence, and Politics," *Brethren in Christ History and Life* 28, no. 2 (2005): 255.

15. Walter Klaassen, ed., *Anabaptism in Outline: Selected Primary Sources* (Scottdale, PA: Herald Press, 1981), 245.

16. Hans Denck, "Concerning True Love," in Klaassen, *Anabaptism in Outline*, 250.

17. Corwin Smidt, "Principled Pluralist Perspective," in Kemeny, *Church, State, and Public Justice*, 131.

18. Ibid., 133.

19. David C. Steinmetz, *Calvin in Context* (New York: Oxford University Press, 1995), 204–5.

20. Ibid., 143–44.

Chapter 10 My Way or the Highway?

1. Marian Wright Edelman, "Say No to This Welfare 'Reform,'" Washington Post, November 3, 1995.

2. Patricia Ireland, "Activists to Demonstrate Start Fasting Over Welfare," National Organization for Women press release, July 31, 1996, http://www.now.org/press/07-96/07-31-96.html.

3. Robert Pear, "G.O.P. Seek Compromise on Welfare Bill," *New York Times*, October 25, 1995.

4. Pete Wilson, "Kicking America's Welfare Habit," *Heritage Lecture #540* (Washington DC: Heritage Foundation), September 6, 1995.

5. Lynn Woolsey, *Congressional Record*, July 18, 1996, H7789.

6. Bill Archer, *Congressional Record*, July 18, 1996, H7796.

7. Francis X. Clines, "Clinton Signs Bill Cutting Welfare; States in New Role," *New York Times*, August 23, 1996.

8. Noah T. Winer, email to moveon.org, February 8, 2007.

9. "Remarks by Senator Hillary Rodham Clinton to the NYS Family Planning Providers," Senator Hillary Rodham Clinton homepage, January 24, 2005, http://clinton.senate.gov/~clinton/speeches/2005125A05.html.

10. "A 21st Century Frame of Reference," Senator Chuck Hagel homepage, December 7, 2006, http://hagel.senate.gov/index.cfm?FuseAction=Speeches.Detail&Speech_id=26&Month=12&Year=2006.

11. Ron Haskins, "The Outcomes of 1996 Welfare Reform," Testimony before the Committee on Ways and Means (Brookings Institution, Washington DC, July 19, 2006).

Chapter 11 Can Christians Honestly Disagree?

1. Randall Balmer, *Thy Kingdom Come: How the Religious Right Distorts the Faith and Threatens America: An Evangelical's Lament* (New York: Basic Books, 2006), 33.

2. Rev. Louis Sheldon, "'Red Letter' Liberal Christians: A New Front Group for Democrats," The Traditional Values Coalition, September 26, 2006, http://www.traditionalvalues.org/modules.php?sid=2867.

3. Mark A. Noll, *America's God: From Jonathan Edwards to Abraham Lincoln* (New York: Oxford University Press, 2002), 387.

4. Ibid., 395. For further detail, see also Mark A. Noll, *The Civil War as a Theological Crisis* (Chapel Hill, NC: University of North Carolina Press, 2006).

5. Daniel J. Treier, "Proof Text," in *Dictionary for Theological Interpretation of the Bible*, ed. Kevin J. Vanhoozer (Grand Rapids: Baker Academic, 2005), 623.

6. One possible resource for further study is Craig Blomberg, *Neither Poverty Nor Riches: A Biblical Theology of Possessions* (Downers Grove, IL: IVP Academic, 2001).

7. Shaun Casey, John Crossin, Eric H. Crump, A. Katherine Grieb, Beverly Mitchell, and Ann K. Riggs, "Love for the Poor: God's Love for the Poor and the Church's Witness to It," The National Council of the Churches of Christ in the United States of America, September 2005, http://www.ncccusa.org/pdfs/LoveforPoor.pdf.

8. The primary formula for calculating poverty statistics is decades old and highly contested. More than likely, the numbers underestimate the income needed to meet basic needs. For the purpose of this short discussion, however, I will rely on these measures.

9. Data from the U.S. Census Bureau, 2006, http://www.census.gov/hhes/www/poverty/histpov/hstpov2.html.

10. Sharon Parrott, Isaac Shapiro, and John Springer, "Selected Research Findings on Accomplishments of the Safety Net," Center on Budget and Policy Priorities, July 19, 2005, http://www.cbpp.org/7-27-05acc.htm.

11. Matthew Ladner, "How to Win the War on Poverty: An Analysis of State Poverty Trends," *Goldwater Institute Policy Report* 215 (November 14, 2006): 18.

12. "President Bush Signs Tax Relief Extension Reconciliation Act of 2005," press release, May 17, 2006, http://www.whitehouse.gov/news/releases/2006/05/20060517-2.html.

13. Jessa Haugebak, "Low-Tax States Cut Poverty Rates: Study," *Budget & Tax News* (February 1, 2007), http://www.newcoalition.org/Article.cfm?artId+20569.

14. Anisha Desai, Scott Klinger, Gloribell Mota, and Liz Stanton, "Nothing to Be Thankful For: Tax Cuts and the Deteriorating U.S. Job Market," United for a Fair Economy (November 2005), http://www.faireconomy.org/press/2006/No_Thanks_Report_01.06.pdf.

15. Food and Nutrition Service, "Child Nutrition Programs—Income Eligibility Guidelines," *The Federal Register* 72, no. 38 (2007): 8687.

16. Jim Wallis, "Budgets Are Moral Documents . . . and There Is Still Time to Speak," *Sojourners*, April 27, 2005, http://www.sojo.net/index.cfm?action=action.display_c&item=051006_BMD_050427.

17. Tony Perkins, quoted in Donald R. Eastman III, "Be Wary of Those Who Claim to Speak for God," *St. Petersburg Times*, April 29, 2005.

18. Brian Sullivan, "Bush Administration Announces Nearly $1.4 Billion to Support a Record Number of Local Homeless Programs Nationwide," Homes & Communities news release, February 20, 2007, http://www.hud.gov/news/release.cfm?content=pr07-017.cfm.

19. For more details about the politics of the faith-based initiative, see Amy E. Black, Douglas Koopman, and David Ryden, *Of Little Faith: The Politics of*

George W. Bush's Faith-Based Initiatives (Washington DC: Georgetown University Press, 2004).

20. Carol Towarnicky, "Why the Budget Is a Moral Document," *Sojourners*, January 17, 2007, http://www.sojo.net/index.cfm?action=news.display_article&mode=s&NewsID=5741.

21. Eastman, "Be Wary."   .

Chapter 12 Behind the Curtain at the Voting Booth

1. The Living Room Candidate: Presidential Campaign Commercials, http://livingroomcandidate.movingimage.us/election/index.php?nav_action=election&nav_subaction=overview&campaign_id=175.

2. Daniel Magleby, David M. O'Brien, Paul C. Light, James MacGregor Burns, Jack W. Peltason, and Thomas E. Cronin, *Government by the People: National, State, and Local Version*, 21st ed. (Upper Saddle River, NJ: Pearson Education, 2006), 294.

3. The Living Room Candidate: Presidential Campaign Commercials, http://livingroomcandidate.movingimage.us/election/index.php?nav_action=election&nav_subaction=overview&campaign_id=178.

4. See Oldmixon, *Uncompromising Positions*.

5. For a list of the DMAs, see http://www.nielsenmedia.com/DMAs.html.

6. Political Advertising Resource Center, "Real Ideas for Change," http://www.umdparc.org/SteeleAnalysisRealIdeas.htm (accessed August 1, 2007).

7. Barack Obama, *The Audacity of Hope* (New York: Crown, 2006), 132.

8. Roberta Combs, "2004 Christian Coalition Voter Guide," Christian Coalition of America, http://www.cc.org/voterguides2004/national.pdf.

Chapter 13 Beyond the Ballot Box

1. Steve Grubbs, quoted in Ian Urbina, "The 2006 Election: Sick of Political Signs, Public Demands Change of Scenery," *New York Times*, November 13, 2006.

2. Sidney Verba, Kay Lehman Schlozman, and Henry Brady, *Voice & Equality: Civic Voluntarism in American Politics* (Cambridge, MA: Harvard University Press, 1995), 37–38.

3. Ibid., 70.

4. Center for Responsive Politics, "Total Raised and Spent—2004 Race: South Dakota Senate," OpenSecrets.org, http://www.opensecrets.org/races/summary.asp?ID=SDS1&cycle=2004&special=N.

5. Alan Cooperman, "Groups Plan Rally on Mall to Protest Darfur Violence," *Washington Post*, April 27, 2006.

6. C. S. Lewis, "The Efficacy of Prayer," in *The Essential C. S. Lewis*, ed. Lyle W. Dorsett (New York: Touchstone, 1996), 381.

Chapter 14 Can We All Get Along?

1. Vaclav Havel, *Art of the Impossible: Politics as Morality in Practice* (New York: A. A. Knopf, 1997), 83.

Suggestions for Further Reading

Religion and Politics—General Discussions

Fowler, Robert Booth, Allen D. Hertzke, Laura R. Olson, and Kevin R. den Dulk. *Religion and Politics in America: Faith, Culture, and Strategic Choices.* 3rd ed. Boulder, CO: Westview, 2004.

Sider, Ronald J. *The Scandal of Evangelical Politics: Why Are Christians Missing the Chance to Really Change the World?* Grand Rapids: Baker Books, 2008.

Wald, Kenneth D., and Allison Calhoun-Brown. *Religion and Politics in the United States.* 5th ed. Lanham, MD: Rowman and Littlefield, 2007.

Religion and American History

Gaustad, Edwin S. *Proclaim Liberty Throughout All the Land: A History of Church and State in America.* New York: Oxford University Press, 2003.

Holmes, David L. *The Faiths of the Founding Fathers.* New York: Oxford University Press, 2006.

Noll, Mark A. *America's God: From Jonathan Edwards to Abraham Lincoln.* New York: Oxford University Press, 2002.

Religion and Contemporary American Politics

From the Ideological Left

Carter, Jimmy. *Our Endangered Values: America's Moral Crisis*. New York: Simon and Schuster, 2005.

Wallis, Jim. *God's Politics: Why the Right Gets It Wrong and the Left Doesn't Get It*. San Francisco: Harper, 2005.

From the Ideological Right

Gerson, Michael J. *Heroic Conservatism: Why Republicans Need to Embrace America's Ideals (And Why They Deserve to Fail If They Don't)*. San Francisco: Harper, 2007.

Land, Richard. *The Divided States of America? What Liberals and Conservatives Are Missing in the God-and-Country Shouting Match!* Nashville: Nelson, 2007.

From the Ideological Center

Danforth, John. *Faith and Politics*. New York: Viking, 2006.

DiIulio, John J. *Godly Republic: A Centrist Blueprint for America's Faith-Based Future*. Berkeley: University of California Press, 2007.

Multiple Perspectives in One Volume

Dionne, E. J., Jean Bethke Elshtain, and Kayla M. Drogosz, eds. *One Electorate Under God? A Dialogue on Religion and American Politics*. Washington DC: Brookings Institution Press, 2004.

Sider, Ronald J., and Dianne Knippers, eds. *Toward an Evangelical Public Policy: Political Strategies for the Health of the Nation*. Grand Rapids: Baker, 2005.

The Religious Right

Gilgoff, Dan. *The Jesus Machine: How James Dobson, Focus on the Family, and Evangelical America Are Winning the Culture War*. New York: St. Martin's, 2007.

Greeley, Andrew, and Michael Hout. *The Truth about Conservative Christians: What They Think and What They Believe*. Chicago: University of Chicago Press, 2006.

Martin, William. *With God on Our Side: The Rise of the Religious Right in America*. New York: Broadway, 2005.

Political Theology

Catechism of the Catholic Church. 2nd ed. Washington DC: U.S. Catholic Conference, 1997.

DiIulio, John J. *The American Catholic Voter*. Program for Research on Religion and Urban Civil Society. Report 06-2. http://www.prrucs.org/pdfs/PRRUCS_AmerCath.pdf.

Kemeny, P. C., ed. *Church, State, and Public Justice: Five Views*. Downers Grove, IL: IVP Academic, 2007.

Klaassen, Walter, ed. *Anabaptism in Outline: Selected Primary Sources*. Scottdale, PA: Herald Press, 1981.

Skillen, James W. *The Scattered Voice: Christians at Odds in the Public Square*. Grand Rapids: Zondervan, 1990.

Steinmetz, David C. *Calvin in Context*. New York: Oxford University Press, 1995.

———. *Luther in Context*. Bloomington, IN: Indiana University Press, 1986.

Contributors

Jennifer L. Aycock is a graduate of Wheaton College, where she studied Christian formation and ministries and political science. She lives in Compiegne, France, serving with Greater Europe Mission.

Jonathan Flugstad is a political science major and history minor at Wheaton College. He is originally from Redmond, Washington, and will graduate in May 2008.

Daniel J. Treier is associate professor of theology at Wheaton College. His recent publications include *Virtue and the Voice of God: Toward Theology as Wisdom* (Eerdmans, 2007) and *Introducing Theological Interpretation of Scripture: Recovering a Christian Practice* (Baker Academic, forthcoming). He is the coeditor of *The Cambridge Companion to Evangelical Theology* (Cambridge University Press, 2007) and an associate editor of the *Dictionary for Theological Interpretation of the Bible* (Baker Academic, 2005).

Index